Integrating
Aging Topics
Into Psychology

Integrating Aging Topics Into Psychology

A PRACTICAL GUIDE FOR TEACHING UNDERGRADUATES

Susan Krauss Whitbourne and
John C. Cavanaugh

In collaboration with the Division 20 Education Committee,
Karen L. Fingerman and Manfred Diehl, Cochairs

American Psychological Association
Washington, DC

Published by
American Psychological Association
750 First Street, NE
Washington, DC 20002
www.apa.org

To order
APA Order Department
P.O. Box 92984
Washington, DC 20090-2984
Tel: (800) 374-2721; Direct: (202) 336-5510
Fax: (202) 336-5502; TDD/TTY: (202) 336-6123
Online: www.apa.org/books/
Email: order@apa.org

In the U.K., Europe, Africa, and the Middle East, copies may be ordered from
American Psychological Association
3 Henrietta Street
Covent Garden, London
WC2E 8LU England

Typeset in Goudy by Page Grafx, Inc., St. Simons Island, GA

Printer: Data Reproductions, Auburn Hills, MI
Cover Designer: Naylor Design, Washington, DC
Technical/Production Editor: Kristen R. Sullivan

The opinions and statements published are the responsibility of the authors, and such opinions and statements do not necessarily represent the policies of the American Psychological Association.

Library of Congress Cataloging-in-Publication Data
Integrating aging topics into psychology : a practical guide for teaching undergraduates / edited by Susan Krauss Whitbourne and John C. Cavanaugh.—1st ed.
    p. cm.
  Includes bibliographical references and index.
  ISBN 1-55798-970-2 (alk. paper)
  1. Aging—Psychological aspects—Study and teaching (Higher) 2. Adulthood Psychological aspects—Study and teaching (Higher) I. Whitbourne, Susan Krauss. II. Cavanaugh, John C.

  BF724.55.A35 .A355 2002
  155.67'1—dc21

                          2002067564

British Library Cataloguing-in-Publication Data
A CIP record is available from the British Library.

Printed in the United States of America
First Edition

CONTENTS

CONTRIBUTORS

Victoria Hilkevitch Bedford, School of Psychological Sciences, Center for Aging and Community, University of Indianapolis, Indianapolis, IN

Ana Begovic, Department of Psychology, University of Akron, Akron, OH

Dean Blevins, Department of Psychology, University of Akron, Akron, OH

Rosemary Blieszner, Department of Human Development, Virginia Polytechnic Institute and State University, Blacksburg

John C. Cavanaugh, President, University of West Florida, Pensacola

Manfred Diehl, Institute on Aging, University of Florida, Gainesville

Karen L. Fingerman, Department of Human Development and Family Studies, Gerontology Center, Pennsylvania State University, State College

Bert Hayslip, Jr., Department of Psychology, University of North Texas, Denton

Karen Kopera-Frye, Department of Human Development and Family Studies & Sanford Center for Aging, University of Nevada–Reno

Antonio E. Puente, Department of Psychology, University of North Carolina at Wilmington

Frank Schieber, Department of Psychology, University of South Dakota, Vermillion

Daniel L. Segal, Department of Psychology, University of Colorado at Colorado Springs

Raymond J. Shaw, Department of Psychology, Merrimack College, North Andover, MA

Aurora M. Sherman, Department of Psychology, Brandeis University, Waltham, MA

Anderson D. Smith, School of Psychology, Georgia Tech, Atlanta

Diane L. Sotnak, Department of Sociology, University of Akron, Akron, OH

Harvey L. Sterns, Department of Psychology, University of Akron, Akron, OH

Susan Krauss Whitbourne, Department of Psychology, University of Massachusetts Amherst

Richard Wiscott, Gerontology Program, Shippensburg University, Shippensburg, PA

Integrating
Aging Topics
Into Psychology

1

INCORPORATING AGING INTO PSYCHOLOGY COURSES: OVERVIEW OF THE ISSUES

JOHN C. CAVANAUGH AND SUSAN KRAUSS WHITBOURNE

That the population of the United States and the rest of the developed world is "graying" is a well-known fact. Over the next few decades, the baby boom generation will roughly double the number of people older than age 65, a situation that will create unprecedented public policy challenges (Binstock, 1999). These changes clearly give rise to a pressing need for the general public to understand the issues pertaining to older adults and for professionals educated to deal with them.

Since the beginning of the scientific field of gerontology in the mid-20th century, psychologists have been at the forefront of research and theory related to older adults. For example, Division 20 (Adult Development and Aging) was the first division in the American Psychological Association (APA) added beyond the initial set of original divisions (in 1947), evidence

Please direct correspondence to John C. Cavanaugh, University of West Florida, Office of the President, 11000 University Parkway, Pensacola, FL 32514; e-mail: jcavanaugh@uwf.edu.

that interest in aging in professional psychology has deep roots (Birren & Stine-Morrow, 1999). The interest continues to grow; in the early 21st century, this is one of the fastest growing subdisciplines in psychology.

Despite the long history of involvement of psychologists in the field of adult development and aging, most psychology students are not exposed to research and theory on the topic. Few psychology programs require a course on adult development and aging, and few psychology courses contain significant coverage of issues related to aging.

As documented in detail throughout this volume, there is a dearth of materials on aging in psychology texts. The lack of course coverage and textbook material creates a serious learning gap given the coming demographic changes in the United States and the world. As described in detail in the chapters, however, this situation can be remedied because many ways are available to incorporate information on aging into core psychology courses without undue difficulty. The purpose of this book is to provide instructors with suggestions for infusing aging into psychology courses and to point them toward the resources necessary to provide their students with an introduction to the key issues in each area.

Division 20 has a long history of promoting ways for instructors to include aging content in their courses. Each year, the Division 20 Education Committee sponsors a teaching symposium at the annual meeting of the APA. The current volume also builds on an earlier volume that was based on the work of the Education Committee of Division 20 (Parham, Poon, & Siegler, 1990), and it provides important updated and expanded material to this previous volume. It is written by leading individuals in the field who not only help create the knowledge but also teach the courses. Most of the authors have been presenters at the annual Division 20 Education Symposia, as well as similar sessions presented at the annual meeting of the Gerontological Society of America. The collection of authors in this volume represents a cross-section of the best teacher–scholars in the field of adult development and aging.

This chapter provides an introduction to the overarching issues confronting an instructor who wants to incorporate aging content into core psychology courses and a summary of each of the constituent chapters. Three main issues related to integrating aging content are discussed: how to organize material on aging, what types of materials can be used, and who should present the material. Each remaining chapter provides specific examples of these issues.

At the outset, we want to make a strong case for including an understanding of aging as one of the learning goals for any course in psychology. We argue that understanding the developmental course of any psychological phenomenon is essential. Anything less than such a treatment means that the issue under study is treated as static throughout life. Few, if any, psychological phenomena remain unchanged throughout adulthood. More important, given the demographic trends in the nation and the world, it is essential that aging content be included in core psychology courses.

HOW SHOULD AGING CONTENT BE PRESENTED?

One of the most challenging issues confronting an instructor is deciding what content to include. Every course presents a conundrum: Should the emphasis be placed on depth of understanding (i.e., cover fewer topics but in more detail) or on breadth of understanding (i.e., more topics but in less depth)? We argue that the inclusion of aging content should not be viewed as a matter of "if" but "how." It is not a dispensable topic but rather one that is vital to every area of psychology.

Aging content can be included as an extension of the depth of coverage of a topic, or it can be approached as a way of expanding the breadth of the course. A course on psychopathology might include clinical interview techniques in diagnostics. If the focus is on depth of knowledge of specific forms of psychopathology, this topic might not be included. In contrast, aging content could still be covered as relevant for understanding differences in symptoms of specific disorders.

Once an instructor decides to include aging content in a course, the first issue is how this content should be presented. Fundamentally, the choice is either treating aging as a separate topic or infusing aging into all topics throughout the course. Conceptually, the former approach is equivalent to having a separate chapter or section of the course on aging in which all of the other topics are viewed developmentally; the latter approach views aging as an inherent component of every topic in the subdiscipline under study.

Aging as a Separate Topic in the Course

Having a separate section of a course devoted to aging is probably the easiest way to add significant aging material, especially for instructors who have little if any background in aging. For example, as described in Anderson D. Smith's chapter on cognitive psychology (chapter 6), a section on aging and cognition could include a developmental perspective on all of the major aspects of cognition (e.g., attention, memory, and resources). Similar inclusive sections can be added not only for the areas discussed in this book but for others as well (e.g., human sexuality, marriage and the family, environmental psychology, and community psychology).

Several advantages of this approach are apparent. The concentration of aging content makes it clear to students that researchers and theorists have examined a broad range of topics from a developmental perspective. By including the content in a separate section, instructors draw more overt attention to aging. As discussed later, having a separate section on aging may facilitate the use of time-limited activities (e.g., class demonstrations) or nontraditional material (e.g., film or music). These supplements may help students better understand the role of aging in the topics under study if they are considered together. Along these lines, if the section on aging is included at the end of the course, then the opportunity to use it as a way to review the entire course is also available, given that all of the key topics are examined developmentally. Finally, it may be easier for instructors who do not have extensive background in aging to create a separate section, which can very closely follow the overall organization of the rest of the course. An instructor can capitalize on the fact that researchers in aging study the same issues as so-called mainstream researchers and bring in an expert on aging as a guest lecturer.

The separate-section approach has downsides. By organizing all of the aging content into one section, it may be difficult for students to understand that age-related changes are an integral part of all psychological phenomena. This issue could be adequately addressed, however, by ensuring that all of the major topics in the course are included in a section on aging. Still, if the aging content is included too early in the course, then some issues may have not yet been discussed in sufficient detail for students to grasp. This is a more serious problem when the section on aging occurs earlier in the course. Finally, including aging as a separate section may make it vulnerable to the extent that an instructor then views it as content that could be deleted to cover fewer topics in more detail. Although, as we have argued, aging content should not be viewed this way, it nevertheless may be considered by some as an "extra" that could be sacrificed.

Aging as Integrated Throughout the Course

The alternative to combining all of the discussion of aging into one section is to integrate it into all sections of the course. As indicated previously, this approach provides the best way for students to understand that aging is an inherent aspect of psychological phenomena. However, integrating aging across the course poses several key challenges.

Integrating aging throughout the course usually requires the instructor to supplement each section of the course, given the few textbooks that actually include any discussion of aging content. In turn, this means that the instructor must do more restructuring of the course compared to simply adding one section on aging. Managing such supplements successfully often requires more expertise in aging-related work.

Including aging content throughout the course has the additional advantage of creating better opportunities for alternative, more protracted supplements such as service learning, discussed in the next section. Such activities take longer to complete and are richer learning experiences if the topic is still relevant throughout the course. This is important to the extent that the instructor has "understanding aging" as a key learning goal for the course.

Using Either Approach

Clearly, either approach (aging as a separate section or aging as integrated throughout the course) can be used effectively to get content on aging into any core psychology course. The choice is more a matter of preference depending on the instructor's comfort and expertise level and the availability of other personnel as guest lecturers or co-instructors. The most important outcome is that aging is included.

WHAT TYPES OF MATERIALS ARE AVAILABLE?

Once an instructor has decided how to cover aging content in his or her course, a much more difficult issue is next: the actual selection of materials to be used as supplements to the core text or readings. Given the enormous volume of journal articles, books, Web sites, literature, film, music, and class activities available on various aspects of aging, the problem is certainly not the lack of material; rather, it is how to choose the best mix for a particular course.

A very common approach is to use supplemental readings as the primary way that aging content is covered. In general, one can use the same guidelines for selecting material on aging as are applicable for other supplements in deciding whether to use primary or secondary source material for coverage of research and theory. The remaining chapters in this book provide several excellent suggestions on where to go for these types of supplements, as well as advice on what types of materials work best in different situations.

A more challenging (and often more compelling) approach to including aging content is to use literature, film, music, and class activities such as writing and research projects (Blieszner & Buffer, 1999; Cavanaugh, 1999a; Fingerman & Bertrand, 1999; McGuire & Zwahr, 1999; Smith & Kohn, 1999; Whitbourne & Collins, 1999a, 1999b). Articles are available that discuss in detail how to select and use these effectively in courses on aging and related topics (e.g., Blieszner, 1999; Cavanaugh, 1999b). Additionally, several authors describe how to create, manage, and integrate service-learning projects into courses in gerontology (Blieszner & Artale, 2001; Brown & Roodin, 2001; Cavanaugh, 2001; Hanks & Icenogle, 2001; Long, Larsen, Hussey, & Travis, 2001; Nichols & Monard, 2001; Peacock, Bradley, & Shenk, 2001; Whitbourne, Collins, & Skultety, 2001). Lessons learned from gerontology courses can be readily applied to other core courses in psychology.

In general, these alternatives to traditional course supplements help students see how research and theory connect to "real-world" phenomena.

This is especially true in the case of class activities, such as writing exercises or research projects, and service-learning projects that are appropriately integrated into classroom content. Interested readers should consult the examples cited previously for specific details about how various supplements are best used and integrated in the course. As noted, these activities are easier to include if aging is integrated throughout the course as writing and service-learning projects take considerable time. Because students would be exposed to aging issues on a regular basis, those who choose aging as the topic for one of these activities would have their topic receive regular review.

OVERVIEW OF THE BOOK

The remaining chapters in this book address how to incorporate aging content into the core courses that are required in most psychology programs in the United States. Each chapter includes specific examples of which aging content could be included, suggestions on how to include it, and examples from the authors' experiences. Chapters are organized by the typical level of the course, from introductory to advanced.

In chapter 2 on introductory psychology courses, Susan Krauss Whitbourne shows how aging can be included in every major section and can be used to demonstrate the importance of topics such as physiological psychology or sensation and perception that students may view as tedious. She offers numerous examples of in-class supplements and other types of activities to supplement the readings. Many of these activities may also be used in more advanced courses. She also provides helpful Web sites that can be used for supplemental material or student assignments.

Antonio E. Puente's chapter on neuropsychology courses (chapter 3) reflects a growing trend in psychology programs to focus on this and other topics that bridge the clinical and neuroscience areas. He argues that knowing about aging is essential to a full understanding of neuropsychology. Puente provides many examples of material that blends clinical diagnosis, cognitive psychology, and physiological psychology. Several suggestions for supplemental material and assignments are offered.

Raymond J. Shaw discusses in chapter 4 several ways that aging can be incorporated into research methods and statistics courses. As he points out, developmental research questions provide much fertile ground for discussing challenges in research (e.g., sampling and representativeness), framing of research questions, and various approaches to data analysis. Shaw provides numerous suggestions for projects that can be used either as in-class demonstrations or actual opportunities for students to collect and analyze data.

In chapter 5, Frank Schieber offers many excellent ways in which aging can be brought into courses on sensation and perception. In this case, aging could also serve as an organizing theme; one could use the question, "How does _____ change with age?" as a way for students to distinguish between those aspects that change with age and those that do not. Schieber provides a link to a superb Web site that contains a wealth of information, links to other sites, and demonstrations of various phenomena.

Because the topic of cognition and aging has been researched more than any other, Anderson D. Smith argues in chapter 6 that aging provides an avenue for understanding all basic cognitive topics. In each section of the course, students can use aging to ask about the relative stability of a process over time and how the study of changes (or lack thereof) in a process enhances our understanding of it. Smith's many examples of demonstrations and course supplements provide ways to make a course in cognitive psychology more engaging and inclusive.

As Manfred Diehl indicates in chapter 7 on personality courses, aging offers an excellent way to introduce students to hotly contested issues such as the relative stability of personality traits and the very definition of personality itself. Diehl also points out that personality courses provide fertile ground for understanding how the continuing evolution of theory drives research. He provides several suggestions for supplemental readings, other materials, and hands-on experiences.

In their discussion incorporating aging into social psychology courses in chapter 8, Karen Kopera-Frye, Richard Wiscott, Dean Blevins, and Ana Begovic present several examples of how phenomena that are well-established in younger adults may differ with older adults (e.g., self processes, prosocial behaviors, intergroup processes, health and politics). Bringing aging into these areas provides several opportunities for introducing supplemental material (e.g., readings, videos) and assignments. Additionally, adding a focus on aging is a powerful way to discuss the effects of stereotypes in a new way.

Aurora M. Sherman notes in chapter 9 that health psychology is an area that is ripe for a focus on aging. As she describes, many phenomena are best exemplified from an aging perspective (e.g., the impact of increased longevity and dealing with chronic illness). This course also provides opportunities to address such key issues as diversity and the quality of and access to health care as well as aging and disease. Sherman offers suggestions on how to apply various criteria to case studies and provides several sources for supplemental material and projects.

Students' inherent interest in abnormal psychology presents both good opportunities and significant challenges for introducing aging, as Daniel L. Segal points out in chapter 10. He presents several reasons why aging content is critical, such as refuting myths about aging and mental health and underuse of mental health services. Segal provides several types of supplemental content, sample case studies, and other activities that will help instructors address a general lack of content in most texts.

Victoria Hilkevitch Bedford points out in chapter 11 that texts for courses on the psychology of gender rarely discuss the issue of aging despite well-grounded data showing that age is an important source of differences. Aging and gender are complementary concepts; one ought not to consider one without the other. Bedford provides a wealth of suggestions for supplemental material, assignments, and activities that demonstrate the true interconnectedness of gender and aging.

Although it may appear that there is little need for suggestions on incorporating aging into courses on life span development (as the topic is included in every text), Karen L. Fingerman shows how to use it more effectively in chapter 12. Because few instructors of this course are gerontologists, the tendency is to overemphasize childhood and adolescence. Through her many examples, Fingerman demonstrates how aging can be used to provide advance organizers for the course and provide a better understanding for the entire life span. Instructors can also use aging to provide a preview of what students may experience in their own future lives. Numerous excellent examples of classic readings and other teaching suggestions are offered.

Harvey L. Sterns, Ana Begovic, and Diane L. Sotnak discuss in chapter 13 how aging can be a critical component in courses on industrial/organizational psychology. Such topics as retraining older workers, the older labor force, human factors, job performance, and the changing nature of work all lend themselves well to including content about aging. This course also permits instructors to address topics such as myths relating to older workers and attitudes toward older workers held by students. Sterns et al. provide an excellent list of supplemental materials.

Bert Hayslip, Jr., provides considerable assistance in chapter 14 for instructors of courses on death and dying so that they can include aging content but not equate aging with death. He presents strong arguments for experiential projects and provides several examples. Hayslip also shows how the course can be used to help students identify their own fears and attitudes toward death and the dying. Several excellent supplemental sources are provided.

Finally, Rosemary Blieszner's chapter on personal relationships courses (chapter 15) provides ideas for challenging students to think about whether key aspects of personal relationships remain constant or change over time. These issues help instructors to get students to think about the future of their own relationships. In addition to many suggestions for supplemental materials and activities, Blieszner provides some Web sites that contain additional ideas for enhancing this course.

We hope that these chapters stimulate your thinking about your own teaching and provide ample evidence that aging is a critical topic in any course in psychology. Should the course you teach not be one specifically discussed, we trust that you will still have enough suggestions from the authors to begin incorporating some topics in any case. Each of the authors asked us to make certain that readers know that they are available for consultation and discussion. Please feel free to contact us.

REFERENCES

Binstock, R. H. (1999). Public policy issues. In J. C. Cavanaugh & S. K. Whitbourne (Eds.), *Gerontology: An interdisciplinary perspective* (pp. 414–447). New York: Oxford University Press.

Birren, B. A., & Stine-Morrow, E. A. L. (1999). A history of Division 20 (Adult Development and Aging): Analysis and reminiscences. In D. A. Dewsbury (Ed.), *Unification through division: Histories of the divisions of the American Psychological Association* (Vol. IV, pp. 35–64). Washington, DC: American Psychological Association.

Blieszner, R. (1999). Strategies and resources for teaching family gerontology. *Teaching of Psychology, 26,* 50–51.

Blieszner, R., & Artale, L. M. (2001). Benefits of intergenerational service-learning to human services majors. *Educational Gerontology, 27,* 71–87.

Blieszner, R., & Buffer, L. C. (1999). Adult development and aging as a writing intensive course: Student evaluation. *Gerontology and Geriatrics Education, 19,* 65–76.

Brown, L. H., & Roodin, P. A. (2001). Service-learning in gerontology: An out-of-classroom experience. *Educational Gerontology, 27,* 89–103.

Cavanaugh, J. C. (1999a). Integrating the humanities into a liberal arts course on adult development and aging. *Teaching of Psychology, 26,* 51–52.

Cavanaugh, J. C. (1999b). Teaching effective undergraduate gerontology courses: Making informed choices. *Gerontology and Geriatrics Education, 19,* 93–100.

Cavanaugh, J. C. (2001). Learning and doing: The importance of service-learning in gerontology. *Educational Gerontology, 27,* 117–124.

Fingerman, K. L., & Bertrand, R. (1999). Approaches to teaching adult development and aging within a life span development course. *Teaching of Psychology, 26,* 55–57.

Hanks, R. S., & Icenogle, M. (2001). Preparing for an age-diverse workforce: Intergenerational service-learning in social gerontology and business curricula. *Educational Gerontology, 27,* 49–70.

Long, A. B., Larsen, P., Hussey, L., & Travis, S. S. (2001). Organizing, managing, and evaluating service-learning projects. *Educational Gerontology, 27,* 3–21.

McGuire, L. C., & Zwahr, M. D. (1999). Tying it together: Two comprehensive projects for adult development and aging courses. *Teaching of Psychology, 26,* 53–55.

Nichols, A. H., & Monard, K. (2001). Designing intergenerational service-learning courses based on student characteristics. *Educational Gerontology, 27,* 37–48.

Parham, I., Poon, L. W., & Siegler, I. (Eds.). (1990). *ACCESS: Aging curriculum content for education in the social sciences.* New York: Springer.

Peacock, J. R., Bradley, D. B., & Shenk, D. (2001). Incorporating field sites into service-learning as collaborative partners. *Educational Gerontology, 27,* 23–35.

Smith, G. C., & Kohn, S. J. (1999). An interdisciplinary team research assignment for use in an introduction to gerontology course. *Gerontology and Geriatrics Education, 19,* 77–91.

Whitbourne, S. K., & Collins, K. J. (1999a). Employing interactive learning methods in a course on the psychology of aging. *Teaching of Psychology, 26,* 48–49.

Whitbourne, S. K., & Collins, K. J. (1999b). Using video and projects to enhance learning in an undergraduate gerontology course. *Gerontology and Geriatrics Education, 19,* 53–63.

Whitbourne, S. K., Collins, K. J., & Skultety, K. M. (2001). Formative reflections on service-learning in a course on the psychology of aging. *Educational Gerontology, 27,* 105–115.

2

INTRODUCTORY PSYCHOLOGY

SUSAN KRAUSS WHITBOURNE

Introductory psychology courses hold an enormous potential for integrating the topic of aging in coverage of fields ranging from methods to social psychology. Unfortunately, introductory psychology texts present a negative view of aging or, at best, mixed messages (Whitbourne & Hulicka, 1990; APA Commission on Ethnic Minority Membership, Recruitment, Retention, and Training–2, in press). Many opportunities are available to integrate aging as a dimension of the course. In this chapter, the intersection of aging and mainstream psychology is explored with a focus on making the material accessible and interesting to students in introductory psychology courses. Each main area of the introductory course is approached from the standpoint of the *aging dimension*, or the developmental implications of the material for incorporating research and theories in the psychology of adult development and aging, as well as social gerontology.

OVERVIEW OF THE COURSE

As a survey course that reaches students from a wide array of majors, introductory psychology presents a special challenge to the instructor. For many students, the course satisfies a general distribution requirement, one

Please direct correspondence to Susan Krauss Whitbourne, Department of Psychology, University of Massachusetts, Amherst, MA 01003; e-mail: swhitbo@psych.umass.edu that may or may not have been chosen on an elective basis. In addition to students representing a diversity of interests and motivations, the course is made more challenging in that it is often a first-year course, and the students lack sophistication in reading, test-taking, and writing skills. However, on the positive side, because the course is so broad, it is possible for the instructor to weave in areas of personal interest as a theme or as a way to give the course more relevance to students. The topic of aging fits perfectly into this framework, because the concept of the developing individual can serve as an integrative theme across many areas within psychology. Moreover, aging is becoming an increasingly relevant topic as the world population grows older. Students will appreciate learning about the aging process because many of them are likely to interact with older adults in the course of their careers, regardless of the field they enter. Furthermore, many students have an inherent interest in the topic because of its relevance to family life, specifically their relationships with parents, grandparents, and other older relatives.

Objectives

The introductory psychology course is intended to provide students with a basic understanding of the principles of behavior. Within this overall objective, the instructor may wish to emphasize the applied utility of knowledge about psychology and its relevance to everyday life. The instructor also may choose to orient students to psychology as a scientific discipline, emphasizing the importance of empirical research methods. The topic of aging fits into these objectives, as it provides students with an appreciation of the way that principles of behavior apply to development in later life, has direct applications, and provides ample opportunities to discuss the need for a scientific approach to understanding behavior. For example, in teaching about the topic of sensation and perception, instructors can make the point that these processes change over adulthood in significant ways. In terms of applications, the topic of aging has relevance to, for example, the area of abnormal psychology. There are important ways in which diagnosis and therapy ideally should be modified to take into account the particular concerns of older adult clients. Finally, in the area of research methods, numerous ways are available in which studies of aging can be used to demonstrate the need for appropriate controls, especially because age is not a true independent variable.

Topics Covered

The syllabus of the introductory psychology courses typically includes a broad representation of the subdisciplines of psychology and the background in the history of psychology and research methods. The majority of instructors set their syllabus on the basis of the textbook they are using, although obviously, it is possible to present chapters in a different order than they appear in the book. Furthermore, a text may be chosen because of its inclusion or exclusion of particular topics. In the case of aging, the instructor may wish to choose a text that has two chapters on developmental psychology, as this increases the chances that aging will be covered in a satisfactory manner within that unit of the course. Because few textbooks now include aging in any chapter other than developmental psychology, it is likely that most of the coverage of aging in other topics requires the introduction of new material during lecture or in the form of additional readings.

One of the challenges of teaching introductory psychology in a one-semester course is that not enough time is available to give sufficient emphasis to every topic, assuming that the instructor wishes to present a balanced approach to the field. Therefore, it may seem difficult to work any new content into a course that is already jammed with information. However, if the instructor wishes to incorporate at least some material on aging into the course, it is possible to do so without sacrificing basic areas. Examples relevant to aging can be used just as readily as examples relevant to any other age group or subtopic, and in this way, no time is lost from the existing course schedule. If the instructor is using multimedia material to enhance the lecture (videotapes, digital video discs, or streaming video), these examples can be sought from movies, television programs, or documentaries that present examples of psychological processes in older adults.

GENERAL CONCERNS REGARDING AGING

As mentioned at the beginning of this chapter, introductory textbooks tend not to do justice to the topic of aging. When material on aging is included in the text, it is often presented in a negative fashion. Stereotypes about aging are then reinforced, and students are not given the opportunity to learn important principles about individual differences and that old age is not equivalent to disease.

A good example of this problem of stereotyping and negative information is the topic of Alzheimer's disease, which may be included either in the chapter on aging or in the chapter on the brain. It is typical for the prevalence of Alzheimer's disease to be overestimated in the popular media as affecting 4 million adults older than age 65 (or about 12% of the population in this age range). These estimates also tend to state that the percentage of adults older than age 85 with the disease is about 50%. More recent estimates of the prevalence of this disease are 2 to 2.5 million among the older population as a whole and perhaps up to 29% in those older than 85 (Brookmeyer & Kawas, 1998; U.S. General Accounting Office, 1998). However, given the ubiquitous nature of the "4 million" estimate, it is likely that introductory textbook authors would use this number as the stated prevalence of the disorder. The problem with using this number is that it perpetuates the myth of old age being equated with senility. The more conservative estimates of prevalence clearly differentiate Alzheimer's disease from normal aging or other forms of dementia. A useful demonstration to illustrate this point would be to ask students to estimate the prevalence of Alzheimer's disease in the population, based on media representations of its prevalence. The instructor can also show a videotape of a recent news item on the disorder, as advances in this field are often covered in nightly network news broadcasts.

Another example of a topic that tends to be treated incorrectly in introductory psychology texts is that of the "mid-life crisis" as a predictable event that primarily affects men in their 40s. Many texts present the Levinson, Darrow, Klein, Levinson, and McKee (1978) chart depicting the "seasons" of a man's life, with the mid-life transition given particular emphasis. The problem with this coverage is that the mid-life crisis is a discounted notion in adult developmental psychology. By presenting the concept in an uncritical fashion, textbook authors perpetuate the mistaken idea that personality changes occur at definite ages in adulthood. An exercise that can be useful in this topic to help instructors convey these points is to ask students whether they think one or both of their parents has had a mid-life crisis. The instructor can then discuss whether these experiences would technically qualify as a mid-life crisis by asking the age of the parents. Most likely, even those parents who fit the criteria will have a wide variety of ages. Excerpts from movies with a mid-life crisis theme can also be shown, such as *American Beauty*.

A reluctance to make large changes from edition to edition of a text presents yet another problem in the presentation of information on aging. Information and theories that were correct at one point in time may fail to be replaced in later editions because textbook authors are not keeping up with the literature on aging, a literature with which they may not be particularly familiar. As a consequence, texts continue to cover data and theories that have long been discarded or replaced.

Disengagement theory provides a good example of the problem of outdated literature remaining in introductory texts. According to disengagement theory, older adults are more satisfied with life if they are allowed to withdraw from social obligations and focus on their inner lives. At one time, this theory was considered to present a viable alternative to activity theory, which presents the opposing view that older adults are more likely to be well-adjusted if they are allowed to remain involved and active in their social roles. The activity versus disengagement theory debate was long ago declared defunct in the field of gerontology (Whitbourne, 2001), but it still breathes life in many introductory psychology texts. Consequently, students are forced to learn (and instructors to teach) an outdated and negative view of the social aspects of the aging process. The situation is even worse in the areas of physical and cognitive aging, in which outdated cross-sectional studies presented uncritically still form the bulk of information presented about older adults. As with the previous examples of inaccurate depictions of aging, instructors can stimulate class discussion around how older adults are portrayed by these studies and question students to determine whether they agree or disagree with these portrayals. Presenting antistereotypical examples of older adults through videos and movies can further reinforce these points. Older adults such as John Glenn who have made remarkable accomplishments can be featured by showing brief video clips.

At best, introductory texts present too little material on aging, and at worst, they present incorrect material. Exacerbating the situation is the tendency to leave aging out of all chapters other than the chapter specifically devoted to aging. This segregation of material that would easily fall into the scope of other areas of substance means that students do not have the opportunity to learn about how the aging process intersects with other topics in the field.

Many of the problems inherent in the current presentation of aging could be remedied if textbook authors presented the more general principles of developmental psychology. These principles include multidirectionality of development, multidimensionality, plasticity, and contextualism. *Multidirectionality* means that development can occur in more than one direction with both gains and losses throughout life. *Multidimensionality* means that it is important to look at more than one facet of the individual, ranging from the biological to the psychological to the social, or as a biopsychosocial process. *Plasticity* is a related concept, meaning that losses in development can be compensated by behaviors in which the individual engages and which maximize functioning. In the case of the brain, for example, plasticity means that although neurons may be lost with aging, new synapses can be formed, and increases in the elaboration of dendrites occur. Finally, *contextualism* means that individual behavior is examined in terms of its social context. Individuals may show losses in environments that deprive them of potential growth experiences and opportunities.

Although textbook authors may fail to do justice to these principles of life span development, instructors can present these ideas in simple and concrete ways as part of the overall orientation to the course. Such a presentation sets the stage for the inclusion of developmental processes, from childhood to old age, as a normal and expectable part of the treatment of psychology as a whole. Individuals are not static in their behavior over time, and continued emphasis on this fact should be as fundamental to the introductory psychology course as are the principles of behaviorism or social psychology.

INCLUSION OF AGING INTO COURSE TOPICS

The typical syllabus in introductory psychology proceeds from background material (history, systems, and research methods) and then moves through the topics of physiological, sensation and perception, learning, intelligence, development, personality, social and abnormal psychology. Health psychology, stress and coping, motivation, and emotion tend to be interspersed in individual chapters throughout this order of topics. As shown in this chapter, instructors can readily incorporate aging into each topic.

History, Systems, and Research Methods

The topic of aging can first be introduced in the course in discussions of contemporary psychology, in which the branches of psychology are described. Within the American Psychological Association, aging is represented by Division 20, Adult Development and Aging, and it is also represented in several other divisions, most notably Section II (Geropsychology) of Division 12, Clinical Psychology. The changing demographics of the United States and the world can be brought into this discussion of the field of psychology to emphasize the need for trained specialists in the field to work with the growing population of individuals older than age 65. Students are invariably impressed and surprised to learn that by the time current undergraduates reach 65, they will constitute about one quarter of the entire U.S. population (U.S. Bureau of the Census, 2002). With the availability of the 2000 Census data, instructors have plentiful resources to document these points.

Because research methods is an area that encompasses all of psychology, aging provides as good a topic as any to use for illustrating principles of the scientific method. Examples relevant to aging can emphasize the need for controls. The fact that cohort differences are linked to age differences in all cross-sectional studies provides a clear-cut example of confounding variables. Furthermore, all studies on aging are, by definition, quasi-experimental. Therefore, studies on aging can be used to illustrate basic points about research design in psychology. Although developmental research designs are a relatively advanced topic and more appropriate for a psychology of aging course, the example of sequential methods provides a good illustration of how researchers attempt to control for cohort and time of measurement effects that either obscure or exaggerate the effects of aging. Examples of documentaries covering major new studies such as the Harvard Medical School New England Centenarian Study (http://www.med.harvard.edu/programs/necs/) and the Nun Study being conducted at the University of Kentucky (http://www.mc.uky.edu/nunnet/) can provide students with concrete examples of fascinating approaches to studies of the aging process.

Statistical procedures can also be taught with examples from geropsychology. Correlational studies on aging can be used to illustrate the relationship between age and other variables. For example, a positive correlation exists between age and reaction time, and a negative correlation exists between age and depression scale scores. Even if instructors do not wish to include examples or studies from the aging field, they should nevertheless explain that the majority of studies in psychology are conducted on college-age samples. This point relates to the problem of sample selectivity, and the need to obtain representative samples of age and other characteristics should be emphasized both in this and in other units of the course.

Brain and Behavior

The brain and behavior unit of the course provides several areas in which aging can be covered. In the area of brain imaging, the instructor can show slides of magnetic resonance imaging or positron emission tomography scans that compare the brains of older adults with those of younger adults. This material is readily available on the Internet at Whole Brain Atlas, which includes aging slides and is located at http://www.med.harvard.edu/ AANLIB/home.html. Examples of research on aging also have provided evidence for plasticity in the nervous system, and animals raised in enriched environments have shown elaborated dendritic and synaptic processes. The topic of Alzheimer's disease also fits in well with this topic to illustrate diseases that can affect the brain and hence behavior (keeping in mind the prevalence statistics mentioned previously).

Circadian rhythms and sleep are often included in the topic of the brain and behavior. Within this topic, instructors can cover sleep disorders, some of which become more pronounced in later life, such as sleep apnea. Decreases in REM sleep occur across the life span, starting in infancy and progressing through old age. Changes in circadian rhythms also take place. Studies on circadian rhythms have shown that older adults are likely to be "morning" people and younger adults to be "evening" people (Li, Hasher, Jonas, Rahhal, & May, 1998). The "Morningness–Eveningness" Questionnaire (Horne & Östberg, 1976) can be administered in class to illustrate this concept and will invariably demonstrate that the majority of college-age students are evening people (expect about 1% of the students to say they are morning people).

The endocrine system is often covered in this unit. Although sufficient time to discuss this system adequately is not available, mention can be made that changes in growth hormone, estrogen, and the androgens occur throughout adulthood (Whitbourne, 2003). As with other topics receiving increased attention in the media, it is likely that the instructor will be able to find a recent example from one of the network news programs on this topic.

Sensation and Perception

The unit on sensation and perception includes many areas, each of which has potential relevance to aging. The topic of vision, which tends to receive the most attention, should include a description of *presbyopia*, the hardening and thickening of the lens with age that leads to loss of accommodation of the eye to focus on near objects. This process begins to be noticed by most adults in their 40s, and it is universal. The type of hearing loss that occurs in middle and later adulthood, called *presbycusis*, should be mentioned in the section on hearing. Several types of presbycusis exist, but the loss is at least in part linked to environmental damage. There is preventative value in including this topic, even if only briefly. Students can be told that the headphones and loud speakers they use to listen to music may very well lead to hearing loss in middle age if not sooner.

Adaptation to visual changes in later life can be illustrated by showing the opening scene from *Driving Miss Daisy*, in which the main character finds that she can no longer drive and now must depend on others to get around. This scene depicts in a sensitive manner the many conflicts around the issue of aging and driving, a matter that draws media attention and the expression of strong opinions from the undergraduates (who will undoubtedly hold negative attitudes toward aging drivers).

In teaching about perception, relevant material on aging is available within the areas of feature analysis theory and top-down versus bottom-up processing. Relatively little information is available on the effects of aging on depth perception or the illusions.

Cognition and Intelligence

The topics of attention, working memory, problem-solving, intelligence, and language have a great deal of relevant information on aging that can potentially be included in the introductory psychology course. Research on memory failure has the greatest applicability to adult development and aging. It is an area in which the instructor can counter myths about aging, such as the belief that young and middle-age people have about memory slips being a sign of Alzheimer's disease. Memory failure is a common occurrence throughout adulthood, and it is only in later adulthood that significant declines are observed. However, these declines are more likely to occur in some memory tasks such as working memory and are not likely to affect other areas such as semantic and procedural memory. Excellent examples can be drawn from Schacter's (2001) book, *The Seven Sins of Memory*.

Some texts already include crystallized-fluid theory and the Seattle Longitudinal Study findings (Schaie, 1996) in the chapter on intelligence; therefore, this is a natural topic to incorporate into lecture. In addition to presenting results on the effects of aging on intelligence, this study has also yielded fascinating data linking lifestyle and personality to intelligence test performance.

Wisdom and creativity in later life are additional topics that can be presented within this section of the course. The model of wisdom developed by Baltes and colleagues (Baltes, Staudinger, Maercker, & Smith, 1995) presents an intriguing view of intelligence in later life. Discussion of studies of creativity throughout adulthood conducted by Simonton (1999) help dispel the myth that older people are not capable of productive output.

Developmental Psychology

Developmental psychology provides the most clear-cut area for application of material on adult development and aging. Instructors can do a real service to their students by presenting the latest information on the field in this area, particularly as it is likely that the introductory textbook (as mentioned previously) is unlikely to present current theories and data.

As stated earlier, instructors who wish to incorporate aging into the introductory psychology course should give preference to textbooks that present material on development throughout the life span rather than just in childhood and adolescence. Emphasis should be given to principles of multidirectionality, multidimensionality, plasticity, and contextualism (Lerner, 1995). The typical introductory textbook presents development from a chronological rather than a process-oriented perspective. A case can be made for taking the chronological approach in an introductory-level course because this is intuitively easier for students to grasp than the more abstract process perspective. If this is the approach taken, then such information should be prefaced by making students aware of the notion of individual differences, both within and across people. Students should also be oriented to the role of sociocultural factors. Development at all ages reflects these processes, not just development in later adulthood, and by taking this approach, the instructor gives emphasis to the important notion of continuity of the individual across periods of the life span.

Finally, because aging is typically presented within the text in the development chapter, the instructor should be sensitive to the tendency of some texts to present stereotyped or unduly negative characterizations of aging. As antidotes to the text, the instructor should seek examples of people who do not fit society's norms and stereotypes of older adults. Multimedia material can be shown during class that highlights such examples, and some of these have already been suggested. Additionally, instructors can draw from segments shown on television magazine programs, which often make available videotapes that focus on unusual older adults. These segments, which can be shown within a certain time limit for educational purposes, often present a story on an older person who has accomplished a remarkable feat, such as climbing a mountain or winning a race. Along the same lines, many popular movies exist in which an older adult is presented as a character demonstrating wisdom, strength, humor, or other positive attributes that defy ageist stereotypes. Some examples of these characters include *Grumpy Old Men*, *Harold and Maude* (which also explores aging and sexuality), and the grandmother in *The Wedding Singer*.

Personality

Personality theories and research provide many potential intersections with aging. Erikson's theory specifically includes adult development and aging in the series of psychosocial issues proposed to occur over the life span (Erikson, 1963). Plentiful examples illustrate themes from Erikson's theory regarding later life. For example, the death scene of Caesar in the film *Gladiator* reflects the processes of generativity and ego integrity.

Within the trait theory tradition, the Five Factor Model (McCrae & Costa, 1990) not only has been examined in terms of aging, but also has received support from cross-sectional and longitudinal studies of personality based on the primary measure derived from the theory, the NEO–PI–R. Data obtained with this instrument are used to reinforce the claims of the theory that personality is stable in adulthood; in addition, cross-national studies have suggested that there is generality of the five factors outside the United States (McCrae et al., 1999). Thus, examining the data in which the Five Factor Model was applied to adults gives students a firmer grounding in the theory.

The teaching of psychodynamic theory in introductory psychology often includes a listing of defense mechanisms along with examples from everyday life. As with trait theory, research on adults that was based on measures of defense mechanisms helps underscore important aspects of the psychodynamic perspective. Older adults use more mature defense mechanisms than do younger adults (Diehl, Coyle, & Labouvie-Vief, 1996). Incorporating this finding into the lecture helps students think of personality in adulthood as changeable and provides an important contrast with the stability approach emphasized by trait theory.

Cognitive theories of personality can also be examined from the standpoint of aging. Studies of the self in adulthood have examined how individuals react to changes in their lives brought about by the aging process (Whitbourne & Collins, 1998). In keeping with the tradition of cognitive psychology, these studies emphasized that it is the interpretation of experiences rather than the experiences themselves that determine the impact on the individual's sense of self.

Motivation and Emotion

In many texts, the topics of motivation and emotion are presented in the same chapter. However, it is difficult to cover both topics in the same lecture, as a variety of theoretical perspectives within each require careful explanation. Traditional approaches to these topics have emphasized alternative theories such as the James–Lange versus Schachter–Singer theories of emotions and the instinct versus incentive theories of motivation.

Research on aging and emotions can provide students with a concrete example of current work in the field of emotions. For example, socioemotional selectivity theory proposes that older adults maximize the positive emotions they experience by spending the limited time they have in life with familiar people rather than strangers (Carstensen, 1992). This fascinating theory has applicability to undergraduates, as the principles of the theory apply equally to younger as to older adults. This theory is of interest because it emphasizes continuity over the life span in basic psychological processes and because it presents an antistereotypic view of older adults as capable of strong, positive emotions. Films depicting loving relationships between older individuals can capture this point; an excellent example is *On Golden Pond*.

A small but noteworthy point that can be made in the area of motivation is that Maslow's theory of self-actualization is more applicable to middle-age and older adults than it is to young adults. Maslow studied more than 3,000 individuals to identify those who were self-actualized, and no one younger than age 50 met the criteria specified by his theory.

Social Psychology

Within the field of social psychology, the topics of attitudes, social cognition, and discrimination in the form of ageism can all be examined from the standpoint of older adults. Older adults are a common target of stereotyped attitudes that mainly are negative (Hummert, Garstka, Shaner, & Strahm, 1994). With concerns over issues such as Social Security and Medicare having become so much a part of the political agenda, attitudes in these areas can be used just as readily as attitudes toward other topics commonly discussed in introductory texts (e.g., attitudes toward abortion).

The targeting of older adults can also be examined in advertisements that portray aging in a negative light. For example, many health advertisements on television depict older characters as having a variety of physical and mental ailments. With proper editing equipment, the instructor can construct a montage of these advertisements, which will illustrate this point effectively. Students can be asked about the impressions that these advertisements make on them about the physical and mental characteristics of older adults.

Characters in movies and television shows also tend to be depicted in a stereotyped manner, and these examples can be shown in class using videotaped examples. One particularly effective example of a negatively portrayed character is the grandmother in *National Lampoon's Christmas Vacation*, who arrives at the door for Christmas dinner with her cat wrapped up as a present. Conversely, the character of Martin Crane (from the television series *Frasier*) is an older adult portrayed in a more realistic light. His relationship with his sons also demonstrates in a favorable manner family relations between adult children and their parents.

Another approach in the area of social psychology is to demonstrate the problems of measuring attitudes by administering scales of attitudes toward older adults among the students in the class. Difficulties with measurement and the actual attitudes expressed by students can be a starting point for discussion of the substantive nature of attitudes toward aging and the technical aspects of measuring these attitudes.

The depiction of nursing homes and institutional life in the popular media is another way to open discussion about attitudes toward older adults. A brief segment in the film *Happy Gilmore* shows a sadistic nurse's aide threatening a new resident, a scene that captures many people's worst fears about what will happen to them in an institution.

Stress and Health Psychology

The topic of stress and coping has become a staple within introductory courses, often in the context of health psychology. Both areas have clear relevance to adult development and aging. The greater proneness of the person with a Type A personality to cardiovascular disease can be discussed as a phenomenon that applies largely to middle-age adults, particularly men. Similarly, the topic of stressful life events applies primarily to individuals in middle age and later who are at greater risk for negative health consequences from experiences such as divorce or death of spouse; loss of job; and the daily hassles of managing roles in home, family, and the community. Although many texts apply these concepts to college students, they were initially developed on adult samples (Folkman & Lazarus, 1980), and a case can be made that these populations are at greater risk for stress-related diseases than are college students.

The field of health psychology has broad applicability to many age groups, ranging from children to older adults. The processes involved in teaching compliance to medical patients can just as readily be discussed using middle-age people who have heart disease as it can with children who have diabetes. Students can gain the most from this topic by selecting a wide range of examples to illustrate how psychologists work with medical health professionals to ensure that patients are able to benefit optimally from medical interventions.

Sexuality and Gender

Although aging is often equated with lack of interest in sexuality, it has long been known that older adults are interested in and able to maintain an active sex life. Nevertheless, a national survey of sexual dysfunction in the United States conducted in the late 1990s indicated that a large percentage of adults experience inhibited sexual responsiveness (Laumann, Paik, & Rosen, 1999). Discussions in this area can include how the expression of sexuality varies throughout the adult years and defining the nature of psychological interventions that can help treat sexual dysfunction.

Abnormal Psychology

Incorporation of material on adult development and aging into the abnormal psychology unit of the course provides an important dimension to a topic, which by its very nature involves an understanding of individual change over time. Just as the topic of childhood disorders is rising to prominence in abnormal psychology, so is a focus on how disorders develop throughout the middle and later adult years (Whitbourne, 2000). The incidence of disorders varies across the adult years and, contrary to myths about aging and mental health, there are lower rates of anxiety and mood disorders. However, depression does occur in later life, and it should be differentiated from normal aging, as it is a treatable disorder.

Diagnosis and treatment also should be examined from the standpoint of the age of the individual. Fascinating issues emerge in examining the dynamics of the therapeutic relationship between a younger therapist and an older adult client. The issue of transference, often discussed in the context of psychoanalytic psychotherapy, therefore takes on a very different form than when the therapist is older than the client. The film *Analyze This* portrays such a relationship in an amusing, if not realistic, manner. Other forms of treatment, such as psychotherapeutic drugs, also require that the clinician take into account the age of the individual.

SUMMARY

Clearly, instructors teaching this course face many choices and demands to cover interesting topics within a limited time frame. However, by including at least some material on the topic of adult development and aging, both the course and the students will benefit from the enriched perspective that such material provides.

REFERENCES

APA Commission on Ethnic Minority Membership, Recruitment, Retention, and Training–2. (in press). *Guidelines for introductory psychology texts for incorporating diversity*. Washington, DC: Author.

Baltes, P. B., Staudinger, U. M., Maercker, A., & Smith, J. (1995). People nominated as wise: A comparative study of wisdom-related knowledge. *Psychology and Aging, 10*, 155–166.

Brookmeyer, R., & Kawas, C. (1998). Projections of Alzheimer's disease in the

United States and the public health impact of delaying disease onset. *American Journal of Public Health, 88,* 1337–1342.

Carstensen, L. L. (1992). Social and emotional patterns in adulthood: Support for socioemotional selectivity theory. *Psychology and Aging, 7,* 331–338.

Diehl, M., Coyle, N., & Labouvie-Vief, G. (1996). Age and sex differences in coping and defense across the life span. *Psychology and Aging, 11,* 127–139.

Erikson, E. H. (1963). *Childhood and society* (2nd ed.). New York: Norton.

Folkman, S., & Lazarus, R. S. (1980). An analysis of coping in a middle-aged community sample. *Journal of Health and Social Behavior, 21,* 219–239.

Horne, J., & Östberg, O. (1976). A self-assessment questionnaire to determine morningness–eveningness in human circadian rhythms. *International Journal of Chronobiology, 4,* 97–110.

Hummert, M. L., Garstka, T. A., Shaner, J. L., & Strahm, S. (1994). Stereotypes of the elderly held by young, middle-aged, and elderly adults. *Journal of Gerontology: Psychological Sciences, 49,* 240–249.

Laumann, E. O., Paik, A., & Rosen, R. C. (1999). Sexual dysfunction in the United States: Prevalence and predictors. *Journal of the American Medical Association, 281,* 537–544.

Lerner, R. M. (1995). Developing individuals within changing contexts: Implications of developmental contextualism for human development, research, policy, and programs. In T. J. Kindermann & J. Valsiner (Eds.), *Development of person–context relations* (pp. 13–37). Hillsdale, NJ: Erlbaum.

Levinson, D. J., Darrow, C. N., Klein, E. B., Levinson, M. H., & McKee, B. (1978). *The seasons of a man's life.* New York: Alfred A. Knopf.

Li, K. Z. H., Hasher, L., Jonas, D., Rahhal, T. A., & May, C. P. (1998). Distractibility, circadian arousal, and aging: A boundary condition? *Psychology and Aging, 13,* 574–583.

McCrae, R. R., & Costa, P. T., Jr. (1990). *Personality in adulthood.* New York: Guilford Press.

McCrae, R. R., Costa, P. T., Jr., de Lima, M. P., Simoes, A., Ostendorf, F., Angleitner, A., et al. (1999). Age differences in personality across the adult life span: Parallels in five cultures. *Developmental Psychology, 35,* 466–477.

Schacter, D. (2001). *The seven sins of memory.* Boston: Houghton-Mifflin.

Schaie, K. W. (1996). Intellectual development in adulthood. In J. E. Birren, K. W. Schaie, R. P. Abeles, M. Gatz, & T. A. Salthouse (Eds.), *Handbook of the psychology of aging* (4th ed., pp. 266–286). San Diego, CA: Academic Press.

Simonton, D. K. (1999). Talent and its development: An emergenic and epigenetic model. *Psychological Review, 106,* 435–457.

U.S. Bureau of the Census. (2002). Projections of the total resident population by 5-year age groups. Retrieved May 13, 2002, from http://www.uscensus.gov/population/projections/nation/summary/hp-t3-e.txt

U.S. General Accounting Office. (1998). *Alzheimer's disease: Estimates of prevalence in the United States* (GAO/HEHS-98-16). Washington, DC: Author.

Whitbourne, S. K. (Ed.). (2000). *Psychopathology in later adulthood*. New York: Wiley.

Whitbourne, S. K. (2001). *Adult development and aging: Biopsychosocial perspectives*. New York: Wiley.

Whitbourne, S. K. (2003). *The aging individual: Physical and psychological perspectives* (2nd. ed.). New York: Springer.

Whitbourne, S. K., & Collins, K. C. (1998). Identity and physical changes in later adulthood: Theoretical and clinical implications. *Psychotherapy, 35*, 519–530.

Whitbourne, S. K., & Hulicka, I. M. (1990). Ageism in undergraduate psychology texts. *American Psychologist, 45*, 1127–1136.

ANNOTATED BIBLIOGRAPHY

Baltes, P. B., Staudinger, U. M., & Lindenberger, U. (1999). Lifespan psychology: Theory and application to intellectual functioning. *Annual Review of Psychology, 50*, 471–507. An excellent summary of the work of Paul Baltes and a contemporary orientation to the field.

Birren, J. E., & Schaie, K. W. (Eds.). (1996). *Handbook of the psychology of aging*. San Diego, CA: Academic Press. A collection of broadly integrative articles by leading researchers in the psychology of aging.

Carstensen, L. L., Isaacowitz, D. M., & Charles, S. T. (1999). Taking time seriously: A theory of socioemotional selectivity. *American Psychologist, 54*, 165–181. Comprehensive summary of current approaches to aging and emotions. Provides a thoughtful discussion of the topic, along with examples of innovative research strategies.

Erikson, E. H., Erikson, J. M., & Kivnick, H. Q. (1986). *Vital involvement in old age*. New York: W.W. Norton. Erikson's last work summarized in this fascinating qualitative study of older adults.

Laumann, E. O., Paik, A., & Rosen, R. C. (1999). Sexual dysfunction in the United States: Prevalence and predictors. *Journal of the American Medical Association, 281*, 537–54. National survey of sexual dysfunction providing information on the extent of sexual difficulties in U.S. adults, along with discussion of correlates and possible causes.

Lerner, R. M. (1995). Developing individuals within changing contexts: Implications of developmental contextualism for human development, research, policy, and programs. In T. J. Kindermann & J. Valsiner (Eds.), *Development of person–context relations* (pp. 13–37). Hillsdale, NJ: Erlbaum. An excellent summary of the emerging field of developmental science that clearly explains principles of contemporary views on the life span.

Simonton, D. K. (1998). Career paths and creative lives: A theoretical perspective on late-life potential. In C. Adams-Price (Ed.), *Creativity and successful aging: Theoretical and empirical approaches* (pp. 3–18). New York: Springer. Summary of the work on creativity across the adult years by the major figure in the field.

U.S. General Accounting Office. (1998). *Alzheimer's disease: Estimates of prevalence in the United States* (GAO/HEHS-98-16). Washington, DC: Author. A somewhat controversial report on the incidence of Alzheimer's disease in the United States; is free.

Ware, M. E., & Johnson, D. E. (Eds.). (2000). *Handbook of demonstrations and activities in the teaching of psychology* (2nd ed.). Mahwah, NJ: Erlbaum. Prepared by members of Division 2 of the American Psychological Association; a guide to activities that can be used in psychology courses. Includes several chapters on developmental psychology, presenting ideas for active learning in the area of adulthood and aging that can be incorporated into introductory psychology courses.

Whitbourne, S. K. (Ed.). (2000). *Psychopathology in later adulthood*. New York: Wiley. An edited volume containing current information on the epidemiology, theories, and treatment of psychological disorders in later adulthood.

Whitbourne, S. K. (2001). *Adult development and aging: Biopsychosocial perspectives*. New York: Wiley. Current reviews of the literature in the areas of brain and behavior, sensation and perception, cognition, personality, social, and abnormal psychology.

Whitbourne, S. K. (2003). *The aging individual: Physical and psychological perspectives* (2nd. ed.). New York: Springer. Comprehensive review of physiological changes associated with the aging process. Detailed information on health, sensation and perception, and the normal aging of major organ systems.

3

NEUROPSYCHOLOGY: INTRODUCING AGING INTO THE STUDY OF BRAIN AND BEHAVIOR

ANTONIO E. PUENTE

Until relatively recently, when the topic of underlying biological sub-strates was discussed in undergraduate and graduate classes of psychology, the course title was either "Physiological Psychology" or "Biological Psychology." With the growth of neuroscience and the application of clinical psychological principles to the assessment and rehabilitation of neurological disorders, neuropsychology has emerged as both the new title for these types of courses and a reconfiguration of the topics discussed. Whereas books such as Kalat's *Biological Psychology* continue to enjoy widespread appeal and acclaim, newer books (e.g., Zillmer & Spiers, 2001) have begun either to replace or change the curricular landscape relative to biological substrates of behavior. As a consequence and together with my own expertise, this chapter focuses on the inclusion of aging issues in neuropsychology.

Please direct correspondence to Antonio E. Puente, Department of Psychology, University of North Carolina at Wilmington, Wilmington, NC 28403; e-mail: puente@uncwil.edu.

Rather than simply provide a personal perspective on the topic, the initial starting point for this chapter was to examine the existing literature on how aging was introduced into courses involving biological substrates of behavior. To do this:

1. A review of the Advanced Placement (AP) psychology course, which is based on an introductory course at a university, was completed.
2. A review of the recently accepted guidelines for the teaching of introductory psychology by the American Psychological Association (APA) was done.
3. A review of the syllabi posted on the Web site of APA's Division 2, the Society for the Teaching of Psychology, was completed.
4. A review of the most recently published book on undergraduate teaching activities (Ware & Johnson, 1996) was accomplished.

LIFE SPAN DEVELOPMENT VS. BRAIN AND BEHAVIOR

The information on the AP course reflected the typical content of a 1-year "Introduction to Psychology" course. Although both life span and biological issues were covered, they were done so separately. For all practical purposes, the newly accepted guidelines for the teaching of "Introduction to Psychology" mirror those of the APA. For example, under the section entitled "Life Span Development," the closest the student would come to underlying neural substrates would be in the illustration of physical and cognitive changes (although those changes are not specified). The focus is clearly on social and behavioral changes. In contrast, under the section entitled "Biological Bases of Behavior," the closest a student would come to discussing developmental issues is presumably in the related discussion of evolution. In the Division 2 database of articles published in the *Teaching of Psychology* between 1974 and 1999, 15 articles were published under "aging" and 32 articles under "psychological." However, again the overlap between developmental issues in general and aging issues in particular with physiological ones were not present. Finally, the same could be said of the Ware and Johnson (1996) book *Handbook of Demonstrations and Activities in Teaching of Psychology*.

In all cases, one point was clearly evident. Aging was almost always introduced in life span development courses or sections of courses. In contrast, aging issues were rarely introduced in sections or courses involving brain and behavior. When aging was introduced into life span courses or sections, the focus was usually on social and emotional issues. More recently, the focus has included or shifted to cognitive issues. However, it is rare for these cognitive issues to be grounded in neural and biological substrates.

The review of information about biologically based courses reflects a paucity of information involving aging. In fact, developmental issues are ignored as a rule. It is as if the organism that is being studied is an adult with no past or future.

As an alternative to this situation, two possibilities exist. In courses involving sections on developmental and biological issues, both could be covered in sequential fashion. Alternatively, an amalgamation of both issues might be in order. In other words, when developmental issues are being covered, they could either include or be grounded in biological or neural substrates. Another possibility would be to flavor an entire course from the other perspective. For example, a neuropsychology course, and not necessarily a developmental neuropsychology course, could be developmentally based.

NEUROPSYCHOLOGY COURSE

Overview

Several assumptions are made in outlining the course. First, the course is not truly a classical developmental course in that it focuses on the adult. Indeed, most neuropsychology courses do not even interface with developmental concepts. When developmental principles have been applied, the assumption is that three distinct and relatively stable developmental periods—child, adult, and aging—exist. Furthermore, although clear developmental changes through the adult cycle are evident, the course assumes that there is relative stability of both psychological and biological phenomena between the 20s and the 50s. Moreover, the most significant developmental changes pertinent to neuropsychologists have traditionally been those that occur in later years. Specifically, the changes during the early and middle adult years are less significant, although still present, than in later years. Thus, developmental perspectives in this and most neuropsychological courses, reflect a comparison between the relatively stable adult and the slowly changing aging years.

The ideas of Benton (Benton & Sivan, 1984) and Costa (1996) outlining the concept of life span neuropsychology and the interface of developmental and neuropsychological perspectives form the foundation for the orientation of a significant portion of such a course. Historically, neuropsychologists were not interested in developmental concepts. Benton and Costa indicated that neuropsychological functioning did not occur in a vacuum and that the organism went through significant developmental changes that affected and were related to neuropsychological processes. Thus, the course reflects the concept that, although some developmental stability occurs for prolonged periods, especially during the adult years, significant changes are present, especially very early and very late in the life span of the person. Additionally, for reasons that are not well-explained in the scientific and professional literatures, early developmental changes and their interface with neuropsychological performance have been of greater interest to school psychologists. However, later developmental changes, especially those in aging, have been more the purview of clinical neuropsychologists.

Objectives

The main objective is to introduce the student to the relationship between psychological activity and neural substrates. Psychological activity primarily focuses on cognitive issues but also addresses emotional and social concerns, although they are less frequently measured in neuropsychology. Biological substrates are almost exclusively neural in scope, and specifically, brain focused. In addition, emphasis is on human rather than animal studies and models. Also, whenever possible, clinical rather than experimental concerns are raised. Thus, this is not a clinical neuroscience or an experimental neuropsychology course; instead, this course could be titled "(Clinical) Neuropsychology."

Another important objective is for the student to understand that the brain (and for that matter, the person) does not live in a vacuum. Thus, specific emphasis is placed on the neural substrates of behavior within a biopsychosocial context (Puente & McCaffrey, 1992). Of particular importance are such factors as medical status, gender, education, and age. Considering the typical clinical activities of the neuropsychologists and the personal experiences with family members of the students, a focus on aging issues is included.

Topics

The course is divided into two main sections: introductory and specific topics. The introductory section involves an introduction to a variety of topics, including educational and theoretical issues. In this section, attention is focused on models of brain functioning, clinical versus actuarial assessment, and historical and biopsychosocial contexts. Throughout, the dichotomy of adult versus aged is provided. The basic portion of the course involves the interviewing, testing, interpretation, diagnosing, and rehabilitation of brain-injured individuals. In the next section, general concerns about the interface between normal and abnormal aging and neuropsychology are addressed.

GENERAL CONCERNS OF AGING
AS APPLIED TO NEUROPSYCHOLOGY

Underlying Neural Substrates

Of utmost importance is the understanding of the biological and physiological changes occurring in the brain of the developing person. Specific focus is placed on understanding the changes between adulthood and aging, both normal and abnormal (Albert & Killiany, 2001). Also, as previously indicated, although these two epochs in a person's life are considered for the purpose of providing generalizations relatively stable, the concept of an evolving neural system is explained. Underlying cellular changes are described, but the primary interest is on macrocellular changes. Thus, attention to specific neural loss and the resulting impact of neurocognitive function would be appropriate. For example, recent evidence (Scheff, Price, & Sparks, 2001) has suggested that synaptic decline occurs in some but not all cortical regions of elderly people's brains. Furthermore, it appears that synaptic decline is seen primarily in individuals with disease process. Thus, when neural substrates are considered, specific attention must be placed on whether one is considering abnormal or normal aging. Attention must also be paid to the concept of neurogenesis across the life span. Related findings (Scharff, 2000) indicate that neuronal production and differentiation continues to occur, although on a smaller scale in most nonhuman animals, through adulthood and aging. Thus, neurogenesis may not be a preadult phenomenon as previously thought.

Of particular importance is the concept of shrinkage of brain volume (combined with the expansion of ventricle volume) and the changes occurring in normal and diseased cerebrovascular function. Indeed, an error typically noted in clinical diagnostic work is the overdiagnosing of shrinkage of brain volume and the indirect assumption of the existence of neuronal tangles. Specific attention is provided to neurofibrillary tangles and senile plaques and their occurrence in the normal aging process. The loss of neurons in the frontal lobes, probably due to tangles and plaques, may be as much as 20% (Greenwood, 2000). At the same time, the majority of the older population does not exhibit appreciable neuronal atrophy. In contrast, there is a reduction of the importance of blood flow and supply to the brain, especially the cerebral cortex (and primarily the frontal and temporal lobes). Recent evidence has suggested that if plaque build-up occurs in any area of the cardiovascular system, there is strong likelihood of the same occurring within the cerebrovascular structures. Finally, it should be noted that the strong possibility exists that in most aging individuals, a decrease in brain volume (or increase in atrophy) and an increase in transient ischemic attacks (TIAs) resulting from cerebrovascular complications are likely to occur simultaneously.

Hence, underlying neural substrates pose a unique challenge for the instructor in that there seems to be an interaction of neurogenesis and disease (over normal aging), along with developmental changes seen in aging.

Cognitive Aging

The question of how aging occurs neurocognitively is a deceptively difficult one in that people do not age in similar manners. Although the aging process is most often categorized by biological or chronological age, aging could be characterized by a cognitive dimension (Park & Schwarz, 2000). Instead of considering a person as having a chronological age (e.g., 70), an alternative would be to consider the individual as having a cognitive quotient that could be understood as the ratio of cognitive abilities over chronological age. Cognitive abilities would be based on t or z scores or percentiles that would be derived from normative tables obtained from the performance of specific cognitive tasks across a relatively wide band of developmental stages (maybe ranging from 18 to 90). Thus, instead of considering a person as having a biological or chronological age, an individual would be considered to have a cognitive age or quotient.

The question remains as to which cognitive abilities would be measured in arriving at a cognitive quotient (Salthouse, 2001). The two most important cortical functions would be those mediated by the frontal and temporal lobes, which, in turn, are most likely to be affected by the aging process anyway. Specifically, frontal functions would be translated into executive functions, which would include but not be limited to, planning, organization, and problem solving, probably combined with persistence, pace, and follow-through. Temporal functions would be almost exclusively learning and memory. It may be worthwhile to consider related cortical functions, including sensory and motor activities. In general, however, the focus would be to present the idea that instead of viewing a person as having an age, the idea would be to consider the possibility that aging is best understood as cognitive capacity. Therefore, to understand a person's age, one should understand his or her cognitive, not chronological, status.

Thus, if the individual had significantly preserved cognitive abilities relative to his or her biological age, then that person would be considered to be cognitively younger. The opposite would also be true. That is, if a person has lost significant cognitive capacity relative to his or her chronological peers, then that person would be considered to be cognitively older. If a person would be cognitively challenged, relatively speaking, then the possibility is that the frontal lobe is compromised. Greenwood (2000) and Kaszniak and Newman (2000) suggested that of all the lobes of the cerebral cortex, the frontal is most sensitive to the aging process. Thus, age-related or normal aging is most quickly affecting frontal rather than other lobe functioning, and thus, the deficits typically seen in older adults would mimic those seen in frontal lobe disorders.

In addition to the concept of cognitive ability (over chronological aging), the idea of cognitive reserve should also be considered. Satz (1993) argued that an individual with significant cognitive capacity before the aging or disease process sets in is more immune to either process. The issue of how to establish or increase such capacity is interesting of itself. The role of education as a prophylactic for the aging or dementing process should be considered. Timiras (1995) suggested that education both lengthens life expectancy and reduces disability and disease in old age. Specifically, he suggested that brain reserve capacity is built up during earlier years and affords the increased threshold to damage seen in both healthy and abnormal aging. In Ardila, Rosselli, and Puente's study (1994), norms for brain-damaged and non-brain-damaged older individuals with and without education were presented. Interestingly, two bell curves emerged when educated and noneducated individuals were compared. Indeed, the two curves (i.e., educated and noneducated) overlapped with brain-injured educated individuals, appearing quite similar to the noneducated and non-brain-injured individuals. Thus, it would appear that education might be a method to increase cognitive capacity or reserve, and therefore, the role of education as predicting and protecting cognitive capacity should be underscored.

In addition, recent evidence from neuropsychological and neuroimaging studies (Grady & Craik, 2000) has suggested that not all cognitive abilities are worse in older adults when compared with younger control individuals. Older adults displayed greater brain activation than their younger counterparts in some memory tasks. Grady and Craik also suggested that specific brain changes may be occurring as a coping mechanism for the effects of aging on cognition. The role of habit and overlearning of tasks as a deterrent to the aging process should be considered.

Although most neuropsychological and cognitive tests tend to favor the measurement of left hemisphere or language-based functions, the right hemisphere–mediated activities such as emotion also draw attention. If education increases cognitive capacity, what increases emotional capital? It would be worthwhile to consider the possibility that cognitive aging is but one part of the aging equation. Discussion at the end of the section on cognitive aging should consider the possibility that just as cognitive aging occurs, so does emotional aging.

Normal vs. Abnormal Aging

The assumption students have is that most people age with problems. Recent research (e.g., Reuter-Lorenz, 2000) has suggested that many adults age with neither significant cortical atrophy nor emotional and physical complications. As a consequence, differences between a normal trajectory for biological aging should be established before understanding the effects of the disease process. Furthermore, aging is sometimes viewed, at least neuropsychologically, as beginning at a cutoff point, typically age 65. Aging is an evolutionary process, whereas disease is a revolutionary one. In other words, normal aging proceeds in a fairly predictable trajectory from a biological perspective, with changes being relatively gradual and in some cases predictable. When a disease process or an injury (e.g., head injury) is introduced, that trajectory is altered, sometimes permanently, resulting in an unstable and less predictable trajectory. If it is a disease process, such as Alzheimer's disease, the trajectory is redefined but still somewhat predictable. Other disease processes such as TIAs are much less predictable and can, at best, be estimated indirectly by examination of other variables such as blood pressure. If an injury occurs, then the trajectory is haltingly altered with a modified S-curve recovery occurring. The question becomes, however, whether the return to preinjury baseline is ever achieved.

It then becomes imperative to establish some type of premorbid understanding of the aging process. In other words, a biopsychosocial history and context of the individual must be understood. If no premorbid trajectory is understood, the best one would be able to do is to use normative samples of diseased or injured cohorts to establish a statistically average estimate of expected trajectory.

Normal aging could also be defined as healthy aging. Tranel, Benton, and Olson (1997) found that health status of older individuals was predictive of cognitive impairments. Aging alone, without an active disease process, does not reduce cognitive or mental capacities. The dichotomy of normal versus abnormal (or diseased) aging might be insufficient in describing very healthy older adults. Thus, instead of presenting a dichotomy, the idea of a third type of aging, healthy or hyper-healthy aging, could be presented. For these individuals a significant component of their aging process includes important cognitive activities such as travel, reading groups, and other creative endeavors. Research on this type of aging is often summarized in *The Positive Aging Newsletter*, available at http://healthandage@newsboomerang.com.

Depression

Estimates suggest that as many as one fourth of individuals referred for neuropsychological evaluation purposes may have direct or indirect symptoms of depression (Holsinger et al., 2002). Although controversial in scope, most neuropsychologists believe that depression affects the measurement of cognitive processes. It would then be prudent to take emotional states into account in the understanding of the aging process.

However, there is a misunderstanding of what could be considered either indirect or direct depression. Depression can be caused by some external or internal situation (e.g., diagnosis of Alzheimer's disease). Whether the depression is long-standing or biologically based (as is often considered in the case of exogenous depression) is not important. Depression could be a direct result of underlying physiological changes, primarily in the right hemisphere, and could be manifested in two ways. First, symptoms that are measured in some scales (e.g., the Beck Depression Inventory; BDI) as apathy could be confounded by what actually is fatigue or lack of stamina. In other situations, a flattening or lack of appreciation of affective information or stimuli is directly caused by right hemisphere dysfunction. In both cases, the clinical presentation appears to be that of depression, but what is actually occurring are specific behavioral changes secondary to neuronal damage. Also as a rule, neuropsychologists are not in a good position to distinguish the two. The three most common tests used to measure these types of changes are Minnesota Multiphasic Inventory, Rorschach, and BDI (Camara, Nathan, & Puente, 2000), and none provide sufficiently detailed data to make the distinction between clinical depression and "depressive" symptoms secondary to neuronal dysfunction. Nevertheless, increasing evidence has shown that depression may not only complicate neuropsychological ability but may actually even predict it (Carmelli, Swan, LaRue, & Eslinger, 1997). Thus, depression may actually be measured incorrectly in that an increase in certain symptoms (e.g., fatigue) is often secondary to a disease process (e.g., multiple sclerosis) and not necessarily truly reflective of depression itself.

INCLUSION OF AGING IN A NEUROPSYCHOLOGY COURSE

Several different topics related to aging are typically included in a neuropsychology course. If the course is clinically focused, then a brief review of the major disorders is in order. Some neuropsychologists are categorizing dementias as being either cortical or subcortical or according to the type of disorder (e.g., anterograde vs. retrograde amnesia), so another approach might be more efficient. The most prudent approach for a course of this type is to provide an overview of the major dementias or disorders that, by definition, involve premature or rapid aging. In many respects, each disorder represents a unique version of how aging might occur if not affected by a disease or illness. In other words, these disorders represent the types of problems that will inevitably occur in the normal aging process.

Alzheimer's Disease

Impairment in cognitive capacity is becoming an increasingly difficult problem with the aging of the American population (Troster, 1998). Of these, progressive dementia or a rapid aging of the brain is clearly the most problematic and frequent. As described earlier, Alzheimer's dementia is secondary to an increase in neurofribillary tangles. Additionally, these tangles are not readily measurable on neuroradiological techniques such as computerized tomography and magnetic resonance imaging. Thus, early detection of Alzheimer's disease is often accomplished by neuropsychological assessment. In fact, there is growing evidence that certain patterns of performance occur in preclinical stages of the disorder. Metamemory appears to be intact in Alzheimer's disease, but a variety of related problems emerge and evolve. Of all the different problems noted in this disease process, the most notable is memory. The most profound difficulty involves the learning of new declarative memory, sometimes referred to as *anterograde amnesia*. For example, individuals have unusual difficulties in learning a short story or a list of 10 words, even when ensuring practice. In contrast, relatively well-stored information such as long term memory tends to remain intact (at least in the initial stages of the disease). Other problems are evident, including word finding and fluency, visual–spatial functioning, and complex problem solving. Less easily measured behaviors such as personality and mood are also affected and in some cases may be the most significant of the behavioral and neurocognitive changes. Finally, the progression of the disease is fairly predictable with faster changes occurring in the later stages.

Cerebrovascular Dementia

What is often diagnosed as Alzheimer's disease is, in reality, probably cerebrovascular dementia. Many of the same problems noted in Alzheimer's disease are seen with this type of dementia. However, there is a prevalence of language and memory problems. A defining characteristic is the progression of the disease and its underlying etiology. In this case, the disease can wax and wane, sometimes even during the course of a day. In some instances, the person appears quite lucid and focused. Additionally, the underlying etiology involves changes in cerebrovasculature rather than anatomic functioning. Peaks, especially extended, of blood pressure or hypertension, for example, are often associated with the development of transient neuropsychological dysfunction. However, the patient does return to a "normal" baseline. Instead, the waning of the significant dysfunction is followed by a change in the original baseline so that although a static state occurs, the resulting plateau is worse than the original baseline functioning. In other words, a return to a baseline never occurs; instead, a slow deterioration of cognitive abilities is marked with peaks and valleys of cognitive abilities.

Related Disease Processes

In addition to the preceding dementias, other disease processes are sometimes seen in older adults. These include Parkinson's, Huntington's, Pick's, and multiple sclerosis (MS). Discovered by James Parkinson 200 years ago, Parkinson's disease is a result of specific degeneration of the motor fibers within the brain. The reduction in dopamine neurotransmitters results in initial but subtle changes in fine motor functioning. As time progresses, the disease evolves into a complex array of dementia-type deficits. These deficits include intellectual and executive function (e.g., organization and planning) problems and what is sometimes referred to as an *inflexible personality*. Also discovered in the last century, Huntington's disease similarly produces unusual changes in motor functioning. Specifically, uncontrolled, spastic, and non-goal-directed motor movements occur. Pick's disease was discovered by a neurologist and psychiatrist who noted that certain patients lost significant cortical cells. This loss resulted in a slow and irreversible reduction in expressive communication.

In contrast to these dementias, MS typically begins in early adulthood, most often in White women, and progresses gradually. Depending on the type of disorders (e.g., relapsing, remitting, or progressive), the symptoms can wax and wane or progress relatively steadily, resulting in early death. MS expresses itself in a variety of ways including motor (fatigue, slowing), sensory (numbness, visual difficulties), and cognitive (memory and executive functions).

CLINICAL NEUROPSYCHOLOGICAL ASSESSMENT

The differentiation between normal and abnormal aging (e.g., resulting from a disease process) almost always involves a clinical neuropsychological evaluation. Furthermore, students often consider the clinical assessment section to be the most interesting and applicable portion of the course. Thus, the most valuable section of the course for the students is the assessment section. At the same time, they are expecting a "cookbook" approach to understanding how assessment is completed. A typical stereotype is that an evaluation consists of matching testing instruments to specific neurological syndromes. In reality, almost nothing of the sort exists. Indeed, almost no neuropsychological test was developed with one specific disorder in mind, and most neuropsychological test items measure a variety of behaviors simultaneously. Hence, it is imperative for the student to come to a realization that the task of an evaluation is most often to have a thorough understanding of the aging and disease process, along with an understanding of the limits of the test instruments themselves.

Instead of thinking of an evaluation of a conglomerate of tests as has historically been the case (e.g., Halstead–Reitan Neuropsychological Battery and Luria–Nebraska Neuropsychological Battery; Reitan & Wolfson, 1993; Golden, Purisch, & Hammeke, 1991), a more prudent approach to the assessment of aging is to consider different categories of behavior to be assessed. Although the major category has traditionally been memory and the most commonly used test for this has been the different editions of the Wechsler Memory Scale, other categories of behaviors should be measured too. Recently, Duke and Kaszniak (2000) proposed the major problems, which should be considered in understanding dementias as the executive control functions. Executive functions would include volition; planning and attention; purposive action/self-regulation, including productivity; cognitive flexibility; and shifting.

Next is the issue of differential diagnoses. Once the data are in, the clinician is faced with the difficult task of determining what type of disorder or syndrome exists. To assist this differential diagnosis, an understanding of the different disorders and syndromes should be obtained. Rosenstein (1998) published a small monograph outlining a summary of neurocognitive functioning among the dementias. For each of the major dementias, the following categories of problems are considered: memory, attention, visuo–spatial functions, language, executive functions, reasoning, sensory–motor functions, psychiatric symptoms, and demographics. Table 1 of the Rosenstein (1998) monograph is invaluable in this regard.

The presentation of a case study and a comprehensive neuropsychological evaluation would assist in the illustration of the complexity of a clinical neuropsychological evaluation. Toward that end, presentations by a practicing neuropsychologist would enhance the information presented in classroom discussions. In addition, presentation of the preceding materials, followed by a carefully orchestrated visit to an adult day care center, assisted living facility, or nursing home, would prove useful in illustrating the different disorders.

SUMMARY

The study of neuropsychology has been applied for the past 2 to 3 decades to clinical settings and more recently to other ones (e.g., legal and sports). Traditionally, the presentation of clinical neuropsychology has focused on the (static) assessment of brain function and dysfunction. However, over the past decade, increasing emphasis has been placed on understanding the numerous variables that affect neuropsychological measurement. This chapter focuses on the increasing importance of a developmental and biopsychosocial perspective in neuropsychology. Of particular importance is the role of aging in this process. This chapter summarizes such issues as the difference between normal and abnormal aging and the concept of cognitive aging. As the population ages and the importance of neuropsychology in understanding the aging population increases, aging and neuropsychology will interface more in the scientific, clinical, and pedagogical realms.

REFERENCES

Albert, M. S., & Killiany, R. J. (2001). Age-related cognitive change and brain-behavior relationships. In J. E. Birren, K. W. Schaie, & K. Warner (Eds.), *Handbook of the psychology of aging* (5th ed., pp. 161–185). San Diego, CA: Academic Press.

Ardila, A., Rosselli, M., & Puente, A. E. (1994). *Neuropsychological evaluation of the Spanish-speaker*. New York: Plenum.

Benton, A. L., & Sivan, A. B. (1984). Problems and conceptual issues in neuropsychological research in aging and dementia. *Journal of Clinical Neuropsychology, 6*, 57–63.

Camara, W. J., Nathan, J. S., & Puente, A. E. (2000). Professional psychological test usage. *Professional Psychology, 31*, 141–154.

Carmelli, D., Swan, G. E., LaRue, A., & Eslinger, P. J. (1997). Correlates of change in cognitive function in survivors from the Western Collaborative Study. *Neuroepidemiology, 16*, 285–295.

Costa, L. (1996). Lifespan neuropsychology. *Clinical Neuropsychologist, 10*, 365–374.

Duke, L. M., & Kaszniak, A. W. (2000, June). Executive control functions in degenerative dementias: A comparative review. *Neuropsychology Review, 10*, 75–99.

Golden, C., Purisch, A., & Hammeke, T. A. (1991). Luria-Nebraska Neuropsychological Battery. Los Angeles: Western Psychological Services.

Grady, C. L., & Craik, F. L. (2000). Changes in memory processing with age. *Current Opinions of Neurobiology, 10*, 224–231.

Greenwood, P. M. (2000). The frontal aging hypothesis evaluated. *Journal of the International Neuropsychological Society, 6*, 705–726.

Holsinger, T., Steffens, D. C., Phillips, C., Helms, M. J., Havlik, R. J., Breitner, J., et al. (2002). Head injury in early adulthood and lifetime risk of depression. *Archives of General Psychiatry, 59*(1), 17–22.

Kalat, J. W. (2001). *Biological psychology* (7th ed.). San Francisco: Wadsworth.

Kaszniak, A. W., & Newman, M. C. (2000). Toward a neuropsychology of cognitive aging. In S. H. Qualls & N. Abelese (Eds.), *Psychology and the aging revolution: How we adapt to longer life* (pp. 43–67). Washington, DC: American Psychological Association.

Park, D. C., & Schwarz, N. (2000). *Cognitive aging: A primer*. Philadelphia: Psychology Press/Taylor & Francis.

Puente, A. E., & McCaffrey, R. (1992). *Handbook of neuropsychological assessment: A biopsychosocial perspective*. New York: Plenum.

Reitan, R. M., & Wolfson, D. (1993). The Halstead-Reitan neuropsychological test battery. Tucson, AZ: Neuropsychology Press.

Reuter-Lorenz, P. A. (2000). Cognitive neuropsychology of the aging brain. In D. C. Park & N. Schwarz (Eds.), *Cognitive aging: A primer* (pp. 93–114). Philadelphia: Psychology Press.

Rosenstein, L. D. (1998). Differential diagnosis of the major progressive dementias and depression in middle and late adulthood: A summary of the literature of the early 1990s. *Neuropsychology Review, 8,* 109–168.

Salthouse, T. A. (2001). Structural models of the relations between age and measures of cognitive functioning. *Intelligence, 29*(2), 93–113.

Satz, P. (1993). Brain reserve capacity on symptom onset after brain injury: A formulation and review of evidence for threshold theory. *Neuropsychology, 13,* 273–295.

Scharff, C. (2000). Chasing fate and function of new neurons in adult brains. *Current Opinion of Neurobiology, 10,* 774–783.

Scheff, S. W., Price, D. A., & Sparks, D. L. (2001). Quantitative assessment of possible age-related change in synaptic numbers in the human frontal cortex. *Neurobiology of Aging, 22,* 355–365.

Timiras, P. S. (1995). Education, homeostasis, and longevity. *Experimental Gerontology, 30,* 189–198.

Tranel, D., Benton, A., & Olson, K. (1997). A 10-year longitudinal study of cognitive changes in elderly persons. *Developmental Neuropsychology, 13,* 87–96.

Troster, A. (1998). *Memory in neurodegenerative disease: Biological, cognitive, and clinical perspectives.* New York: Cambridge University Press.

Ware, M., & Johnson, D. E. (1996). *Handbook of demonstrations and activities in teaching of psychology.* Mahwah, NJ: Erlbaum.

Zillmer, E. A., & Spiers, M. V. (2001). *Principles of neuropsychology.* Belmont, CA: Wadsworth.

ANNOTATED BIBLIOGRAPHY

LaRue, A. (1992). *Aging and neuropsychological assessment.* New York: Plenum. Provides one of the first comprehensive (and authored) presentations on the topic of neuropsychological assessment of normal and abnormal aging.

Nussbaum, P. D. (1997). *Handbook of neuropsychology and aging.* New York: Plenum. A "reference source" for the understanding, assessment, and treatment of older adults.

Parks R. W., & Zec, R. F. (1993). *Neuropsychology of Alzheimer's disease and other dementias.* New York: Oxford University Press. Provides a somewhat outdated review of most of the dementias and their pathophysiology and assessment.

Poon, L. W. (1986). *Handbook of clinical memory assessment.* Washington, DC: American Psychological Association. An important initial publication on many of the topics discussed in this chapter.

Woodruff, D. S. (1997). *The neuropsychology of aging.* Malden, MA: Blackwell. Analyzes the impact of aging on brain function.

4

USING AND CONDUCTING AGING RESEARCH IN EXPERIMENTAL METHODS AND STATISTICS COURSES

RAYMOND J. SHAW

A variety of psychological theories of learning support the value of active participation in learning. Piagetian notions of learning by doing, levels-of-processing (Craik & Lockhart, 1972) and encoding-specificity notions (Tulving, 1983) that what one learns depends on how one learns it, and Rogoff's (1990) notion of guided participation all help psychologists understand that learning occurs best through activity on the part of the learner. This chapter starts from the active learning perspective of teaching the experimental methods or statistics course. The specific applications described for incorporating aging into such courses all involve active participation in learning by conducting research.

The author thanks Diane Aprile for comments on an earlier version of this chapter. This chapter is dedicated to the memory of Sandra K. Beck. Please direct correspondence to Raymond J. Shaw, Department of Psychology, Merrimack College, North Andover, MA 01845; e-mail: raymond.shaw@merrimack.edu.

The value of aging research in this context comes in several forms. First, there are several statistical and methodological concerns that are well-illustrated by considering aging research, including issues of sampling, representativeness, validity, reliability, and research design. Second, aging is inherently an interesting topic, as is evident in the other chapters in this volume. Learning about one's future holds a certain fascination, even for the most jaded undergraduate. Nontraditional students are perhaps even more interested because of their greater awareness of their own aging. Third, an excellent source of research participants for class projects is the family members of the students in the class, including grandparents or other older family members. Students enjoy having a reason to interact with their grandparents, and the grandparents enjoy the interest and attention of their grandchildren. Finally, anything that livens up a methods and statistics course is a good thing, and incorporating aging research works well in that regard.

The chapter is organized into two sections. First, four methodological and statistical issues that are well-illustrated by aging research are discussed. These issues are particularly appropriate for methods and statistics courses and are excellent illustrative material for lectures and discussion. They can also be of use in psychological testing or assessment courses and laboratory-based courses in experimental psychology. That section concludes with some illustrations of statistical methods using aging research. Then, a case study illustrating the use of aging research into teaching a methods course is presented, followed by some concluding remarks.

The material described in this chapter is relevant to courses that go by different names with various differences in content and organization (e.g., "Experimental Psychology," "Methods," "Statistics"). Therefore, although statistics and methods are taught in a variety of courses, the material in this chapter is relevant to the majority of them. Except where the distinction is important, the term *methods course* is used as the generic course name.

METHODOLOGICAL AND STATISTICAL ISSUES

Many psychology departments teach basic statistics and methods courses, even though the math department of the same institution may teach a course that is nearly identical. One rationale usually offered for that duplication is that psychology students learn statistics more easily if the examples used in the text and by the instructor are psychological ones. Because the various students in the course are going to be interested in or may resonate with different areas of psychology, it is useful to give examples from a variety of subfields in psychology. Several important statistical and methodological issues are well-described with examples from aging. Specifically, four issues that are central to a course on methods are discussed with aging as examples: (a) sampling and representativeness (external validity), (b) identifying what is measured (internal validity), (c) reliability, and (d) developmental or quasi-experimental designs.

Sampling and Representativeness

One of the basic messages to convey to students in a statistics or methods course is the careful work required to ensure that the results of research are valid and to be believed. An important type of validity is the ability of the researcher to generalize to the population from which she or he sampled, which is sometimes referred to as *external validity*. Aging researchers are particularly concerned with that element of external validity. When researchers want to learn about a particular characteristic of older adults, they will collect a sample of older adults that they believe is typical of older adults so that their research will be informative about older adults in general. As with all published research, articles describing an aging study always include a description of how the older adult sample was obtained. The most common source is "independently living, community-dwelling older adults." That source is most representative of older adults and thus most likely to lead to a representative sample (see Hertzog, 1996, and Salthouse, 2000, for excellent discussions of sampling issues in aging research).

There are two elements of that description that are valuable in a methods course. First, it provides a good example of how to get a representative sample. It can serve as a helpful supplement to more typical examples using undergraduate students as representative of young adults. Second, it is often a surprise to some students; many people believe that older adults are likely to be in nursing homes rather than living independently at home. Thus, it is more memorable as an example. However, it is also worth noting to students that for some studies, recruiting older adults from nursing homes, geriatric outpatient clinics, retirement communities, or fitness centers may be appropriate sampling for particular research questions. The variety of circumstances in which older adults are found make them an interesting source for a discussion of sampling.

Internal Validity Issues

There is another important layer to the sampling issue described previously that is particularly useful in a methods course. That is, whenever one does developmental research, there is an additional concern for the comparability of age group samples. When generalizing the results, the samples only validly generalize to their true parent populations. Thus, in making conclusions about the results of aging research, researchers need to know not only about the external validity for each sample but also about the internal validity issues involved in comparing two samples.

Internal validity refers to whether a variable measures what the researcher thinks it is measuring. In an aging study, the critical internal validity issue
is the true cause of the difference between research participants from two different age groups. Technically, because aging research is quasi-experimental
in design (discussed later in this chapter), the true cause cannot be ascer-
tained, but researchers need to be careful to minimize other possible explanations besides age group. When making a comparison between two age groups,
therefore, not only must each age group sample be representative of its population, but the two samples must also be as comparable to each other as are
the populations. That is, aging researchers must attempt to ensure that the
only difference between the young adult sample and the older adult sample is
their age. Otherwise, the explanation for any obtained difference cannot be
clearly attributed to age group. Although this is true for any developmental
research project, it is particularly important in aging research. The issue can
be phrased as the following question: What is the effect of age?

For example, a study of financial decision making comparing younger
and older adults may find differences between the two groups. A simple conclusion is that age is the cause of the difference. However, as Schaie (1988)
and Cavanaugh and Whitbourne (1999) have pointed out, there are three
classes of causes that may explain the effects. First, age may indeed be the
cause—through biological (e.g., changes in the brain), psychological, or sociocultural mechanisms (Birren & Cunningham, 1985). Second, cohort may
be the cause. Cohort is roughly equivalent to the generation to which one
belongs (see chapter 3 in Salthouse, 1991, for a thorough analysis of the cohort concept). The older adults in the financial decision-making study may
have experienced the Great Depression and may make decisions differently
as a result, compared with younger adults who have grown up in the recent
history of economic boom times. Third, what theorists call *time-of-measure-
ment* effects may be the cause; that is, the economic, sociocultural, political
context during the time when the data are collected may influence the outcome. Older adults are likely to have more investments than younger adults,
and the economic climate at the time of the study may make that difference
the cause of the difference in decision-making behavior. In other words, the
older adults may act more cautiously in an economic downturn but not differently from younger adults in an economic upturn.

A variety of developmental research designs exist that attempt to dis-
entangle these effects (see, e.g., Hertzog & Dixon, 1996). Fortunately for the
professor teaching research methods, the three effects are an excellent vehicle
for explaining the concept of confounding. For example, the behavior of 60-
year-olds is determined in part by the fact that they have aged 60 years and
that they are members of the cohort born 60 years ago. Their aging and cohort
are confounded. If a researcher conducts a longitudinal study and tests people
at age 40 and then 20 years later at age 60, the results are attributable to both
age and time of measurement, which are thus confounded. Again, although

this pattern is true in any developmental research, it is particularly dramatic in aging research. Students are likely to have a clearer understanding of cohort effects if they compare themselves with their grandparents than if the first-year students compare themselves with fourth-year students, for example.

Reliability

A reliable measure is one that measures the same variable each time it is used. Therefore, a reliable measure would measure the same variable regardless of the type of person being tested. For example, when younger and older adults are asked to respond to a set of verbal materials, researchers may be tempted to assume that the materials and the tasks mean the same to both age groups. However, if an experimenter asked younger and older adults to write down the first word that starts with *cel*, for example, she would find that the younger adults will be more likely to write *cellular* than the older adults will (Shaw, Thornton, & Iorio, 2000; see also Table 4.1). Because of different experiences with words throughout the life course, words have different meanings to younger and older adults and different degrees of familiarity. Given that meaning and familiarity are important variables in verbal memory performance, a memory test with words may not be equivalent for the two age groups and the task is not necessarily a reliable measure of memory for both groups. There are many examples of variables that lack age equivalence

TABLE 4.1
Completion Frequencies to the Word Stem *cel_____* for Older and Younger Adults (Shaw, Thornton, & Iorio, 2000) and Normative Word Frequency per Million (Kucera & Francis, 1967)

Completion	Old (N = 63)	Young (N = 63)	Frequency per million
celebrate	4	12	4
celebrity	1	3	3
celery	28	7	4
celestial	1	1	8
cell	5	15	65
cellar	8	6	26
cello	4	0	0
cellophane	2	0	1
cells	1	2	81
cellular	5	12	3
cellular phone	0	1	0
cellulite	1	0	0
cellulose	1	2	10
no or invalid response	2	2	N/A

Note. N/A = not available.

in measurement, from depression (e.g., Cavanaugh & Blanchard-Fields, 2002) to reaction time (e.g., Rogers, Hertzog, & Fisk, 2000). Salthouse (2000) provides a useful guideline on how to deal with such measurement equivalence issues that is more appropriate for advanced courses.

Quasi-Experimental Design

Another topic in methods courses is the concept of a "true experiment." In a true experiment, the levels of the experimenter-manipulated independent variable are randomly assigned to participants. Otherwise, the cause of the effect cannot be attributed necessarily to the independent variable. Age, of course, is not a variable that can be assigned randomly to people; the experimenter cannot assign one participant to be age 20 and another to be age 80. People are whatever age they are, and age is thus an observed variable rather than a manipulated one. Thus, aging research studies are quasi-experimental (Hertzog & Dixon, 1996; Schaie, 1988). As Schaie (1988) noted, the quasi-experimental nature of aging research means that "the issue of the validity of such studies looms large" (p. 242).

Aging researchers and theorists have explored these issues extensively. Although any developmental research design is quasi-experimental, it is perhaps more obvious in aging research because of all the potential alternative explanations that come from the large differences in life experience between younger and older adults from different historical periods. Thus, aging examples serve well for getting the point across to students. Many variables can be identified as ones that researchers treat as if they were experimental variables rather than observed ones (e.g., sex, age, the section in which a student is enrolled, class year), but age is an easy one to identify and is helpful for students. The consequence is that it illustrates issues of determining the cause of an effect; age cannot unambiguously be identified as a cause of differences in behavior (see chapter 2 in Salthouse, 1982, for a lucid description of this idea). This is a particularly important point for teaching students to be intelligent consumers of research. Quasi-experimental studies are often seductive about apparent causes.

Aging and Specific Statistical Procedures

In teaching various statistical techniques, aging provides rich opportunities for simple data collection and analysis. As mentioned at the outset, students can collect data from parents, grandparents, other relatives, roommates, and friends. Each student can collect data from a few people, and then all the data can be combined as one study for data analysis.

Typical topics in statistics courses include tests of differences (e.g., *t* tests, analysis of variance) and tests of association (e.g., correlation, regression, and chi-square). Aging research uses all of these techniques, of course, and the methodological issues raised earlier can be integrated with practical work with each technique.

Tests of differences are perhaps the easiest to generate and conceptualize, particularly for simple research questions. For example, t tests can be used to answer questions about age-related differences in a wide variety of psychological issues. Do age differences occur in memory? In problem solving? In attention? Reaction time? Students can generate (or the instructor can provide) simple tests of each of these abilities and administer them to relatives and friends as described previously. In the context of a more traditional lecture course, such examples can be added to other examples of tests of differences.

For the analysis of variance (ANOVA), collecting data on aging can provide a good context for discussing quasi-experimental designs. If there is an experimental manipulation (e.g., varying the rate of presentation for a memory experiment) along with aging, there can be a discussion of factorial ANOVA, with one true and one quasi-experimental factor. Aging research also often includes repeated-measures designs, and the literature can be mined for many examples.

Correlational research on aging can be a bit more complex, particularly for a beginning undergraduate course in statistics. There are basically two options for correlational research. In one case, students can collect data on several variables from younger and older adults (e.g., the various mental abilities mentioned previously) and can assess correlations among them separately for young and old adults. Alternatively, students can collect a continuous age sample, including participants of all ages across adulthood, and calculate correlations between age and a variable of interest.

For more advanced courses, relatively complex ANOVA models can be described with aging examples, and multiple regression models with age group as a bivariate indicator variable can be described and tested. Again, the research literature on aging is replete with studies using these methodologies.

Finally, a note of caution is in order: If students are to collect data from relatives and friends, the instructor should avoid assessing mental health variables. Students generally lack the expertise to interpret the data appropriately, the clinical skills to counsel family members, and the emotional strength to cope when tests suggest poor mental health functioning in such participants. However, such domains as depression and anxiety provide excellent research areas to discuss in more traditional (and removed) contexts as lecture courses.

A similar note of caution is in order for cognitive measures. Older adults are often quite concerned about their mental abilities and may question how well they performed on a cognitive task. Students should be instructed to tell their participants that the tests are not diagnostic of mental functioning and are intended to be difficult for everyone. If their relatives do poorly on a test, the students should know that there are multiple reasons for poor performance, including the general difficulty of the tests. Of course, if someone does particularly poorly, that participant should be encouraged to consult with a physician.

In generating research ideas for projects, two excellent types of sources are general undergraduate textbooks in aging (e.g., Cavanaugh & Blanchard-Fields, 2002; Schaie & Willis, 2002; Whitbourne, 2001) and any of the editions of the *Handbook of the Psychology of Aging* (e.g., Birren & Schaie, 2001). Other chapters in this volume can also provide research ideas.

IN-CLASS RESEARCH:
A CASE STUDY

Combining an active learning approach to statistics and methodology with aging research can be done relatively simply. One option, of course, is to have each student generate a research question, go and collect data, and so forth. This assignment can place a heavy burden on students and instructors, so a better approach is to have students work together to collect data.

A useful strategy is to have all students work together on the same research question, with each student collecting data from a small number of participants. The data are then combined and analyzed together (or in parallel) by the students to give them practice at statistical techniques. From the instructor's perspective, there is only a single research topic, which can simplify the work. Also, the project can be discussed in class, minimizing out-of-class office meetings with student teams and maximizing opportunities for teaching about research design and development. From the students' perspective, when the instructor provides the topic, the stress of generating a research idea is removed. Also, the instructor is generally enthusiastic about the project (because it is likely to be within his or her area of interest), and that raises student interest in the work as well. Additionally, student workload is reduced. They can work together on finding relevant research articles for their reviews, they have fewer participants to test, and the instructor is more knowledgeable about their work and thus a more supportive resource. It is also helpful to point out these benefits to the students in this era of the strong influence of student evaluations. Finally, with large classes in particular, the combined data can produce a large study (e.g., 60 students collecting data from only 2 younger adults and 2 older adults produce 240 participants).

This approach can be used to collect data appropriate for the entire range of analytical techniques taught in methods and statistics courses in practically any domain of psychological research of interest to the instructor. However, an alternative approach for incorporating aging research into methods courses is to use existing data, as in the following case study. The case illustrates several statistical techniques to address the same research question.

The project examined age differences in word stem completion. A total of 63 older and 63 younger adults had been given 150 word stems to complete with the first word that came to mind (Shaw et al., 2000). An example word stem is *cel_____*. The task is important in memory research, particularly in studies of implicit memory. Many studies have examined whether there are age differences in implicit memory (e.g., LaVoie & Light, 1994; Park & Shaw, 1992; see also Zacks, Hasher, and Li, 2000, for a review).

One problem with such studies is that older and younger adults may differ in the baseline completion rate for particular word stems. For example, older adults are much less likely than younger adults are to complete the stem *cel_____* with the word *cellular* (Shaw et al., 2000). Thus, if *cellular* were selected as a studied word in an implicit memory experiment, age differences in the likelihood of generating it would have the potential to bias the results on age differences in implicit memory.

The data were organized as follows. For each stem, all the different responses were tallied up; that is, for each response, the number of older adults and younger adults who wrote it were both listed. Table 4.1 shows an example. Students in the course were assigned two word stems each and were required to find the normative word frequency of each response, according to Kucera and Francis (1967), copies of which were on reserve in the library.

Students engaged in a series of analyses of the data as the course progressed. The same data were used throughout the semester, providing practical experience with a variety of statistical techniques. The first assignment was to calculate and report on the means and standard deviations for word frequency separately for each age group and word stem. (Note that the mean word frequency for older adults in Table 4.1 is 12.79; the mean for younger adults is 23.64.) Students also created and examined frequency distributions of word frequency. The second project was to conduct *t* tests comparing the age groups on mean word frequency. Here, then, they were asking the actual research question: Were there any age differences in word stem completion?

For the final project, students had several options. One option was a regression analysis, in which the regression model was to predict the frequency with which people would use a particular completion with word frequency as the predictor variable. Alternatively, students could use word length as a predictor; for a more advanced course, both variables could be used in a multiple regression analysis. At an even more advanced level, rather than conduct separate regression analyses for each age group, age could be used as an indicator variable to test directly whether there were age differences in the relations among word frequency, word length, and the word chosen for completing the stem.

A second option for the final project was to conduct a χ^2 analysis. Students were told to group the responses into low-, medium-, and high-frequency words. The result was a 2 (age group) × 3 (word frequency category) χ^2. That analysis provided another way to test whether there were age differences in the kinds of completions people use in the task.

Clearly, the data were appropriate for a variety of analysis techniques, at many levels of sophistication. In each case, students were learning different ways of asking the basic research question about age differences in stem completion. Along the way, they were learning about how older and younger adults differ in the way they think about and use words and also laid the groundwork for thinking about the possibility that experiments may not always measure what experimenters think they are measuring.

Making a series of projects work as in this case study depends on a set of data that can be analyzed in several ways. One value of such a project is that students do not have to understand a series of different studies, one for each type of data analysis they are learning. They can focus on the data analysis itself while learning about how different data analysis techniques can address the same overall question. A further value is that the instructor can also talk about the sorts of methodological issues described earlier in this chapter in the context of the projects on which the students are working.

OTHER RESOURCES FOR AGING AND METHODS COURSES

There are many supplemental materials that instructors can use for incorporating aging research into methods and statistics courses. On the active learning side, there are several Web sites that contain data involving aging that students can analyze. The U.S. Bureau of the Census (available at http://www.census.gov) and the Administration on Aging (available at http://www.aoa.dhhs.gov) are two organizations that maintain such databases. On the more traditional side, there are several films that can be used to illustrate research and methodological issues. The APA's Division 20 (Adult Development and Aging) maintains a Web site (http://aging.ufl.edu/apadiv20) with an extensive list. Only a few of them contain much useful material, but it is a good place to start.

IN CONCLUSION

An active learning approach to teaching a methods or statistics course in psychology enhances the experience for students and for the instructor. This chapter presented four fundamental methodological and statistical issues (external and internal validity, reliability, and quasi-experiments) that are well-illustrated by examples from aging research. Students find such

examples helpful and interesting. One approach to using the examples is straightforward: The instructor merely adds the material to lectures. Aging examples clarify the issues because of the dramatic differences between people at different points in the life span. Also, aging examples offer an excellent opportunity for critical thinking: Age differences seem simple at first glance, but the subtleties of the issues demand that students take a much closer look.

A more integrated approach to incorporating aging examples into methods courses was also illustrated in this chapter. A case study of using actual research data was presented. Students can analyze existing data to make the issues more immediate. An even more active learning approach was also described, in which students can go and collect the data themselves, gaining a firsthand understanding of the subtleties of research methods. From simply adding examples to existing lectures to having students experience the issues by collecting data, instructors can use aging to enhance the learning process in methods courses and to produce more sophisticated researchers and consumers of research.

REFERENCES

Birren, J. E., & Cunningham, W. R. (1985). Research on the psychology of aging: Principles, concepts, and theory. In J. E. Birren & K. W. Schaie (Eds.), *Handbook of the psychology of aging* (2nd ed., pp. 3–34). New York: Van Nostrand Reinhold.

Birren, J. E., & Schaie, K. W. (Eds.). (2001). *Handbook of the psychology of aging* (5th ed.). San Diego, CA: Academic Press.

Cavanaugh, J. C., & Blanchard-Fields, F. (2002). *Adult development and aging* (4th ed.). Belmont, CA: Wadsworth.

Cavanaugh, J. C., & Whitbourne, S. K. (1999). Research methods. In J. C. Cavanaugh & S. K. Whitbourne (Eds.), *Gerontology: An interdisciplinary perspective* (pp. 33–64). New York: Oxford University Press.

Craik, F. I. M., & Lockhart, R. S. (1972). Levels of processing: A framework for memory research. *Journal of Verbal Learning and Verbal Behavior, 11,* 671–684.

Hertzog, C. (1996). Research design in studies of aging and cognition. In J. E. Birren & K. W. Schaie (Eds.), *Handbook of the psychology of aging* (4th ed., pp. 24–37). San Diego, CA: Academic Press.

Hertzog, C., & Dixon, R. A. (1996). Methodological issues in research on cognition and aging. In F. Blanchard-Fields & T. M. Hess (Eds.), *Perspectives on cognitive change in adulthood and aging* (pp. 66–121). New York: McGraw-Hill.

Kucera, H., & Francis, W. N. (1967). *Computational analysis of present-day American English.* Providence, RI: Brown University Press.

LaVoie, D., & Light, L. L. (1994). Adult age differences in repetition priming: A meta-analysis. *Psychology and Aging, 9,* 539–555.

Park, D. C., & Shaw, R. J. (1992). Effect of environmental support on implicit and explicit memory in younger and older adults. *Psychology and Aging, 7*, 632–642.

Rogers, W. A., Hertzog, C., & Fisk, A. D. (2000). An individual differences analysis of ability and strategy influences: Age-related differences in associative learning. *Journal of Experimental Psychology: Learning, Memory, and Cognition, 26*, 359–394.

Rogoff, B. (1990). *Apprenticeship in thinking.* Cambridge, MA: Harvard University Press.

Salthouse, T. A. (1982). *Adult cognition: An experimental psychology of human aging.* New York: Springer-Verlag.

Salthouse, T. A. (1991). *Theoretical perspectives on cognitive aging.* Hillsdale, NJ: Erlbaum.

Salthouse, T. A. (2000). Methodological assumptions in cognitive aging research. In F. I. M. Craik & T. A. Salthouse (Eds.), *Handbook of aging and cognition* (2nd ed., pp. 467–498). Mahwah, NJ: Erlbaum.

Schaie, K. W. (1988). Internal validity threats in studies of adult cognitive development. In M. L. Howe & C. J. Brainerd (Eds.), *Cognitive development in adulthood* (pp. 241–272). New York: Springer-Verlag.

Schaie, K. W., & Willis, S. L. (2002). *Adult development and aging* (5th ed.). New York: Prentice Hall.

Shaw, R. J., Thornton, D. M., & Iorio, D. M. (2000, April). *Age differences in word-stem completion.* Poster presented at the 8th Cognitive Aging Conference, Atlanta, GA.

Tulving, E. (1983). *Elements of episodic memory.* Oxford, England: Clarendon Press.

Whitbourne, S. K. (2001). *Adult development and aging: Biopsychosocial perspectives.* New York: Wiley.

Zacks, R. T., Hasher, L., & Li, K. H. Z. (2000). Human memory. In F. I. M. Craik & T. A. Salthouse (Eds.), *Handbook of aging and cognition* (2nd ed., pp. 293–357). Mahwah, NJ: Erlbaum.

ANNOTATED BIBLIOGRAPHY

Birren, J. E., & Schaie, K.W. (Eds.). (2001). *Handbook of the psychology of aging* (5th ed.). San Diego, CA: Academic Press. Includes several excellent chapters on research methods. Each volume in the series includes at least one chapter on research methods. They are often quite tutorial in nature and are readily accessible to instructors of methods and statistics courses. The series also can be an excellent source of research ideas for class projects.

Cavanaugh, J. C., & Whitbourne, S. K. (1999). Research methods. In J. C. Cavanaugh & S. K. Whitbourne (Eds.), *Gerontology: An interdisciplinary perspective*

(pp. 33–64). New York: Oxford University Press. A graduate-level textbook on gerontology and a thorough tutorial review of research designs and methods in developmental research. Designed for beginning-level graduate student audiences and therefore an easy read for instructors of methods and statistics classes.

Hertzog, C., & Dixon, R. A. (1996). Methodological issues in research on cognition and aging. In F. Blanchard-Fields & T. M. Hess (Eds.), *Perspectives on cognitive change in adulthood and aging* (pp. 66–121). New York: McGraw-Hill. A very thorough textbook on aging and cognition aimed at advanced undergraduates and beginning graduate students. Along with a detailed treatment of methodological issues and research designs, the chapter provides a conceptual basis for the methods.

Salthouse, T. A. (2000). Methodological assumptions in cognitive aging research. In F. I. M. Craik & T. A. Salthouse (Eds.), *Handbook of aging and cognition* (2nd ed., pp. 467–498). Mahwah, NJ: Erlbaum. This chapter is fairly high level but thorough. Salthouse is an exceptionally clear writer and has written extensively on research methods. Any of his works on methods are worth reading. Ideal for instructors but too intense for undergraduates.

Schwarz, N., Park, D., Knäuper, B., & Sudman, S. (Eds.). (1999). *Cognition, aging, and self-reports*. Philadelphia: Psychology Press. Chapters work at two goals: First, they describe age-related changes in cognition, and second, they discuss the implications for survey and self-report research on aging in general. That is, the chapters are quite tutorial about age-related changes in cognition and discuss possibilities for further research. At the same time, they consider the consequences of those changes for conducting research on aging, particularly survey research. Thus, the substantive material can provide some ideas for research projects in class, and the survey material is helpful for working with research projects. Issues of age equivalence of measures are highlighted. Park and Schwarz (2000) published an updated version of the substantive material, with additional chapters as *Cognitive Aging: A Primer*.

5

INTEGRATING HUMAN AGING INTO THE UNDERGRADUATE SENSATION AND PERCEPTION COURSE

FRANK SCHIEBER

The undergraduate course in sensation and perception offers many opportunities to incorporate major findings from the field of gerontology. Most of these opportunities revolve around the links between structure and function that play such a critical role in the pedagogy of both disciplines. As such, this chapter is organized around this central theme. For each of the five sense modalities, the major age-related structural changes are briefly summarized. A synopsis of the significant age-related changes in functional capacity that result from these structural developments is then offered to the readers to use as they may choose in their own class curricula.

In addition to structure–function relationships, other important themes from gerontology can be woven into the undergraduate sensation and perception class with relative ease. These include but are not limited to (a) pathways to successful aging, (b) mechanisms of compensation for

Please direct correspondence to Frank Schieber, Department of Psychology, University of South Dakota, Vermillion, SD 57069; e-mail: schieber@usd.edu diminished functional capacity, (c) consideration of the attentional or cognitive "costs" of such compensation for low-level sensory deficits, and (d) opportunities for intervention at the level of the individual or environmental design. Web-based demonstrations and several pages of integrative exercises are included to provide guidance in the selection of activities that may help incorporate these themes into the typical undergraduate course experience.

VISION

Age-Related Structural Changes in the Eye

Lens

Beginning in early childhood, the ability of the lens to increase its refractive power through the process of accommodation declines linearly with advancing age. By the mid-40s, the accommodative power of the lens has become so weak that most people begin to experience difficulty reading text at typical working distances (e.g., shorter than arm's length). This age-related loss in near vision is commonly referred to as *presbyopia* (from the Greek for old and sight). Fortunately, the lost refractive power of the senescent lens can be replaced through the use of bifocal adjustments to existing eyeglasses or through the use of inexpensive reading glasses.

A more serious age-related change in the lens involves its progressive loss of clarity, which is often accompanied by a distinctive yellowing and the accumulation of opacities that contribute to significant increases in intraocular light scattering. In many older individuals, the opacity of the lens becomes so severe that visual acuity declines significantly; this is a clinical condition known as *cataract*. The incidence of cataract is so high among the growing senior population that surgery to remove cataracts and to replace them with fixed-focus intraocular lens implants has become the fourth most commonly performed operation in the United States today (Desai, Pratt, Lentzne, & Robinson, 2001). Despite popular misconceptions to the contrary, outpatient cataract surgery does not involve the use of lasers.

Pupil

The pupil is an aperture formed by the muscles of the iris. By changing its diameter (2–8 mm), it can regulate the amount of light reaching the retina over a 16:1 range (Lowenfeld, 1979). When observed under dim to moderate lighting conditions, the typical older person will present with pupils that are significantly reduced in their diameter. This systematic age-related reduction in the diameter of the pupil is known as *senile miosis*. Because of this decrease in the diameter of the pupil (together with the lenticular opacification discussed previously), it has been estimated that the retina of the typical 60-year-old receives only one third of the light falling on a 20-year-old counterpart. Hence, visual disability among older adults tends to be exacerbated at low to moderate illumination levels.

Retina

Classical studies of the retina reported significant losses in the number of photoreceptors (rods and cones) and retinal ganglion cells and optic nerve fibers. However, a wave of more recently published studies challenges this view. The more modern findings suggest that the number of cones in the fovea is invariant with advancing adult age. Yet, there appears to be a significant loss (30%) of rods in the central and midperipheral areas of the retina (Curcio, Millican, Allen, & Kalina, 1993). The implications of these findings has yet to be well-understood.

Visual Cortex

Classic studies have reported significant age-related declines in the number of cells in the primary (striate) visual cortex. Reductions as large as 25% have been reported as early as age 60 (Devaney & Johnson, 1980). The assumption of significant brain cell loss with advancing age has had a profound influence on theory building and the direction of research in gerontology. More modern studies, however, again appear to be challenging this view. For example, a recent influential review of literature such as Spear (1993) concluded that "the available results suggest that there are no massive losses of striate neurons" (p. 2600) in the brains of older adults.

Age-Related Changes in Visual Function

Absolute Threshold

Given the reduction in the amount of light reaching the older retina as a result of changes in the lens and pupil, it should be no surprise that the minimum amount of energy needed to detect the presence of a small light stimulus increases systematically with age. Between ages 60 and 90 years, dark adapted observers demonstrate an elevation in the absolute threshold for light that proceeds at a rate of approximately 25% per decade of the life span. Fortunately for older adults, very few tasks of daily life are determined by absolute sensitivity for light.

Acuity

The ability to resolve high-contrast spatial detail (at a distance of 20 feet or farther) begins to decline as early as age 30, and the rate of loss accelerates thereafter (see Schieber, 1992). However, much of this age-related decline in visual acuity can be recovered when individuals are fitted with their best ophthalmic correction (i.e., a freshly prescribed pair of eyeglasses or contact lenses). Remarkable changes in "corrected" visual acuity are not typically observed until after age 65. In fact, approximately 92% of those between ages 65 and 75 can achieve acuity levels of 20/25 (1.25 minarc) or better when refracted to their best level of performance. Similarly, fully 69% of those between ages 75 and 85 can be refracted to this same high level of acuity. Yet because of common age-related pathologies (e.g., glaucoma and macular degeneration), many older adults cannot achieve an acuity level of 20/40 (2 minarc); the most common minimum acuity standard for obtaining an unrestricted driver's license in the United States. Approximately 13% of those ages 75 to 85 demonstrate best corrected visual acuity of 20/40 or worse. Even the best available eyeglasses cannot compensate for pathological deterioration of the retina and related neural structures. Age deficits in visual acuity in both healthy and pathological eyes are exacerbated under low contrast, low luminance, and glare conditions. Unlike distance vision, uncorrected acuity for near objects such as the printed page begins to deteriorate rapidly during one's 40s. As discussed, these deficits result from presbyopic changes in the lens that are most commonly ameliorated through reading glasses or bifocal modifications to existing refractive aids (see Exhibit 5.1).

Color

Normal observers are capable of distinguishing between more than 100,000 pairs of adjacent hues that are generated from various combinations of three primary color light sources. Numerous studies (Gilbert, 1957; Dalderup & Friedrichs, 1969; Knoblauch et al., 1987) have revealed that only modest reductions in color naming accuracy and color discrimination appear to accompany advancing adult age. These deficits are minimized under optimized lighting conditions (e.g., high illumination with minimal opportunity

EXHIBIT 5.1
Fine Print and Presbyopia

Human eyes are constructed to focus on objects that are 20 feet (or farther) away. To clearly focus light coming from objects closer than 20 feet, the crystalline lens within each eye needs to increase its light refracting power by bending itself into a more convex shape (i.e., accommodation). As the eye ages, the crystalline lens becomes less capable of bending. Consequently, by the mid-40s, people begin to have difficulty focusing on printed text closer than an "arm's length" away. This condition is presbyopia. What is it like to have presbyopia? To get a bit of an idea, hold this page at arm's length (little accommodation is required at this distance) and try reading the "fine print" presented in the paragraph below.

Very fine print viewed at arm's length will subtend such a small visual angle
that it will fall below the acuity limit. If you move the fine print closer
to your eye, it will eventually subtend a large enough visual angle to exceed the
visual acuity limit. However, to read text at very close distances, your lens
must increase its radius of curvature to bring the retinal image of the text into focus.

Exhibit continues

EXHIBIT 5.1 (Continued)

If you have normal visual acuity, you will have difficulty reading the small text in the previous paragraph when viewed at arm's length. This is because at arm's length, the 3-point Times Roman font used to render the fine print subtends a visual angle just below the 5-minarc nominal acuity limit. If you do not yet have presbyopia, you will be able to read the text by moving it closer to your eyes. However, moving the text closer will not help if you have presbyopia because the lenses within your eyes will not bend to accommodate near stimuli. Hence, for those with presbyopia, close work with fine visual stimuli yields a lot of blurry-looking objects. Yet, holding small text at arm's length so that it can be accommodated results in a retinal image that is too small to be of practical use. Fortunately, for individuals hoping to survive through their 40s and beyond, presbyopia is easily circumvented by the increased refractive power provided by bifocals or simple reading glasses.

The traditional college-age student (ages 18–30) has enough accommodative reserve capacity to resolve fine-print text by bringing it close enough to his or her eyes to exceed the acuity limit. However, this same student has significantly less accommodative reserve of his or her 10-year-old counterpart—that is, a person in his or her 20s has already lost a significant amount of accommodative capacity. To demonstrate this fact, measure your accommodative reserve, or near-point, as follows: (a) Hold a sheet of typical printed text at arm's length; if you have normal vision, you should be able to easily read this text. (b) Gradually bring the sheet of text closer to your eyes until the text becomes fuzzy-looking or out of focus. (c) Measure the distance from your eyes at which the text first becomes fuzzy. (d) The reciprocal of this distance, measured in meters (i.e., 1/m), is your near-point, or amplitude of accommodation in units of refractive power, called diopters. Repeat this measurement with a cooperative 10-year-old friend, sibling, or relative. You will find that younger observers can bring textual materials much closer to their eyes before they exceed their maximum amplitude of accommodation and become blurred. In fact, you should be able to predict this age difference in the near-point of accommodation using the classic data of Donders (1864), reproduced in Table 5.1.

TABLE 5.1

Near-Point and Amplitude of Accommodation as a Function of Age

Age (years)	Near-Point (cm)	Accommodative amplitude (diopters)
10	7	14
15	8	12
20	10	10
25	12	8.5
30	14	7
35	18	5.5
40	22	4.5
45	28	3.5
50	40	2.5
55	51	1.75
60	100	1
65	200	0.50
70	400	0.25

Note. Data from On the Anomalies and Accommodation and Refraction of the Eye by F. C. Donders, 1864, London: The Sydenham Society. Reported in Physiological Optics (p. 79), by W. D. Zoethout, 1939, Chicago: Professional Press. Copyright 1939 by The Professional Press, Inc.

for glare). The modest nature of these age-related changes is surprising, given the distinct yellowing process that characterizes the senescent lens (see Exhibit 5.2). When age-related deficits have been reported, they are primarily limited to the blue-green (short wavelength) region of the spectrum. Such observations are consistent with the fact that the yellowed senescent lens differentially absorbs short wavelength light.

Temporal Resolution

Older observers are less sensitive in the detection of temporally modulated (i.e., flickering) light stimuli. This decline in flicker sensitivity is especially robust for targets in the periphery and suggests that visual events in peripheral vision may be less perceptually salient for older observers. Similarly, the ability to detect oscillatory motion in small visual targets also declines markedly among middle-age and older adults. Several studies (Schiff, Oldak, & Shah, 1992; Scialfa, Guzy, Leibowitz, Garvey, & Tyrrell, 1991) have also demonstrated systematic age differences in the ability to judge the speed of automobiles. Older women, in particular, appear to exhibit pronounced errors in estimating the time of arrival of approaching vehicles. The underlying cause of these age-related declines in the temporal resolving power of the visual system remain uncertain. The potential significance of an age-related weakening in the bottom-up signaling of transient events is explored in Exhibit 5.3.

EXHIBIT 5.2
Functional Effects of Rapid Color Adaptation

Despite the fact that advanced adult age is associated with a strong, persistent yellowing of the crystalline lens within our eyes, older observers experience relatively minor changes in color perception. How can this be when such yellow lenses are known to absorb much of the short wavelength (bluish) light entering the eye? The simple explanation for this robust maintenance of color appearance phenomena appears to be a result of color adaptation mechanisms mediated within the photoreceptors and at the highest levels of the visual nervous system. The demonstration available at the link listed below will enable you to experience how color perception remains relatively robust and genuine even when looking through yellow or blue lenses. Try the demo and experience the profound effects of color adaptation for yourself: Color Adaptation Demo, available at http://www.usd.edu/psyc301/coloradapt.htm.

The maintenance of color perception through some sort of adaptation mechanism is one of many examples of how the perceptual systems can compensate for degraded sensory input. Can you think of any other examples of compensatory mechanisms that might reduce the deleterious effects of degraded sensory inputs associated with advanced adult aging?

The line between where perceptual processes give way to higher-order cognitive processes is undoubtedly a fuzzy one. As we learn more about the complexities of perceptual processes, it has become apparent that even the most fundamental perceptions are heavily influenced by top-down mechanisms based on goals, knowledge and experience of the individual observer. Nonetheless, it is important to remember that the perceptual systems have evolved over millions of years to use environmental information in the service of the survival of a species. Despite the fact that they have often been ignored by the juggernaut of modern cognitive psychology, strong bottom-up perceptual processes continue to provide powerful guidance to the attentional/cognitive layers that lay above or beside them in the chain or network of information processing. Schieber (2000) has hypothesized that some of these critical perceptual mechanisms become weakened with age and masquerade as cognitive/attentional deficits because their failures ultimately present themselves as problems with search, selection, or working memory capacity. This hypothesis is consistent with the recent observation that older drivers are overrepresented in the looked-but-didn't-see class of traffic accidents.

The hyperlink listed below points to an online computer simulation of what your situational awareness of a changing visual scene might be like if the bottom-up perceptual mechanisms that automatically and effortlessly localize sources of change were blocked using a simple but effective masking procedure. This demonstration has become known as the change blindness paradigm. Once you have experienced visual search under the special circumstances of this paradigm, you should gain a new appreciation for the powerful role of primitive bottom-up mechanisms in optimizing the deployment of higher-order but resource-limited cognitive/attentional processes. In addition, experiencing the change blindness demonstration also serves to simulate functional difficulties that might emerge among older observers if advancing age was indeed associated with decrements in transient event detection mechanisms (Kline & Schieber, 1981). Try the demo and see for yourself: Change Blindness Demo, available at http://www.usd.edu/psyc301/ChangeBlindness.htm (demonstration requires a Java-enabled Web browser).

HEARING

Hearing loss, to the degree that it interferes with the daily tasks of living, is undoubtedly the most common and problematic form of sensory disability occurring in older adults. Approximately one third of those between the ages of 65 and 75 and fully one half of those ages 85 or older demonstrate significant hearing related problems (Ries, 1985). The hearing losses commonly experienced by older adults can significantly interfere with social interaction and the ability to meaningfully and efficiently interact with one's environment.

Age-Related Structural Changes in the Ear

Anatomical studies of aging have tended to find degenerative changes at virtually every level of the auditory system. In the outer ear, there is often excessive accumulation of ear wax (cerumen), which can completely block the auditory canal. In the middle ear, the joints and connective tissues linking the ossicular bone chain (i.e., malleus, incus, and stapes) become calcified and less elastic, thus contributing to the conductive hearing loss commonly observed among older adults. Changes in the inner ear are dominated by the loss of inner hair cells, the very site of the transduction of acoustic energy into nervous system impulses. Significant age-related cell loss has also been reported in the ascending auditory pathway up to and including the auditory cortex (Corso, 1981).

Age-Related Functional Changes in Hearing

Absolute Sensitivity

An individual's sensitivity for detecting acoustic energy in the air varies as a function of stimulus frequency. Hence, auditory sensitivity is usually represented as an audiogram, which graphically depicts one's detection thresholds for a range of stimulus frequencies ranging from 200 to 8,000 hertz (Hz). Threshold sensitivity is usually expressed in terms of a difference score, relative to a standard observer, in decibel (dB) units. Age-related losses in hearing sensitivity for pure tone stimuli are essentially universal. However, the pattern of age-related loss is heavily dependent on stimulus frequency, gender, and long-term noise exposure history. Age-related hearing loss, when it first occurs, is usually limited to high-frequency stimuli (8,000 Hz). This age-related high-frequency hearing loss is commonly referred to as *presbycusis* (from the Greek term *presbus* for *old* and *akouo* for *hearing*). This loss at 8 kilohertz (kHz) progresses at a constant rate of approximately 1 dB per year from ages 20 to 80. Beyond age 60, age-related reductions in auditory sensitivity begin to encroach on lower-stimulus frequencies (1–4 kHz), declining at a rate of approximately 1.4 dB per year thereafter.

As presbycusis advances, its most debilitating effects involve a reduction in the ability to understand speech. There is a significant body of scientific research that has suggested that the lion's share of age-related hearing loss results from an accumulation of sensory damage resulting from lifelong exposure to high levels of environmental (i.e., industrial) noise. For example, several studies have shown that older individuals among socially and economically isolated ethnic groups with little or no life-span exposure to industrial noise demonstrate only a small fraction of the age-related hearing loss typically seen among age-matched individuals living in modern industrialized areas (see Willott, 1991).

Finally, the magnitude of age-related hearing loss observed among women tends to be considerably less than that experienced by their male counterparts. This finding may merely reflect gender differences in lifelong exposure to high levels of environmental noise.

Sound Localization

The ability to localize the source of a sound is usually studied in the laboratory by determining the amount of interaural delay or interaural intensity difference required to accurately specify the spatial source of the stimulus. Using such techniques, several studies (Herman, Warren, & Wagener, 1977; Tillman, Carhart, & Nicholls, 1973) have demonstrated that sound localization performance declines with advancing age. However, such losses appear to be significant only for interaural time delay cues. This suggests that older adults may have difficulty locating the source of low-frequency sounds but may be relatively unimpaired in their ability to localize high-frequency sources.

Speech Perception

Many studies have been conducted to examine the effects of advancing age on speech recognition ability. Under quiet laboratory conditions, small to modest reductions in speech recognition accuracy have been reported among those ages 60 and older (Jerger, 1973). However, under less optimal conditions (e.g., background noise, reverberation, hurried speech), much more robust age-related deficits are typically observed (Jokinen, 1973). For example, 70-year-old observers may fail to recognize up to 20% of the stimulus words presented at an electronically sped-up rate of 300 words per minute, whereas their 20-year-old counterparts achieve performance levels approaching 100% accuracy (Gordon-Salant & Fizgibbons, 1997). Similar decrements in performance are observed for target words embedded in noisy backgrounds. In the quiet laboratory setting the speech recognition deficits can be attributed almost entirely to the peripheral mechanisms typically thought to mediate presbycusis (e.g., hair cell loss in the cochlea). However, the mechanisms mediating the dramatic decrements in speech recognition performance under challenging listening conditions may result from age-related changes in centrally mediated processes such as selective attention. Despite such apparent difficulties with central mechanisms, several studies have demonstrated that the size of the age-related speech recognition deficit observed under noisy background conditions was markedly reduced when target words were preceded by prompts that provided a rich, linguistic context (i.e., predictive redundancy; Gordon-Salant & Fizgibbons, 1999; Holtzman, Familitant, Deptula, & Hoyer, 1986). Such outcomes strongly suggest that older observers may be able to use higher-order cognitive processes to compensate for peripheral sensory deficits.

The Chemical Senses

Structural Changes

Unlike the case for vision and hearing, the chemical sense organs in the nose and mouth require direct contact with the molecular structure of the stimulus. In the case of the taste sense, stimulus molecules must be soluble in saliva to reach the taste receptors embedded in taste buds distributed across the dorsal surface of the tongue. To stimulate olfactory receptors, stimulus molecules must be vaporous and soluble in fat to reach and then penetrate the mucous-covered olfactory epithelium located deep within the nasal passages leading from the nose. Modern research has indicated that, although intraindividual differences in the number of taste buds may vary more than tenfold from one person to the next, there is little evidence that their numbers systematically change with advancing adult age. However, there is clear evidence that structures responsible for the transduction and sensory coding of odor molecules are susceptible to profound age-related degeneration. As early as age 30, clear age-related losses in the number of olfactory receptor cells is evident in the olfactory epithelium. Electron microscopy reveals massive losses by age 65. Such cellular disruption in the olfactory system extends to the olfactory bulb, whereas few as 25% of the glomeruli may remain intact by age 75. Little is known about age-related changes in the number or structure of olfactory-binding proteins known to play a critical role in the olfactory transduction process.

Threshold and Suprathreshold Sensitivity

Results from psychophysical studies are consistent with the age-related structural changes noted earlier. Between ages 20 and 80, absolute thresholds for the detection of salty and bitter substances increase by 1 and 0.5 log units, respectively. Yet, little or no reliable age differences are observed for the minimum concentrations needed to detect sweet or sour taste stimuli (Weiffenbach, 1984). At stimulus concentration levels exceeding 0.5 to 1.0 log units above absolute threshold, little or no age differences in the magnitude of taste sensations are typically reported (Murphy, 1979). In other words, suprathreshold taste sensation is relatively unaffected by advancing adult age (when prescription drug use, smoking and periodontal disease are factored out of consideration). The picture that emerges for olfactory perception is bleaker. Between ages 20 and 70, absolute sensitivity for the detection of olfactory stimuli declines by approximately 0.15 log units per decade of age, representing a nearly tenfold reduction in sensitivity across the period of adulthood (Doty et al., 1984). Precipitous declines in the accuracy of suprathreshold odor identification are observed by age 65; by age 80 performance is cut in half. Similarly, psychophysical scaling studies suggest that the growth in the apparent magnitude of a smell with increases in stimulus intensity advances at a diminished rate among older observers (see Murphy, 1986).

Flavor Perception

What we colloquially refer to as taste is more formally referred to as flavor perception in the sensory sciences. Both taste and olfactory inputs mediate flavor perception, with the olfactory component being most heavily weighted. This is why food loses much of its appeal during nasal congestion or a head cold. Despite the fact that pure taste perception (i.e., from the taste buds alone) remains relatively unaffected by aging, flavor perception has consistently been found to deteriorate markedly beyond age 65. Based on their flavor alone, older adults usually can correctly identify only about half as many common foodstuffs as their younger counterparts. However, when olfactory input is diminished through the use of "nose clips," age differences in flavor identification performance are virtually eliminated, because performance among the young observers deteriorates to match that typically demonstrated by older ones. Such results clearly suggest that diminished flavor experiences reported by many older adults are primarily the result of age-related changes in suprathreshold olfactory sensitivity. It should not come as a surprise, then, that efforts aimed at enhancing the gustatory experience of older consumers have found that both rated flavor and the amount of food consumed increases most when odor enhancement (rather than taste enhancement) optimizations are applied in the kitchen.

TOUCH

Structural Changes

Numerous age-related changes in the properties of the skin and its embedded sensory receptors have been reported. The skin becomes less elastic with age and as a result must, by inference, have a negative effect on the efficacy of stretch receptors used to modulate grip and related manual behavioral functions. Systematic reductions in the number and the structural integrity of both Meissner's corpuscles and Pacinian corpuscles have been documented. Some deleterious changes in both the *lemniscal* (touch and vibration) and the *extralemniscal* (pain and temperature) pathways to the brain have been reported. However, a reliable characterization of how these ascending neural pathways change with advancing age has yet to be established.

Touch Sensitivity

Studies of age-related changes in touch sensitivity have primarily involved the use of punctate stimuli delivered to the glabrous skin surfaces of the hands and feet (i.e., pads of the fingers and soles of the feet). These investigations have consistently reported that touch sensitivity declines continuously between ages 20 and 90. These age differences have been on the order of 0.5 to 1.0 log unit in size (Thornbury & Minstretta, 1981). Such age-related decrements in cutaneous touch sensitivity have consistently been found to be associated with concomitant declines in the number (density) of Meissner's corpuscles in the skin regions being stimulated (e.g., Kenshalo, 1986). Vibrotactile sensitivity declines, which is indicative of Pacinian corpuscle atrophy, have also been reported among those older than age 55 (Verrillo & Verrillo, 1985).

INSTRUCTIONAL EXERCISES

Cumulative Energy Exposure of Sensory Organs Across the Life Span

Sekuler and Blake (1987) stated that "by age 60 our eyes have been exposed to more light energy than would be unleashed in a nuclear blast" (p. 51). In fact, all of the sensory organs experience a cumulative exposure to massive amounts of energy over the course of the normal human life span. Using plausible assumptions, estimate the annual dosage of energy (watts/m^2) reaching the retina and cochlea. Use these annual values to construct a cumulative dosage curve from ages 1 through 100. Relate these cumulative energy values to real-world phenomena or events (e.g., environmental noise exposure, ultraviolet light from the sun, and so on). Speculate about the potential damage that may be associated with such cumulative exposures.

Design Guidelines

Generate a checklist or set of guidelines for designing a document, house, or appliance using principles that compensate for common age-related changes in sensory or perceptual abilities. Several excellent resources are available for this exercise; see Fisk and Rogers (1997), Pirkl (1994), Schieber, Fozard, Gordon-Salant, and Weiffenbach (1991). For select Web resources, see *Effective Color Contrast* (http://www.lighthouse.org/color_contrast.htm), *Environments for the Elderly* (http://www.homemods.org/library/life-span/sensory.html), *Text for the Visually Impaired* (http://www.lighthouse.org/print_leg.htm), and *Universal Design* (http://www.asaging.org/am/cia2/design.html).

Simulating Age-Related Sensory Deficits

It has often been said that the best way to understand others is to walk a mile in their shoes. This same empathic strategy is also worth observing when one is attempting to appreciate the functional costs of the deficits that accumulate in the various sense modalities of growing older. Try performing a host of sensory domain-relevant tasks while implementing any or all of the following approaches to simulating sensory aging in otherwise robust individuals.

Vision Simulation

The loss of transparency, blue light absorption (i.e., yellowing), and light scatter introduced by the senescent lens can be simulated by using a pair of yellow sunglasses with lenses that have been subjected to a light abrasion using fine sandpaper. (A light coating of petroleum jelly can be used instead of sandpaper if a nondestructive approach is preferred.) Try performing several tasks while wearing this visual aging simulator, such as reading in bright versus dim light, judging colors, walking outside at night, and so on. Especially noteworthy is your change in performance during the presence of a bright, glaring source. Catalog your findings. Discuss the implications of your observations as they relate to the ability of older adults to perform the activities of daily life (see Pastalan, 1982, for practical suggestions and examples related to the construction of a visual aging simulator).

Hearing Simulation

It is very challenging to implement a scientifically valid simulation of sensory aging in the auditory system without recourse to real-time signal processing equipment. However, some degree of empathy for the plight of people experiencing sensory–neural hearing loss can be obtained by wearing ear stopples and by introducing a moderate volume background noise source such as static generated by a radio or television tuned to a channel to which no local broadcaster has been assigned. Try having a discussion with others, watching television, talking on the telephone, and so on while implementing the auditory simulation of sensory aging. Catalog your findings. Discuss the implications of your observations as they relate to the ability of older adults to perform the activities of daily life. If you have tried the visual simulation described above, compare the degree of disability encountered under each situation.

After completing the Hearing Simulation exercise, you may want to chronicle your experience by taking the Self-Assessment Hearing Test available online at *Self Help for Hard of Hearing* (http://www.shhh.org/About/self.cfm).

Touch Simulation

A reasonable simulation of age-related declines in cutaneous sensitivity and manual dexterity can be achieved by wearing a pair of thin latex surgical gloves (readily available at your local pharmacy or in any science or medical department of your local college or university). If you cannot find a pair of thin surgical gloves, you can use regular household rubber gloves. Keep in mind, however, that household rubber gloves will attenuate your sensitivity to much greater degree than would be expected as a result of normal adult aging. Try performing several typical manual tasks while wearing the gloves; for example, pick up a dime, apply a postage stamp to an envelope, adjust the dial on a telephone, type on your computer, try to discriminate objects on the basis of their texture, and so on. Summarize your observations and rate the overall degree of functional decline with or without the gloves in place.

Flavor Perception Simulation

The flavor of food is mediated by a combination of sensory inputs from the tongue and mouth (taste) and the olfactory epithelium located at the top of your nasal passages (smell). A reasonable simulation of commonly experienced degrees of age-related declines in flavor perception can be simulated by packing small amounts of sterile cotton into both nostrils. (Caution: Use small amounts of cotton, and do not pack it too deeply or too densely. Remember you will want to remove this cotton from your nostrils when the simulation exercise has been completed.) With the cotton in place and partially blocking vaporous access to your olfactory epithelium, try tasting a variety of foods and beverages. An especially powerful simulation experience will be achieved if you have a colleague give you small samples of food or drink and then have you try to identify the items by name. Small restrictions in olfactory input can have a profound impact on flavor experience. Record your observations and discuss their implications.

Specifications for a "Third-Age" Suit

The *Third Age*, taken from the French *troisième age*, refers to the final stage of maturity following one's release from the *other*-directed responsibilities of midlife (e.g., career building and child rearing). In recent years, designers from the automotive industry have adopted the practice of using what has become known as a *third-age suit* to help them identify and appreciate those age-related sensory and motor changes that might impact the ability of people to interact with the designed environment. The ambitious but achievable goal of this exercise is to design such a suit and develop a plan for using it in the evaluation of product designs. The truly ambitious individuals among you may actually consider building a prototype as part of a class or group project.

Some Web-based resources to help get you started include Project Taurus at Loughborough University (http://www.lboro.ac.uk/research/taurus/simulation.html) and Ford Motor Company's Third Age Suit (http://www.wired.com/news/technology/0,1282,46818,00.html).

Age-Related Changes Across the Major Sense Modalities

Do age-related declines in visual sensitivity develop at the same rate as age-related losses in hearing sensitivity? What about touch, taste, or smell? To address the question as to whether the senses age at similar or independent rates, try the following exercise. Identify classic studies of sensory acuity/sensitivity from different modalities that sample participants over a wide age range. Normalize the data from these experiments and plot the normalized sensitivity data for each modality as a function of age. Do the curves overlap, or do the various sense modalities appear to follow independent aging trajectories? Discuss the theoretical significance of your conclusions.

Suggested data sets for use in this exercise are as follows: visual acuity (Burg, 1966; Pitts, 1982), odor identification (Doty et al., 1984), and speech intelligibility (Jerger, 1973).

Controlling Extraneous Sensory Influences on Cognitive Research

A working knowledge regarding the major age-related changes in sensory–perceptual capacity is necessary if one is interested in isolating these effects from higher-order attentional or cognitive explanations of age-related changes in behavior. List the major age-related changes in vision and hearing that might influence performance on cognitive tasks and develop strategies that would experimentally control for these sources of extraneous variance. A valuable resource to guide this exercise is Schieber and Baldwin (1996).

REFERENCES

Burg, A. (1966). Visual acuity as measured by dynamic and static tests. *Journal of Applied Psychology, 50,* 460–466.

Corso, J. F. (1981). *Aging, sensory systems and perception.* New York: Praeger.

Curcio, C. A., Millican, C. L., Allen, K. A., & Kalina, R. E. (1993). Aging of the human photoreceptor mosaic: Evidence for selective vulnerability of rods in central vision. *Investigative Ophthalmology and Visual Science, 34,* 3278–3296.

Dalderup, L. M., & Friedrichs, M. L. C. (1969). Color sensitivity in old age. *Journal of the American Geriatrics Society, 17,* 388–390.

Devaney, K. O., & Johnson, H. A. (1980). Neuron loss in the aging visual cortex of man. *Journal of Gerontology, 35,* 836–841.

Desai, M., Pratt, L. A., Lentzne, H., & Robinson, K. N. (2001). Trends in vision and hearing among older Americans. *Aging Trends; No. 2.* Hyattsville, MD: National Center for Health Statistics.

Donders, F. C. (1864). *On the anomalies and accommodation and refraction of the eye.* London: Sydenham Society.

Doty, R. L., Shaman, P., Applebaum, S. L., Giberson, R., Sikorski, L., & Rosenberg, L. (1984). Smell identification ability: Changes with age. *Science, 226,* 1441–1443.

Fisk, A. D., & Rogers, W. A. (Eds.). (1997). *Handbook of human factors and the older adult* (pp. 27–54). New York: Academic Press.

Gilbert, J. G. (1957). Age changes in color matching. *Journal of Gerontology, 12,* 210–215.

Gordon-Salant, S., & Fizgibbons, P. J. (1997). Selected cognitive factors and speech recognition performance among young and elderly listeners. *Journal of Speech, Language, and Hearing Research, 40,* 423–431.

Gordon-Salant, S., & Fitzgibbons, P. J. (1999). Profile of auditory temporal processing in older listeners. *Journal of Speech, Language and Hearing Research, 42,* 300–311.

Herman, G. E., Warren, L. R., & Wagener, J. W. (1977). Auditory lateralization: Age differences in sensitivity to dichotic time and amplitude cues. *Journal of Gerontology, 32,* 187–191.

Holtzman, R. E., Familitant, M. E., Deptula, P., & Hoyer, W. (1986). Aging and the use of sentential structure to facilitate word recognition. *Experimental Aging Research, 12,* 85–88.

Jerger, J. (1973). Audiological findings in aging. *Advances in Otorhinolaryngology, 20,* 115–124.

Jokinen, J. (1973). Presbycusis. VI: Masking of speech. *Acta Otolarygologica, 76,* 426–430.

Kenshalo, D. R. (1986). Somesthetic sensitivity in young and elderly humans. *Journal of Gerontology, 41,* 732–742.

Kline, D. W., & Schieber, F. (1981). Visual aging: A transient/sustained shift? *Perception and Psychophysics, 29,* 181–182.

Knoblauch, K., Sanders, F., Kusuda, M., Hynes, R., Podgor, M., Higgins, K. E., & de Monasterio, F. M. (1987). Age and illuminance effects in Farnsworth-Munsell 100 hue test. *Applied Optics, 26,* 1441–1448.

Lowenfeld, L. E. (1979). Pupillary changes related to age. In H. S. Thompson (Ed.), *Topics in neuro-ophthalmology* (pp. 124–150). Baltimore: Williams and Wilkins.

Murphy, C. (1979). The effect of age on taste sensitivity. In S. S. Han & D. H. Coons (Eds.), *Special senses in aging* (pp. 21–33). Ann Arbor, MI: Institute of Gerontology, University of Michigan.

Murphy, C. (1986). Taste and smell in the elderly. In H. L. Meiselman & R. S. Rivlin (Eds.), *Clinical measures of taste and smell* (pp. 343–371). New York: Macmillan.

Pastalan, L. A. (1982). Environmental design and adaptation to visual environment. In R. Sekuler, D. Kline, & K. Dismukes (Eds.), *Aging and human visual function* (pp. 323–333). New York: Liss.

Pirkl, J. J. (1994). *Transgenerational design: Products for an aging population.* New York: Van Nostrand Reinhold.

Pitts, D. G. (1982). The effects of aging upon selected visual functions: Dark adaptation, visual acuity, stereopsis and brightness contrast. In R. Sekuler, D. Kline, & K. Dismukes (Eds.), *Aging and human visual function* (pp. 131–160). New York: Liss.

Ries, P. W. (1985). The demography of hearing loss. In H. Orlans (Ed.), *Adjustment to adult hearing loss* (pp. 3–21). San Diego, CA: College Hill Press.

Schieber, F. (1992). Aging and the senses. In J. E. Birren, R. B. Sloane, & G. Cohen (Eds.), *Handbook of mental health and aging* (pp. 251–306). New York: Academic Press.

Schieber, F. (2000). What do driving accident patterns reveal about age-related changes in visual information processing? In K. W. Schaie & M. Pietrucha (Eds.), *Mobility and transportation in the elderly* (pp. 207–211). New York: Springer.

Schieber, F., & Baldwin, C. L. (1996). Vision, audition and aging research. In F. Blanchard-Fields & T. Hess (Eds.), *Perspectives on cognitive change in adulthood and aging* (pp. 122–162). New York: McGraw-Hill.

Schieber, F., Fozard, J. L., Gordon-Salant, S., & Weiffenbach, J. (1991). Optimizing the sensory–perceptual environment for older adults. *International Journal of Industrial Ergonomics, 7,* 133–162.

Schiff, W., Oldak, R., & Shah, V. (1992). Aging persons' estimates of vehicular motion. *Psychology and Aging, 7,* 518–525.

Scialfa, C. T., Guzy, L. T., Leibowitz, H. W., Garvey, P. M., & Tyrrell, R. A. (1991). Age differences in judgments of vehicle velocity and distance. *Psychology and Aging, 6,* 60–66.

Sekuler, R., & Blake, R. (1987). Sensory underload. *Psychology Today, 21,* 48–53.

Spear, P. D. (1993). Neural basis of visual deficits during aging. *Vision Research, 33,* 2589–2609.

Thornbury, J. M., & Minstretta, C. M. (1981). Tactile sensitivity as a function of age. *Journal of Gerontology, 36,* 34–39.

Tillman, T. W., Carhart, R., & Nicholls, S. (1973). Release from multiple maskers in elderly persons. *Journal of Speech and Hearing Research, 16,* 152–160.

Verrillo, R. T., & Verrillo, V. (1985). Sensory and perceptual performance. In N. Charness (Ed.), *Aging and human performance* (pp. 1–46). New York: Wiley.

Weiffenbach, J. M. (1984). Taste and smell perception in aging. *Gerontology, 3,* 137–146.

Willott, J. F. (1991). *Aging and the auditory system: Anatomy, physiology and psychophysics.* San Diego, CA: Singular.

Zoethout, W. D. (Ed.). (1939). *Physiological optics.* Chicago: The Professional Press.

ANNOTATED BIBLIOGRAPHY

American Speech–Language–Hearing Association, *Speech, Hearing, and Aging,* available at http://www.asha.org/hearing/disorders/prevalence_adults.cfm. The

American Speech-Language-Hearing Association (ASHA) is the professional, scientific, and credentialing association for more than 103,000 audiologists, speech-language pathologists, and speech, language, and hearing scientists. Their Web site is a rich source of information regarding the prevalence and treatment of age-related hearing loss.

Kline, D. W., & Scialfa, C. T. (1997). Sensory and perceptual functioning: Basic research and human factors implications. In A. D. Fisk & W. A. Rogers (Eds.), *Handbook of human factors and the older adult* (pp. 27–54). New York: Academic Press. This textbook chapter contains an up-to-date review of age-related changes in vision and hearing along with checklists detailing intervention strategies for ameliorating age-related deficits in sensory function.

National Aging Information Center, *Low Vision and Aging*, available at http://www.aoa.gov/NAIC/notes/lowvision&aging.html; *Hearing Loss and Aging*, available at http://www.aoa.gov/NAIC/notes/hearingloss.html. The NAIC Web site is a very comprehensive source of information on age-related changes in health and functional status. Its pages on vision and hearing loss are extensive and contain many links to other related sources of information.

National Institute on Deafness and Other Communication Disorders, *Smell and Taste*, available at http://www.nidcd.nih.gov/health/st.htm. The NIDCD Web site contains information on age-related disorders of taste and smell as well as links to generic taste and smell organizations.

Schieber, F. (1992). Aging and the senses. In J. E. Birren, R. B. Sloan, & G. Cohen (Eds.), *Handbook of mental health and aging* (pp. 251–306). New York: Academic Press. This textbook chapter describes the major age-related changes in the structure and function of the five major senses: vision, hearing, touch, taste, and smell. The underlying mechanisms thought to mediate these changes are also discussed.

6

INCORPORATING COGNITIVE AGING INTO COGNITIVE PSYCHOLOGY COURSES

ANDERSON D. SMITH

There is ample opportunity for instructors in cognitive psychology classes to include information about adult age differences in cognition. This chapter discusses cognitive aging content that could and should be included in courses on basic memory and cognition. As is demonstrated here, much of the content is already found in cognition textbooks, but texts differ greatly in both breadth and depth of coverage. This chapter describes two types of cognitive topics for which aging content could be useful to instructors. First, certain cognitive topics should include aging content because that content actually helps define the phenomena to be discussed, such as expertise or creativity. Second, aging content would provide excellent pedagogical examples or illustrations of more general cognitive phenomena such as memory systems or brain mechanisms.

The coverage of memory and cognition is an important part of undergraduate educational curricula in psychology. At least one course in

Please direct correspondence to Anderson D. Smith, School of Psychology, Georgia Tech, Atlanta, GA 30332; e-mail: Anderson.Smith@cos.gatech.edu cognition is found in essentially all undergraduate psychology curricula, with most schools having multiple courses. A simple survey was conducted using college Web pages to see how many cognitive psychology courses are actually taught in the typical psychology curriculum. The 10 highest rated national liberal arts colleges and the 10 highest rated national research universities were selected from the 2001 *U.S. News and World Report* online college ratings (http://www.usnews.com/usnews/edu/college/corank.htm). The Web pages from these colleges and universities were then surveyed to determine the representation of cognition in each of their course listings. The survey revealed that the top 10 liberal arts colleges had an average of 4 different cognitive psychology courses in their course listings and that the top 10 national research universities had an average of more than 7 courses that dealt in some way with cognition. It is clear, therefore, that cognitive psychology has become a major and important component of the undergraduate curriculum in psychology.

The study of cognition by researchers interested in aging has also been popular. In fact, an analysis of the content found in the *Journal of Gerontology: Psychological Sciences*, one of the major publication outlets for aging research in psychology over the past 50 years, indicated that most of the articles published in this interdisciplinary journal have dealt with cognition to some extent. Figure 6.1 shows the number of articles that dealt with cognitive aging and those that did not.

In 1985, the American Psychological Association (APA) established the journal *Psychology and Aging*; this journal, typical of APA journals, has become the primary publication outlet for the psychology of aging. In

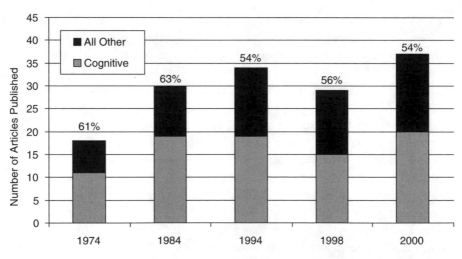

Figure 6.1. Articles in the Journal of Gerontology: Psychological Science that deal with cognitive aging compared with articles representing all the other research areas in psychology.

Volume 14 (1999), more than 65% of its published articles dealt with cognition in some way. Again, in 2000 (Volume 15), 67% of the published articles dealt with cognitive aging.

Just as it is clear that cognitive psychology has become a major component of the undergraduate psychology curriculum, it is also clear that cognitive aging represents a major research activity in the psychology of aging. One purpose of this chapter is to determine the extent to which aging research is found in current introductory memory and cognition texts. A second purpose is to provide course instructors some interesting ways in which aging content can enrich their introductory courses in memory and cognition regardless of the coverage in the text they select for the course. Examples are discussed that already have captured the attention of text writers, along with examples rarely included in introductory texts but that could enhance the student experience in these courses.

COVERAGE OF AGING IN COGNITION TEXTS

Given the abundance of research dealing with cognitive aging and the apparent resultant number of opportunities to incorporate cognitive aging into introductory cognitive psychology classes, it first should be determined to what extent cognitive aging research actually is represented in introductory cognition books. To determine this, a sample of introductory cognition or memory textbooks was selected (see the 17 introductory cognition or memory texts listed in Exhibit 6.1). These books were then reviewed to determine whether cognitive aging research was represented in the content of these texts. Results showed that 14 of the 17 textbooks did include at least some information about cognitive aging. Only 3 texts failed to discuss any aspect of cognitive aging research. In fact, a majority of the texts had major sections devoted to a discussion of adult age differences in cognition. Six of the 17 texts had extensive coverage of cognitive aging research, often

EXHIBIT 6.1
Introductory Memory and Cognition Textbooks Surveyed

Anderson (2000)	Hampson & Morris (1996)
Ashcraft (1994)	Jahnke & Nowaczyk (1998)
Baddeley (1998)	Matlin (1999)
Benjafield (1997)	Medin & Ross (1996)
Ellis & Hunt (1993)	Parklin (1993)
Eysenck & Keane (2000)	Reisberg (1997)
Guenther (1998)	Searleman & Herrman (1994)
Haberlandt (1997)	Sternberg (1999)
Haberlandt (1999)	

including separate coverage of aging and cognition as a part of the text. Four other texts included at least one section devoted to cognitive aging research, and the other 3 containing aging content included discussion of individual topics.

Unlike other areas of psychology represented in this book, the argument in this chapter is that cognitive aging has become integrated into mainstream cognitive psychology. As further evidence, two recent major edited reference monographs dealing with memory were reviewed (Bjork & Bjork, 1996; Tulving & Craik, 2000). The Bjork and Bjork book had 1 chapter on memory and aging out of 15 chapters in total (Light, 1996). The more recent Tulving and Craik memory handbook contained 39 chapters. Four chapters explicitly dealt with memory aging research topics. Chapters included 1 on memory changes in healthy aging (Balota, Dolan, & Duchek, 2000), 1 on memory in the aging brain (Anderson & Craik, 2000), 1 on very long retention intervals or long-term maintenance of knowledge (Bahrick, 2000), and 1 on memory and dementia (Hodges, 2000). In addition, 7 other chapters discussed memory aging research in some form. This analysis revealed that almost 30% of the chapters in the handbook had at least some aging content.

Why Is Cognitive Aging Being Integrated Into Cognition Texts?

There are several reasons why cognitive aging content is increasingly finding its way into mainstream memory and cognition texts. First, some topics seen as important to understanding human cognition inherently require consideration of cognition in older adults. Some phenomena important in cognitive psychology require consideration of aging because the phenomena are seen in older adults. Four such topics are maintenance of long-term knowledge, the development of expertise, extraordinary creativity, and Alzheimer's disease. These phenomena are seen in older adults, and often, the development of these phenomena take major portions of the adult life span.

In addition to aging content being built in to certain cognitive content areas, another reason that cognitive aging research has been incorporated into most introductory textbooks is that many research leaders in basic cognitive psychology are also cognitive aging researchers. To name a few, scientists such as Fergus Craik, Dan Schacter, Lynn Hasher, Rose Zacks, Marcia Johnson, and Larry Jacoby are well-recognized because of their contributions to cognitive psychology. They are also major contributors to the literature on cognitive aging, and their research on age differences has often served as a testing ground for their theoretical ideas. Because cognitive phenomena change across the adult life span, undergraduate instructors in cognitive psychology will be missing important content if they do not cover cognitive aging in their courses.

The study of age differences, for example, has been a major component in Lynn Hasher's and Rose Zacks's research about inhibition of attention being an important mechanism in understanding working memory capacity (see Hasher, Zacks, & May, 1999, for a review). According to their ideas, efficient working memory requires attention to relevant information and active inhibition of irrelevant information for the cognitive task at hand. The Hasher and Zacks theory also stated that older adults with normal aging lose their ability to inhibit irrelevant information. Their research has provided support to the hypothesis that there are age differences in the failure to inhibit, thus reducing the older adult's working memory capacity and efficiency.

Likewise, the study of adult age differences has been used by Larry Jacoby to support the distinction between deliberate recollection and familiarity revealed by his process dissociation procedures (see Kelley & Jacoby, 2000, for a review). Process dissociation is a methodological technique that permits the simultaneous computation of remembering produced by intentional, deliberate recollection and remembering based simply on familiarity or habit. Jacoby and his colleagues demonstrated that adult age differences in memory are a result of differences in deliberate recollection and that there are no age differences in memory based on the more automatic process of familiarity or habit (Hay & Jacoby, 1999).

Cognitive aging papers are frequently found in basic cognitive journals such as the *Journal of Experimental Psychology: Learning, Memory, and Cognition*; the *Journal of Experimental Psychology: General*; or *Memory and Cognition*. This occurrence means that understanding of age-related effects on memory and cognition is important to understanding cognition in general. Dissociations with age often can provide evidence for construct distinctions found in the cognitive literature. As just discussed, the distinction between intentional recollection and automatic familiarity is supported by the finding that older adults have deficits in one process (deliberate recollection) but not the other (habit or familiarity; Hay & Jacoby, 1999). In fact, aging research is often used to validate the theoretical meaningfulness of the construct distinctions found in cognitive psychology (Lockhart, 2000). For this reason, as seen in the next section of this chapter, instructors can use patterns of age differences to better illustrate many theoretical distinctions important to memory and cognition.

What Cognitive Aging Research Should Be Included in Introductory Cognition Courses and How?

Often, those teaching cognitive courses do not have a background in aging research, and for this reason, aging content would be limited to topics found in whatever textbook was selected for the course. As discussed earlier, however, textbooks differ significantly in what aging content is included, and instructors may need to supplement the textbook material to adequately represent aging research in their course. A case has been made that aging content provides an excellent mechanism to illustrate important phenomena and theoretical distinctions in the cognitive literature. Two excellent edited primers on cognitive aging have been published recently. Blanchard-Fields and Hess (1996) and Park and Schwarz (2000) are both aimed at research coverage for undergraduate students and are excellent resources for instructors as they prepare their course material.

Of those cognitive psychology texts that cover only certain topics in cognitive aging, for the most part, the aging content deals with just six topics. Four of these topics were listed previously as areas of cognition explicitly dealing with older adults: maintenance of long-term knowledge, the development of expertise, extraordinary creativity, and Alzheimer's disease. The other two topics of aging research that sometimes appear are the consideration of memory systems and psychometric intelligence. These six topics are described together here with suggestions of how aging research can best be incorporated into their discussion.

Maintenance of Long-Term Knowledge

The maintenance of long-term knowledge has become a popular topic to be covered in cognition texts. Maintenance of long-term knowledge, however, requires testing memory for acquired information after very long retention intervals (Bahrick, 2000). Retention is typically tested after long retention intervals for domains of knowledge acquired earlier in life for which there is some control over rehearsal, salience, and accuracy for the material originally learned. Such domains have included memory for high school or college classmate names, retention of high-school algebra, and retained knowledge from second-language learning. Because these long retention intervals of years are totally confounded with age, aging and memory becomes an important aspect of this research. It is interesting to note that only a few studies have explicitly separated aging from retention interval (e.g., Conway, Cohen, & Stanhope, 1992), even though Bahrick (2000) pointed out that most retention functions from such studies likely reflect interactions between the effects of normal aging and characteristics of the domain-specific content. The distinction between forgetting because of retention interval and forgetting as a result of aging should be discussed when covering this material.

As a class exercise, the instructor could ask the students to list all of their elementary school teachers and then ask whether they expect the same level of performance 40 years from now, when they are 60 years old. Then, a discussion could follow on why they would expect to do worse when they are 60. Is it because forgetting occurs with delay and without rehearsal, or is it because episodic memory is worse in older adults?

Expertise

A second area found in some introductory cognition texts that forces at least some discussion of aging content is in the area of expertise. Once skills have been acquired and expertise has been developed, the cognitive operations involved in executing these skills become more automatic and thus less influenced by normal aging (Jenkins & Hoyer, 2000).

Interesting work on typing skill, interpreting medical images, chess playing, musical instrument performing, and piloting aircraft has shown that older experts maintain a high level of performance in these skills when compared with older adults with less expertise (Bosman & Charness, 1996).

This research has also shown that expert skilled performance is often maintained by implicitly emphasizing cognitive abilities that are not affected by aging as "compensation" for abilities that are affected by aging (for a review, see Charness, 2001).

For instructors, an excellent classic study to demonstrate the relationship between aging and development of expertise is the research by Salthouse (1984a) on expert typists. Salthouse found that some expert typists were able to maintain fast typing speeds even with age-produced decreases in perceptual speed and reaction time. The older typists simply looked farther ahead in the text, giving themselves more time to plan for typing movements and thus compensating for the slower decision-making speed and movement time. Fortunately, this research also appeared as a *Scientific American* article (Salthouse, 1984b), making the research highly accessible to undergraduates.

Exceptional Creativity

A similar line of research that is popular in mainstream cognition is consideration of exceptional creativity, the creation of great works of art, music, or scholarship. The construct of aging enters into this research when trying to determine the "peak" age for such creativity. Research has reported that the production of exceptional creative works peaks at age 40 but differs considerably, according to the area of expertise (e.g., earlier in mathematics, later in history) and the number of years spent in the enterprise (Simonton, 1996). This research shows that many creative works have been produced later in life.

Instructors could compare extraordinary creativity to ordinary creativity (i.e., divergent thinking), which does show age declines on most psychometric tasks that measure it (e.g., word fluency, different uses of a single object such as a newspaper). Given that exceptional creativity indicates how people can be highly creative in one domain and not in others, measures of ordinary creativity are probably not indicative of great works that most would consider were produced by creative people such as those in art or scholarship. The issue of defining creativity is discussed in a student resource book that discusses controversies in aging research (Moody, 2000).

Alzheimer's Disease

Another research area that includes a consideration of aging because of its very nature is Alzheimer's disease. Symptoms are primarily cognitive, and amnesia and other cognitive pathologies are appropriate topics for courses in cognitive psychology. Alzheimer's disease accounts for more than two thirds of all cases of dementia and is a popular topic of discussion because of the large amount of research that has been conducted on this disorder. A consideration of Alzheimer's disease forces a discussion of aging because it is associated with old age. It has been said that if young adults forget, it is considered absent-mindedness; if older adults forget, it is Alzheimer's disease.

It is important to point out to students that Alzheimer's disease is a disease and not the cognitive end-product of aging. Few informed aging researchers believe that dementia will occur if we live long enough, and the myth of equating aging with eventual dementia needs to be addressed. In fact, as Whitbourne indicated earlier in this book, only a small percentage of older adults ever experience serious dementia. Often the cognitive deficits of dementia are contrasted with those found in healthy aging. Moderate Alzheimer's disease, for example, shows major deficits in semantic memory, deficits not seen in normal older adults (Hodges, 2000).

Neuroimaging techniques now allow comparisons of brain activities when normal adults and those with pathology perform various cognitive tasks. Because Alzheimer's disease is seen in older adults, the cognitive deficits of dementia are often contrasted with those found in healthy aging.

Many excellent films and videotapes are available for instructors to demonstrate the cognitive deficits associated with Alzheimer's disease. Seeing patients in different stages of the disease promotes students' understanding of differences in cognitive functioning. For example, the APA Division of Adult Development and Aging Web page (http://aging.ufl.edu/apadiv20) lists and describes 60 different films on Alzheimer's disease and the other dementias.

Memory Systems

Most cognitive psychology texts include a discussion of the different types of memory, and research on memory and aging is an excellent pedagogical tool for conveying the differences in the various memory systems. As mentioned previously, because normal aging has significant effects on some memory systems but minimal, if any, effects on other memory systems, discussion of age research provides an excellent illustration of the different systems. There are large age differences in episodic memory and working memory but no significant age effects on procedural memory or semantic memory (for reviews, see Craik, 1999, or Smith, 1996). Episodic memory involves remembering by reconstructing a previous perceived experience (retrieval by context), and semantic memory involves retrieving world knowledge (retrieval by concept). Procedural memory involves remembering without conscious recollection and without awareness. Working memory involves online information processing, the ability to process and store information temporarily in conscious mind. The fact that age differences vary significantly on the different types of memory is often used as evidence for the validity of the distinctions.

The recent explosion of research using neuroimaging is now providing physiological support for the memory systems approach. Much of this new research in cognitive neuroscience examines participants of different ages (Schacter, Wagner, & Buckner, 2000).

Psychometric Intelligence

When intelligence is discussed, instructors should include discussion of changes in psychometric IQ test performance across the adult life span. For example, aging research is often represented by a discussion of the distinction between crystallized and fluid intelligence. There are increases across the life span with tests of crystallized intelligence (e.g., tests of acquired knowledge) but decreases across the life span with tests of fluid intelligence (e.g., tests of reasoning ability; for a review, see Horn and Noll, 1997).

To assist students in understanding this distinction, a Web-based self-test is available that demonstrates how fluid and crystallized intelligence are measured. The test is part of a study guide used with a science exhibit on aging. Secrets of Aging was developed by the Boston Museum of Science and has been touring around the country since September 2000 (http://www.secretsofaging.org). The different demonstrations of intelligence types and the several memory tests are included in the "Mind" section of the Web site.

Discussion of intelligence across the adult life span should include a discussion of longitudinal studies and cross-sectional comparisons. Research from the Seattle Longitudinal Study, for example, has shown an overestimation of age changes in intelligence when using cross-sectional designs. The Seattle study indicated more stability across the middle ages with significant declines only in old age (Schaie & Willis, 1996).

Other Suggested Topics

The discussion now turns from aging topics that can be found in some cognition texts to those that are typically not found but should be considered when covering memory and cognition. These topics include (a) wisdom, a cognitive process associated with aging; (b) cognitive neuroscience of aging, the interaction between aging, brain, and cognition; (c) cognitive aging in social contexts, the relationship between aging, culture, and cognition; and (d) applied cognitive aging, which includes research-based applications of cognitive aging to improve the everyday life of older adults. All of these areas are receiving considerably more interest by cognitive aging researchers and are areas listed as major research opportunities by a recent study of cognitive aging research conducted by the National Academy of Sciences (Stern & Carstensen, 2000)

Wisdom

Until recently, there was little research on the cognitive construct most identified with older adults, the construct of wisdom. Yet, students are aware of wisdom as a construct and would expect it to be included in any discussion of higher mental processes. Wisdom could be contrasted with other better-researched mental functions such as intelligence and creativity. Paul Baltes and colleagues have now produced empirical studies demonstrating the characteristics of "wise" behavior by examining the decisions of older individuals who are nominated as wise people (Baltes, Staudinger, Maeker, & Smith, 1995; Staudinger & Baltes, 1994). In the Baltes et al. (1995) study, for example, wisdom nominees, with a mean age of 64 years, were more likely to give the very best judged responses (most wise) when responding to real-life personal dilemmas such as how to deal with a friend who says he or she is going to commit suicide. The wisdom nominees made significantly more of the top 20% wise responses than either young or old control participants.

Most students associate wisdom with old age, but an excellent discussion topic is for students to consider whether aging is a necessary prerequisite of wisdom. This debate is also highlighted in the student resource book dealing with aging issues mentioned earlier (Moody, 2000).

Cognitive Neuroscience

Because of developments in functional neuroimaging, cognitive psychologists are now able to examine brain activity while subjects are performing various cognitive activities. These techniques allow researchers to determine whether the observed dissociations between aging and various types of memory, for example, are due to differences in parts of the brain that are differentially changed by aging. Prull, Gabrieli, and Bunge (2000) provided a review of cognitive neuroscience research on aging and memory. They discussed evidence that shows how age effects on the brain (primarily in the medial–temporal lobe) are associated with age-related losses in recent episodic memory. Likewise, age differences in the activity of the frontal lobes are associated with age-related declines on tasks that involve strategic processes and tasks involving working memory.

The Center for the Neural Study of Cognition, a collaborative center between Carnegie–Mellon University and the University of Pittsburgh, has a

Web site with links to many resources for the instructor to use in developing this material (http://www.cnbc.cmu.edu/other/homepages.html).

Aging and Memory in Context

Cognition is determined by the brain, but it is also determined by the sociocultural context in which cognition occurs. It is recognized that language and cultural experiences can influence memory and thinking, and aging research provides an excellent mechanism for discussing the role culture plays in shaping the ways in which individuals attend to, process, and interpret information. Park, Nisbett, and Hedden (1999), for example, have shown cultural differences in the ways in which people process information. Eastern cultures tend to process information in a more contextual fashion, whereas Western cultures tend to be more analytical in their processing. They also suggested, however, that as individuals get older, cultural effects may not have greater influence, even though older adults have many years of greater exposure to the culture. Older adults in different cultures may actually become more alike in their cognitive function because of age-related limits placed on cognitive resources that result from more universal neurobiological aging. These limits reduce the strategic differences that can be attributed to culture.

Applied Cognitive Aging

Students like practical examples showing how theory and research findings can be applied to real world problems. The student's understanding of cognitive principles and constructs can be enhanced by demonstrations of how the principles of cognition are applied to problems faced by older adults as they live their lives. There is growing literature on how theory-guided cognitive aging research is being applied to help older adults function in their everyday lives (Rogers & Fisk, 2000). Just to list a few examples, recent research has applied what is known about cognitive aging to improve older adults' medication adherence, use of computer technology including the internet and ATM machines, understanding medical instructions, understanding of warning labels, and driving. Human factor researchers use both training and environmental design to improve the relationship between older adults and their environment. Cognitive aging research has shown that much of behavior is malleable and can be improved by training and practice (e.g., Schaie & Willis, 1996). "Elderdesign" also offers ways to better match the tasks that need to be performed on a daily basis to the cognitive capabilities of adults of different ages (Rogers & Fisk, 2000). For example, I have published a chapter explicitly directing designers of health care interventions how research principles of cognitive aging can inform their designs (Smith, 2001).

An interesting class project would be to have students indicate how they would change a grandparent's house to better accommodate his or her memory and cognitive changes. Then the student would justify suggestions using principles of cognitive psychology. Discussion of specific applications of cognitive psychology and human factors to solve problems for the older adults (e.g., medication compliance, computer use, new health care technology) can be found in a handbook on the topic by Fisk and Rogers (1997).

SUMMARY

Cognitive aging research, unlike many of the content areas of psychology, is being discussed increasingly in textbooks dealing with basic memory and cognition. Opportunities remain, however, for better use of this research to illustrate the principles of cognition. Differences in cognition between young and old adults can be used to illustrate and validate distinctions between cognitive constructs. Cognitive aging research can also provide numerous examples of applications of cognitive psychology to real world problems. Examples, illustrations, and applications are common pedagogical tools used by instructors to increase understanding by students as they are exposed to psychological science.

REFERENCES

Anderson, J. R. (2000). *Cognitive psychology and its implications* (5th ed.). New York: Worth.

Anderson, N. D., & Craik, F. I. M. (2000). Memory in the aging brain. In E. Tulving & F. I. M. Craik (Eds.), *Oxford handbook of memory* (pp. 411–425). Oxford, England: Oxford University Press.

Ashcraft, M. H. (1994). *Human memory and cognition* (2nd ed.). New York: HarperCollins.

Baddeley, A. (1998). *Human memory: Theory and practice* (rev. ed.). Boston: Allyn & Bacon.

Bahrick, H. P. (2000). Long-term maintenance of knowledge. In E. Tulving & F. I. M. Craik (Eds.), *Oxford handbook of memory* (pp. 347–362). Oxford, England: Oxford University Press.

Balota, D. A., Dolan, P. O., & Duchek, J. M. (2000). Memory changes in healthy older adults. In E. Tulving & F. I. M. Craik (Eds.), *Oxford handbook of memory* (pp. 395–409). Oxford, England: Oxford University Press.

Baltes, P. B., Staudinger, U. M., Maeker, A., & Smith, J. (1995). People nominated as wise: A comparative study of wisdom related knowledge. *Psychology and Aging, 10,* 155–166.

Benjafield, J. G. (1997). *Cognition* (2nd ed.). New York: Prentice-Hall.

Bjork, E. L., & Bjork, R. A. (Eds.). (1996). *Memory*. San Diego, CA: Academic Press.

Blanchard-Fields, F., & Hess, T. M. (Eds.). (1996). *Perspectives on cognitive changes in adulthood and aging*. New York: McGraw-Hill.

Bosman, E. A., & Charness, N. (1996). Differences in skilled performance and skill acquisition. In F. Blanchard-Fields & T. M. Hess (Eds.), *Perspectives on cognitive changes in adulthood and aging* (pp. 428–453). New York: McGraw-Hill.

Charness, N. (2001). Can acquired knowledge compensate for age-related declines in cognitive efficiency? In S. H. Qualls & N. Abeles (Eds.), *Dialogues about aging: Psychology responds to the aging revolution* (pp. 99–117). Washington, DC: American Psychological Association.

Conway, M. A., Cohen, G., & Stanhope, N. (1992). Very long-term knowledge acquired at school and university. *Applied Cognitive Psychology, 6,* 467–482.

Craik, F. I. M. (1999). Age-related change in human memory. In D. Park & N. Schwarz (Eds.), *Cognitive aging: A primer* (pp. 75–92). Philadelphia: Psychology Press.

Ellis, H. C., & Hunt, R. R. (1993). *Fundamentals of cognitive psychology* (5th ed.). Madison, WI: Brown & Benchmark.

Eysenck, M. W., & Keane, M. T. (2000). *Cognitive psychology* (4th ed.). New York: Psychology Press.

Fisk, A. D., & Rogers, W. A. (Eds.). (1997). *Handbook of human factors and the older adult*. San Diego, CA: Academic Press.

Guenther, R. K. (1998). *Human cognition*. New York: Prentice-Hall.

Haberlandt, K. (1997). *Cognitive psychology* (2nd ed.). New York: Prentice-Hall.

Haberlandt, K. (1999). *Introduction to human memory: Exploration and applications*. Boston: Allyn & Bacon.

Hampson, P. J., & Morris, P. E. (1996). *Understanding cognition*. Oxford, England: Blackwell Science.

Hasher, L., Zacks, R. T., & May, C. P. (1999). Inhibitory control, circadian arousal, and age. In D. Gopher & A. Koriat (Eds.), *Attention and performance XVII: Cognitive regulation of performance: Interaction of theory and application* (pp. 653–675). Cambridge, MA: MIT Press.

Hay, J. F., & Jacoby, L. L. (1999). Separating habit and recollection in young and elderly adults. Effects of elaborative processing and distinctiveness. *Psychology and Aging, 14,* 122–134.

Hodges, J. R. (2000). Memory in the dementias. In E. Tulving & F. I. M. Craik (Eds.), *Oxford handbook of memory*. Oxford, England: Oxford University Press.

Horn, J., & Noll, J. (1997). Human cognitive abilities: Gf–Gc theory. In D. P. Flanagan, J. L. Gershaft, & P. L. Harrison (Eds.), *Contemporary intellectual assessment* (pp. 53–91). New York: Guilford Press.

Jahnke, J. C., & Nowaczyk, R. H. (1998). *Cognition*. New York: Prentice-Hall.

Jenkins, L., & Hoyer, W. J. (2000). Instance-based automaticity and aging: Acquisition, reacquisition, and long-term retention. *Psychology and Aging, 15,* 551–565.

Kelley, C. M., & Jacoby, L. L. (2000). Recollection and familiarity: Process–dissociation. In E. Tulving & F. I. M. Craik (Eds.), *The Oxford handbook of memory* (pp. 215–228). Oxford, England: Oxford University Press.

Light, L. L. (1996). Memory and aging. In E. L. Bjork & R. A. Bjork (Eds.), *Memory* (pp. 444–490). San Diego, CA: Academic Press.

Lockhart, R. S. (2000). Methods of memory research. In E. Tulving & F. I. M. Craik (Eds.), *Oxford handbook of memory* (pp. 45–57). Oxford, England: Oxford University Press.

Matlin, M. (1999). *Cognitive psychology* (3rd ed.). New York: Harcourt Brace.

Medin, D., & Ross, B. H. (1996). *Cognitive psychology.* New York: Harcourt College.

Moody, H. R. (2000). *Aging: Concepts and controversies* (3rd ed.). London: Pine Forge Press.

Park, D. C., Nisbett, R., & Hedden, T. (1999). Aging, culture, and cognition. *Journal of Gerontology B: Psychological Sciences, 54,* P75–P84.

Park, D. C., & Schwarz, N. (Eds.). (2000). *Cognitive aging: A primer.* Philadelphia: Psychology Press.

Parklin, A. (1993). *Memory.* Oxford, England: Blackwell Science.

Prull, M. W., Gabrieli, J. D. E., & Bunge, S. A. (2000). Age-related changes in memory: A cognitive neuroscience perspective. In F. I. M. Craik & T. A. Salthouse (Eds.), *The handbook of aging and cognition* (2nd ed., pp. 91–153). Mahwah, NJ: Erlbaum.

Reisberg, D. (1997). *Cognition: Exploring the science of the mind.* New York: Norton.

Rogers, W. A., & Fisk, A. D. (2000). Human factors, applied cognition, and aging. In F. I. M. Craik & T. A. Salthouse (Eds.), *The handbook of aging and cognition* (2nd ed., pp. 559–591). Mahwah, NJ: Erlbaum.

Salthouse, T. A. (1984a). Effects of age and skill in typing. *Journal of Experimental Psychology: General, 113,* 345–371.

Salthouse, T. A. (1984b). The skill of typing. *Scientific American, 250,* 128–135.

Schacter, D. L., Wagner, A. D., & Buckner, R. L. (2000). Memory systems of 1999. In E. Tulving & F. I. M. Craik (Eds.), *Oxford handbook of memory* (pp. 627–643). Oxford, England: Oxford University Press.

Schaie, K. W., & Willis, S. L. (1996). Psychometric intelligence and aging. In F. Blanchard-Fields & T. M. Hess (Eds.), *Perspectives on cognitive change in adulthood and aging* (pp. 293–322). New York: McGraw-Hill.

Searleman, A., & Herrman, D. (1994). *Memory from a broader perspective.* New York: McGraw-Hill.

Simonton, D. K. (1996). Creative expertise: A life-span developmental perspective. In K. A. Ericsson (Ed.), *The road to excellence: The acquisition of expert performance in the arts and sciences* (pp. 227–253). Mahwah, NJ: Erlbaum.

Smith, A. D. (1996). Memory. In J. E. Birren & K. W. Schaie (Eds.), *The handbook on the psychology of aging* (4th ed., pp. 236–250). New York: Academic Press.

Smith, A. D. (2001). Consideration of memory factors in health care interventions with older adults. In W. Rogers & A. D. Fisk (Eds.), *Human factors interventions for the health care of older adults* (pp. 31–46). Mahwah, NJ: Erlbaum.

Staudinger, U. M., & Baltes, P. B. (1994). The psychology of wisdom. In R. J. Sternberg (Ed.), *Encyclopedia of intelligence* (pp. 1143–1152). New York: Macmillan.

Stern, P. C., & Carstensen, L. L. (2000). *The aging mind: Opportunities in cognitive research.* Washington, DC: National Academy Press.

Sternberg, R. J. (1999). *Cognitive psychology* (3rd ed.). New York: Harcourt Brace.

Tulving, E., & Craik, F. I. M. (Eds.). (2000). *The Oxford handbook of memory.* Oxford, England: Oxford University Press.

ANNOTATED BIBLIOGRAPHY

Birren, J. E., & Schaie, K. W. (Eds.). (2001). *Handbook of the psychology of aging* (5th ed.). San Diego, CA: Academic Press. Now in its fifth edition and is published every 5 or 6 years. Although not devoted to cognitive aging research alone, each edition has had a chapter on aging and memory as well as chapters on intelligence, neuropsychology, and language. The fifth edition, published in 2001, includes chapters on attention, speed, memory, motor control, cognition and brain function, language, and wisdom. Provides up-to-date reviews of research and has become a major reference resource for aging research.

Blanchard-Fields, F., & Hess, T. M. (Eds.). (1996). *Perspectives on cognitive changes in adulthood and aging,* New York: McGraw-Hill. An excellent edited book covering cognitive aging but written as a text for advanced undergraduate classes in cognitive aging. Includes four introductory chapters on methods and theory, four chapters on memory and basic cognitive processes, three chapters on intelligence, and four chapters on cognition in context (e.g., skill acquisition, social cognition, memory self-efficacy).

Craik, F. I. M., & Salthouse, T. A. (Eds.). (2000). *The handbook of aging and cognition* (2nd ed.). Mahwah, NJ: Erlbaum. Intended for more advanced audiences. Serves as one of the very best sources for advanced reviews of research areas in cognitive aging. Chapters, written by research leaders in cognitive aging, cover the standard topics such as attention, memory, and language but also include emotion and cognition, cognitive neuroscience, metacognition, human factors, personality and social cognition, and cognition in the very old.

Park, D. C., & Schwarz, N. (Eds.). (2000). *Cognitive aging: A primer.* Philadelphia: Psychology Press. Provides excellent coverage to basic areas of cognitive aging including attention, memory, and language. Includes chapters not typically found in textbooks on applications of cognitive aging, self-report measures, and circadian rhythms.

Tulving, E., & Craik, F. I. M. (Eds.). (2000). *The Oxford handbook of memory*. Oxford, England: Oxford University Press. This excellent advanced handbook contains four chapters dealing with memory aging and seven others that discuss various aspects of aging and memory research. Chapters written by acknowledged research leaders in the topics being discussed.

ANDERSON D. SMITH

7

PERSONALITY PSYCHOLOGY AND AGING: UNDERSTANDING AND INTEGRATING CONTINUITY AND CHANGE

MANFRED DIEHL

The teaching of personality psychology lends itself very naturally to an integration and discussion of aging-related topics. Why is that so? A cogent answer to this question was recently provided by Funder (2001) when he stated, "Personality psychology seeks to bring together the contributions of developmental, social, cognitive and biological psychology into an understanding of whole persons and the dimensions of difference that allow them to be psychologically distinguished from one another" (p. 198). This statement serves as an important reminder that in the field of psychology, theories and research on personality have always assumed an integrative function. This integrative function is a direct result of the very subject of inquiry, which is the *whole person* rather than specific psychological processes (Allport, 1937; McAdams, 2001).

Personality psychologists have always focused on constructs (e.g., drives, motives, traits, goals) that try to explain why humans behave in certain

Please direct correspondence to Manfred Diehl, Institute on Aging, University of Florida, P. O. Box 103505, 1329 SW 16th Street, Gainesville, FL 32610-3505; e-mail to mdiehl@ufl.edu. Work on this chapter was in part supported by grant R03 AG19328-01.

ways. Moreover, they have investigated how these constructs develop; how their development is influenced by biological, social, and cultural forces; and how these constructs work together as a unified whole (Allport, 1937; Freud, 1923/1961; Jung, 1933; Lewin, 1935; Murray, 1938; Stern, 1924). Thus, all major theories of personality incorporate basic propositions about *personality development* and make assumptions about the major developmental milestones, the temporal stability, and potential endpoints of personality development. Whether an individual's personality is mostly established by the end of childhood as suggested by Freud (1905/1953) or in early adulthood as suggested by trait theorists (McCrae & Costa, 1999), or whether personality development continues into middle and later adulthood as suggested by life span–oriented theorists (Erikson, 1950, 1982; Jung, 1933) has been the subject of a vigorous and ongoing debate. Today, this debate is more lively and better informed than ever before, and recent theorizing (Bandura, 1999; McCrae & Costa, 1999; Mischel & Shoda, 1999) has infused the field with new energy and momentum. This newly gained momentum is, among others, exemplified by the way in which issues of adult development and aging are incorporated into scholarly reflections on personality.

This chapter focuses on how instructors can incorporate aging-related topics into an undergraduate core curriculum course on human personality.[1] The chapter consists of three major parts. The first part describes the general objectives, the substantive topics, and the organizational structure of such a course. The second part identifies and discusses some of the basic issues with regard to adult development and aging that can be addressed in such a core course. In addition, this part introduces several unifying themes that can serve as an organizational framework for instructors. Finally, the third part presents specific exercises that instructors can incorporate into their classroom teaching. For many instructors and students, these exercises are a sort of road test for the theories and themes discussed in the classroom. Thus, these exercises are explicitly designed to make the person in personality psychology come alive.

COURSE OBJECTIVES, TOPICS COVERED, AND ORGANIZATIONAL STRUCTURE

Most instructors would probably agree that a core curriculum course in personality psychology has three major objectives. First, students need to

---

[1]In general, the suggestions made in this chapter apply to a course at the junior or senior level and a class size that can range anywhere from about 50 to more than 150 students, depending on the size of the academic institution. Although most colleges and universities do not specify any prerequisites for this course, the author's teaching experiences have led to the conclusion that instructors should advise students to complete the introduction to psychology and a course on life span development before taking a course in personality psychology.

become familiar with the most important theories of personality. Second, students need to learn about normal personality development and maladaptive personality processes as outlined by the different theories. Third, students need to become familiar with the most important empirical research findings related to the different theories and need to be able to compare and contrast research findings from different studies and theoretical frameworks.

In terms of course organization, these objectives are usually accomplished by presenting four or five sets of *theories* that share a number of basic assumptions (i.e., theory-focused approach). Thus, most personality textbooks start with the presentation of psychodynamic theories (e.g., theories by Freud, Jung, Adler, Horney, Sullivan, Erikson) and their basic propositions. These theories are often followed by trait theories (e.g., theories by Allport, Cattell, Eysenck), including the most recent extension in terms of the Big Five personality factors. These theoretical frameworks are often contrasted against learning theories of personality (e.g., theories by Watson, Dollard and Miller, Skinner) because this juxtaposition illustrates that different theoretical frameworks differ in their emphasis of internal or external influences as constituents of personality. In the context of learning theories of personality, increasing attention is given to social-cognitive learning theories (e.g., theories by Rotter, Bandura, Mischel) because they emphasize the proactive and agentic nature of humans and their theoretical statements are supported by a large body of empirical research. Cognitive schema theories (e.g., theories by Kelly, Fiske, Markus); humanistic theories (e.g., theories by Maslow, Rogers, Csikszentmihalyi); and narrative approaches to personality (e.g., theories by Hermans, McAdams), which emphasize the plasticity and creative potential of individuals, usually complete the sequence.

An alternative to this theory-focused approach is the *thematic approach* that organizes the course content around major themes of human behavior, such as the biological bases of personality, self-concept and identity, emotion, social relationships, stress and illness, or disorders of personality (Derlega, Winstead, & Jones, 1999). Compared with the theory-focused approach, this way of exploring human personality has the advantage that students tend to relate to these themes more readily than to the theories that have been developed to explain these behaviors. An additional advantage of this approach is that it lends itself more naturally to the use of a variety of media (e.g., newsprint, popular music, movies and videos, the World Wide Web) that facilitate and support the learning process. For example, in the context of discussing aggressive or altruistic behavior, instructors can effectively use short newspaper or magazine articles about prominent personalities (e.g., Timothy McVeigh versus Mahatma Gandhi) or short clips from movies (e.g., *Schindler's List*) to underscore the theoretical discussions in the classroom.

Regardless of what approach an instructor chooses, effective teaching of personality psychology incorporates from the beginning the basic assumptions regarding *personality development*, along with a description of established research methods. This emphasis is important because it establishes from the outset that certain assumptions about the nature of human personality have major implications for how personality development is conceptualized and what criteria are applied to assess the developmental level of individual personalities. In addition, it is advisable to emphasize from the beginning that there are a number of *unifying themes* (e.g., the nature versus nurture controversy) that cut across theories and can be fruitfully used to incorporate topics related to adult development and aging into the course content.

A LIFE SPAN APPROACH TO PERSONALITY: UNIFYING THEMES

Because the predominant method to teaching personality psychology is the *theory-focused approach*, the previously mentioned unifying themes are described in more detail here. Additionally, how instructors can draw on these themes to include adult development and aging in their courses is also discussed. Most instructors will find that introducing these unifying themes early in the course not only provides an organizing framework to students but also sets the stage to discuss these themes in the context of different theories and within a framework that advocates the study of personality across the entire life span. Furthermore, the continued revisiting of these themes results in an increasingly deeper level of processing and a thorough understanding of key issues in personality research.

The first unifying theme concerns the definition of the term *personality* itself and proposes that human personality is a *complex system* that develops out of the interplay of biological, physical, social, and psychological processes. Starting early on in the course, instructors should emphasize that each theory of personality addresses the basic building blocks and processes of this system in a slightly different way, and it is therefore important to look for commonalties across theories. Furthermore, instructors should point out that every theory describes to a certain extent how the building blocks and processes and the interactions among them change across the life span.

This definition of personality leads naturally to a second unifying theme, the *nature versus nurture controversy* (Ceci & Williams, 1999). A long tradition in psychology has examined the genetic and environmental influences on different personality characteristics. In general, this controversy has focused on the relative influence of genes and the environment on a variety of human behaviors and has resulted in statistics such as the heritability quotient (HQ). Research in behavioral genetics, however, has suggested that the influences of genetic makeup and environment are not constant across the life span and are more fluctuating than previously assumed (McCartney, Harris, & Bernieri, 1990; Plomin, DeFries, McClearn, & Rutter, 1997). Thus, instructors may use this general finding to show that with advancing age, genetic influences become increasingly moderated by environmental influences (e.g., nonnormative life events), resulting in decreasing HQs over the course of the adult life span, even for identical twins. On the other hand, in very old age, when social and psychological variables may become secondary to the effects of serious physical changes, biological influences may become again more important and may override the influences of the social and psychological environment (Baltes, Staudinger, & Lindenberger, 1999). Overall, instructors can use the nature versus nurture controversy as a theme to illustrate how the influences of genetics and environment on personality wax and wane across the life span and how they contribute to the great interindividual variability that can be observed in older adults.

A third unifying theme that instructors might use to incorporate topics of adult development and aging in their course concerns the debate about the *continuity versus discontinuity* of personality characteristics (Caspi, 2000; Caspi & Roberts, 2001). This debate focuses on the extent to which behaviors that characterize individuals during childhood and adolescence continue to be important characteristics of their personality when they are adults. Prime examples for the continuity versus discontinuity debate are styles of temperament, such as shyness or impulsiveness (Caspi & Silva, 1995), or styles of emotional attachment that can be observed in young children's behavior. In particular, Bowlby's (1979) *attachment theory* provides an ideal illustration for the continuity versus discontinuity debate, because he stated that attachment was an integral part of human behavior "from the cradle to the grave" (p. 129). Bowlby thought that the attachment relationship that a child forms with the primary caregiver results in a generalized way of relating to others and that this generalized way of relating is activated in all close relationships for the remainder of a person's life (Bowlby, 1988; Hazan & Shaver, 1994). Thus, Bowlby (1979) postulated that continuity in attachment behavior occurs from early childhood into later periods of the life span, and research on adult attachment styles provides some support for this proposition (Hazan & Shaver, 1994).

A fourth unifying theme concerns the debate about *stability versus change* of personality across the adult life span. This debate dates back to the beginnings of personality psychology and occupies a prominent place in current discussions (Ardelt, 2000). For example, Sigmund Freud postulated that the major components of a person's character are established by the end of childhood, whereas Carl Gustav Jung argued that important challenges are presented with regard to personality development in adulthood. Jung (1939/1959) referred to these challenges as the *process of individuation*, a process that leads to the realization of a person's true self. Moreover, Jung contrasted the individuation process, which he saw as the main developmental task during the second half of life, against the process of socialization that takes place during the first half of life. Similarly, Erik Erikson (1950, 1982) described several distinct stages of adult personality development that he considered important for happiness and psychological well-being in old age.

Although these early theorists tended to base their arguments on a limited number of observations, several large-scale longitudinal studies are currently available, providing evidence for both the stability and malleability of adults' personality (Costa & McCrae, 1997; Helson, 1993). Indeed, as of this writing, most researchers tend to support a "paradigm of tension between stability and change" (Helson, 1993, p. 93). Instructors need to emphasize that this tension between stability and change extends even into very old age and that it contradicts some of the existing stereotypes about older adults (Field & Millsap, 1991; Troll & Skaff, 1997). This latter point is important because the so-called *old-old* (i.e., adults age 85 and older) are the fastest-growing segment of the over-65 U.S. population, and knowledge about their physical, social, and psychological functioning is crucial so that the larger society can appropriately draw on the potentials and prepare for the special needs of this age group.

A last unifying theme that instructors can fruitfully incorporate into their course is the issue of *gains and losses* in personality development (Baltes, 1987). Although the notion that human development is a complex tradeoff between acquiring new behaviors (i.e., gains) and giving up or losing earlier behaviors (i.e., losses) has been mostly promoted in the area of cognitive development (Labouvie-Vief, 1977), it can also be used to describe important changes in personality in adulthood. For example, Carstensen's (1993) theory of socioemotional selectivity postulates that in later life, adults' social relationships are mostly motivated by the desire to experience positive and gratifying emotions. This goal increasingly motivates older adults to limit or select out those relationships in their social network that serve other purposes and to focus on those relationships that maximize the experience of mutually gratifying emotions. Similarly, Whitbourne (1999) has developed a theoretical model according to which individuals negotiate the main challenges to their personal identity through processes of accommodation and assimilation.

These examples illustrate that the self is resourceful, proactive, and intentional in adapting to the challenges of the aging process. These adaptations include the selection of appropriate levels of performance, the optimization of existing strengths, and the compensation for age-related losses (Baltes & Baltes, 1990). Thus, in combination with other examples from the adult development and aging literature (Aldwin, 1994; Brandtstädter & Greve, 1994; Diehl, Coyle, & Labouvie-Vief, 1996), these highlights show that personality psychologists can enrich their perspective by adopting a life span–theoretical framework and by paying attention to the dynamics between gains and losses.

In summary, instructors can use these unifying themes to anchor the course and encourage students to discuss and evaluate the presented theories with regard to these broader themes. Such an approach explicitly links the different units of the course, provides a sense of continuity, and sensitizes students to the fact that certain basic elements apply to each theory regardless of the theory's specific content.

INCORPORATING ISSUES OF ADULT DEVELOPMENT AND AGING INTO COURSE TOPICS

Even if instructors follow the suggestions just outlined, incorporating adult development and aging into a course on personality psychology is by no means an easy task. What are some of the reasons for this difficulty? First, traditional college students are young adults who are at a stage in their life when issues of aging are usually not of great personal relevance. Unless they have an older adult family member with whom they have or used to have a close relationship, old age is a period of the life span that is experientially so far away that it may be difficult for them to relate in meaningful ways to the process of growing older.

Second, this situation is exacerbated by the generally negative stereotype that exists in our society with regard to the aging process. It is a widely known fact that our society is very youth-oriented and that the mass media, for example, portray older adults mostly in negative terms. These stereotypes are often expressed in our everyday language, where terms such as *old fart*, *grumpy old man*, or *greedy geezer* have become part of regular vocabulary, or they are shown when older individuals are consistently referred to as *granny* or *grandpa*. Instructors need to be aware that their students are exposed to these negative stereotypes and that they very likely have internalized most of them—at least to a certain extent.

Third, even if students have personal experiences with older family members, relatives, or neighbors, rarely do they focus on the positive aspects of the aging process. Rather, they are much more likely to remember the negative sides of growing old. Instructors should not deny that for some people, growing older is associated with decline and illness, but they should use their students' personal experiences as the opportunity to correct the negative stereotypes by providing accurate information and highlighting some of the positive things that are part of the aging process. For example, instructors should share with their students research findings from those areas that have shown how for many adults, aging is associated with positive rather than negative changes. Good examples that drive home this point are research on emotion experience and emotion regulation, the development of coping strategies, subjective well-being, or wisdom.

Although this is a good starting point, instructors need to understand that presenting research findings that contradict students' current opinions does not suffice in the long run. To get students more deeply interested in issues of adult development and aging, it is necessary to create *personalized learning experiences* that actively engage students in contents related to aging. Such experiences serve, to a certain extent, as a preparation for developmental tasks students will face as they grow from young into middle adulthood. The following are a number of exercises and materials that instructors can use at different points throughout their course to incorporate issues of adult development and aging into their teaching activities.

LEARNING ACTIVITIES RELATED TO ADULT DEVELOPMENT AND AGING

The first set of exercises can be incorporated in the section on psychodynamic theories of personality and focuses on the continuity of attachment styles from childhood into adulthood. The second exercise can be used when instructors present trait-theoretical approaches and discuss the stability and change controversy. Finally, the third group of exercises can be incorporated when instructors cover approaches that emphasize the proactive, intentional, and self-determined aspects of personality.

These assignments and exercises were designed to make students struggle with the idea that for the majority of adults, growing older is actually not as negative an experience as the commonly held stereotypes suggest. Through these exercises, young adults increasingly understand that many positive personality-related developments are associated with the normal aging process, such as improved coping skills, better understanding of one's own emotions, and perhaps wisdom and serenity. As research studies have shown, for the overwhelming majority of adults, these positive changes outweigh the negative biological and physical changes that they may experience as they grow older.

Adult Attachment Styles

As pointed out previously, the topic of adult attachment styles (Cassidy & Shaver, 1999) is ideally suited to address issues of *continuity and discontinuity* in personality. Several assignments can make it easier for students to relate the content of this section to their own lives and experiences in close, interpersonal relationships.

The first assignment consists of three related parts. First, students fill out and score the *Relationship Style Questionnaire* (RSQ) (Griffin & Bartholomew, 1994), one of the most commonly used self-report measures in adult attachment research. Subsequently, students code their responses to the questions, derive their scores for the four attachment styles (i.e., secure, preoccupied, dismissive, and fearful attachment) assessed by the RSQ, and determine their primary attachment style.

In the second part, students write a brief essay (1 to 3 pages) explaining in their own words how their primary attachment style has developed and how it influences their current relationship with a romantic partner. For this part, students are encouraged to think about those attachment-related behaviors and emotions that they perceive as having remained the same from childhood to adulthood and those that they perceive as having changed. Furthermore, students are encouraged to include in their assignment their thoughts on how current relationship experiences may have modified or reaffirmed earlier relationship experiences.

The third part of the assignment draws on examples from the media and asks students to describe the attachment styles of one prominent character in a popular television show or movie. Current television shows that instructors can consider for this part of the assignment are *Seinfeld*, *Sex and the City*, *Friends*, *ER*, or *Providence*. Popular movies suitable for this exercise are *When Harry Met Sally*, *You've Got Mail*, *The English Patient*, *Fried Green Tomatoes*, *Driving Miss Daisy*, and many others. These examples are only a selection from a larger pool of shows or movies. The important part is that the instructor chooses a show or movie that deals in detail with close relationships so that students have sufficient opportunity to observe how attachment styles are expressed in the day-to-day interactions of the different characters. Overall, students need to be able to observe a number of behaviors so that they can comment on a pattern that may be indicative of the character's attachment style.

Another assignment that instructors might use when discussing adult attachment styles builds on the *Adult Attachment Interview* (AAI; George, Kaplan, & Main, 1985). Like the AAI, this assignment asks students to come up with five adjectives that best describe their relationship with each parent during childhood and then to provide an account of a particular episode or event from childhood illustrating each adjective. In addition, students are asked to think of specific childhood situations and how their parents reacted to these situations. For example, to which parent did they turn when they were upset or injured as a child? How did the parents express their feelings of emotional closeness and to which parent did they feel closer? How has the relationship with the parents changed over time? How may the early experiences with their parents have affected the ways in which they relate to other people as adults? These instructions tend to generate very interesting papers, and students report a great variety of experiences reported in their assignments. Moreover, this assignment permits students to engage in a good deal of self-analysis and thus helps students to gain considerable insight into their own attachment behavior.

Instructors can further enhance this learning experience by adding another component to this exercise. In addition to simply thinking in a self-reflective way about their relationships with their parents, students may want to interview their parents and query them about their views of how the attachment relationship has changed (or stayed the same) as a son or daughter has grown into a young adult. Gathering information from the parents serves as a complement to the students' own views and gives them the opportunity to gain some insight into their parents' experiences and perceptions, which may foster a greater intergenerational understanding.

The Stability Versus Change Controversy

For most instructors, discussion of the trait-theoretical approaches to personality includes an in-depth treatment of the stability versus change controversy. A three-part writing assignment can be used to personalize the different aspects of this controversy. In the first part, students draw a *life graph* that depicts all the positive and negative life events that they have experienced up to their current age and all the positive and negative events that they expect to happen to them up to age 80. With regard to the future events, students are instructed to think about both normative (i.e., events that occur in every person's life) and nonnormative (i.e., events that are unexpected and do not occur in every person's life) life events. In addition, they are instructed to think about how different people may have played or might play a role in the occurrence of the listed life events.

The life graph is then used to complete the second and third parts of the assignment. The second part of the assignment asks students to describe their main personality characteristics and to reflect on how they have changed (or stayed the same) up to now. In addition, they are asked to reflect on whether certain individuals (e.g., parents, siblings, teachers, friends) or events in their lives may have influenced their personality development up to now. This exercise continues in Part Three of the assignment, where students look into the future and describe how they think they will change (or stay the same) over the remainder of the adult life span up to age 80. Again, students are asked to reflect on whether they anticipate that certain individuals (e.g., spouse, children, friends, colleagues) may influence how they develop over this period and whether their influences may be positive or negative.

This writing assignment challenges students to think more personally about the stability versus change controversy and leads to a deeper level of processing of the research findings presented in the classroom. While completing this assignment, students think about periods of their own lives during which they may expect a good deal of change compared with periods during which they mostly expect stability. Interestingly, students often raise and discuss the same basic questions in their assignments that are debated in the professional journals and in the empirical literature. In contrast to the general literature, however, in the assignments, these questions are embedded into the context of their personal lives.

Successful Aging

At the end of the semester, when all major personality theories have been presented, one or two class sessions are dedicated to discussions related to the following questions: What is optimal personality development? Should theories of personality define desirable developmental endpoints and how could these endpoints be evaluated? How does personality contribute to successful aging?

These questions are raised to make students reflect on how optimal personality development may be defined by different theories and to think about what a desirable endpoint of personality development could be. Of course, this is not the first time during the semester that these questions are raised. At earlier points in the semester, the instructor discussed, for example, that Freud defined a mentally healthy individual as a person who has resolved the sequence of psychosexual conflicts in an appropriate way and who is able to love and work. Thus, students already have had the opportunity to reflect on these issues, and they are now required to synthesize some of their thoughts into a coherent and informed opinion.

With regard to the issue of a desirable endpoint of personality development and the role of personality in successful aging, instructors can draw a good deal on Erikson's theory of psychosocial development and incorporate it into a three-part writing assignment. For the first part, students are required to develop a set of questions for an interview with an older adult of their choice (e.g., a grandparent or great-grandparent, a neighbor, a friend of their family). The questions included in the interview need to focus on the three major psychosocial stages of the adult life span as described by Erikson (1950, 1982). Thus, students generate questions related to issues of interpersonal intimacy (young adulthood), generativity (middle adulthood), and ego integrity (old age) to find out what a person may have done or is doing with regard to these psychosocial crises. After the students have received feedback on their questions from the instructor, they then use these questions to conduct an interview with an older adult who is familiar to them and who consents to the interview. If possible, students tape their interview and transcribe selected parts for inclusion in their papers in which they summarize the important points that they learned from the interview. In writing this summary of the interview, students are specifically instructed to pay attention to and comment on whether the person they interviewed experienced crisis-like periods during his or her adult years and what this person did to avoid the negative developmental outcomes that Erikson described in his theory. Students who cannot interview an older adult are referred to a number of movies and videos (a complete listing of such videos and movies is available on the APA Division 20 Web page, available at http://www.aging.ufl.edu/apadiv20/vidlist.htm and http://www.aging.ufl.edu/apadiv20/cinema.htm) to use to complete this assignment.

Conducting one-on-one interviews with older adults and writing summaries of the stories and experiences that these seasoned individuals share with the students are probably the best routes to counteracting the negative stereotypes that students hold with regard to the aging process. Students who are sufficiently inspired by the interview may continue to visit the older adult and form a friendship with this person that lasts beyond their coursework. Alternatively, each semester, some students decide to form or join a visitation program for residents in assisted care facilities or housing for low-income older adults. Often, these students become seriously interested in the life stories of their new older adult friends and are inspired to pursue a professional career in the aging field.

SUMMARY

The objective of this chapter was to describe ways in which topics related to adult development and aging can be incorporated into an undergraduate core curriculum course on personality psychology. On the one hand, instructors face a number of challenges as they try to incorporate issues related to adult development and aging in their courses. On the other hand, personality psychology lends itself to a natural integration of aging-related themes if the instructor chooses to adopt a life span approach. The main challenge that instructors face in teaching personality psychology is how to create learning situations that connect the abstract content of the theories with the personal experiences and lives of their students. Throughout this chapter, assignments and ideas were suggested that instructors can easily adopt for their purposes or that may stimulate their own thinking and creativity. These assignments have been tested and fine-tuned in the classroom and have been found helpful in creating a personalized learning experience for students.

REFERENCES

Aldwin, C. M. (1994). *Stress, coping, and development: An integrative perspective*. New York: Guilford.

Allport, G. W. (1937). *Personality: A psychological interpretation*. New York: Holt.

Ardelt, M. (2000). Still stable after all these years? Personality stability theory revisited. *Social Psychology Quarterly, 63*, 392–405.

Baltes, P. B. (1987). Theoretical propositions of life-span developmental psychology: On the dynamics between growth and decline. *Developmental Psychology*, 23, 611–626.

Baltes, P. B., & Baltes, M. M. (1990). Psychological perspectives on successful aging: The model of selective optimization with compensation. In P. B. Baltes & M. M. Baltes (Eds.), *Successful aging: Perspectives from the behavioral sciences* (pp. 1– 34). New York: Cambridge University Press.

Baltes, P. B., Staudinger, U. M., & Lindenberger, U. (1999). Lifespan psychology: Theory and application to intellectual functioning. *Annual Review of Psychology*, 50, 471–507.

Bandura, A. (1999). Social cognitive theory of personality. In L. A. Pervin & O. P. John (Eds.), *Handbook of personality: Theory and research* (2nd ed., pp. 154–196). New York: Guilford.

Bowlby, J. (1979). *The making and breaking of affectional bonds*. London, United Kingdom: Tavistock.

Bowlby, J. (1988). *A secure base: Parent-child attachment and healthy human development*. New York: Basic Books.

Brandtstädter, J., & Greve, W. (1994). The aging self: Stabilizing and protective processes. *Developmental Review*, 14, 52–80.

Carstensen, L. L. (1993). Motivation for social contact across the life span: A theory of socioemotional selectivity. In J. E. Jacobs (Ed.), *Nebraska Symposium on Motivation 1992: Vol. 40. Developmental perspectives on motivation* (pp. 209–254). Lincoln, NE: University of Nebraska Press.

Caspi, A. (2000). The child is father to the man: Personality continuities from childhood to adulthood. *Journal of Personality and Social Psychology*, 78, 158–172.

Caspi, A., & Roberts, B. W. (2001). Personality development across the life course: The argument for change and continuity. *Psychological Inquiry*, 12, 49–66.

Caspi, A., & Silva, P. (1995). Temperamental qualities at age three predict personality traits in young adulthood: Longitudinal evidence from a birth cohort. *Child Development*, 66, 486–498.

Cassidy, J., & Shaver, P. R. (Eds.). (1999). *Handbook of attachment: Theory, research, and clinical applications*. New York: Guilford.

Ceci, S. J., & Williams, W. M. (Eds.). (1999). *The nature–nurture debate: The essential readings*. Malden, MA: Blackwell.

Costa, P. T., Jr., & McCrae, R. R. (1997). Longitudinal stability of adult personality. In R. Hogan, J. Johnson, & S. Briggs (Eds.), *Handbook of personality psychology* (pp. 269–290). San Diego: Academic Press.

Derlega, V. J., Winstead, B. A., & Jones, W. H. (Eds.). (1999). *Personality: Contemporary theory and research* (2nd ed.). Chicago: Nelson-Hall.

Diehl, M., Coyle, N., & Labouvie-Vief, G. (1996). Age and sex differences in strategies of coping and defense across the life span. *Psychology and Aging*, 11, 127–139.

Erikson, E. H. (1950). *Childhood and society*. New York: Norton.

Erikson, E. H. (1982). *The life cycle completed*. New York: Norton.

Field, D., & Millsap, R. E. (1991). Personality in advanced old age: Continuity or change? *Journal of Gerontology: Psychological Sciences, 46*, P299–P308.

Freud, S. (1953). Three essays on the theory of sexuality. In J. Strachey (Ed. & Trans.), *The standard edition of the complete psychological works of Sigmund Freud* (Vol. 7, pp. 126–243). London: Hogarth Press. (Original work published 1905)

Freud, S. (1961). The ego and the id. In J. Strachey (Ed. & Trans.), *The standard edition of the complete psychological works of Sigmund Freud* (Vol. 19, pp. 12–66). London: Hogarth Press. (Original work published 1923)

Funder, D. C. (2001). Personality. *Annual Review of Psychology, 52*, 197–221.

George, C., Kaplan, N., & Main, M. (1985). *An adult attachment interview: Interview protocol*. Unpublished manuscript.

Griffin, D. W., & Bartholomew, K. (1994). The metaphysics of measurement: The case of adult attachment. In K. Bartholomew & D. Perlman (Eds.), *Advances in person relationships: Attachment processes in adulthood* (Vol. 5, pp. 17–52). London: Jessica Kingsley.

Hazan, C., & Shaver, P. (1994). Attachment as an organizational framework for research on close relationships. *Psychological Inquiry, 5*, 1–22.

Helson, R. (1993). Comparing studies of adult development: Toward a paradigm of tension between stability and change. In D. C. Funder, R. D. Parke, C. Tomlinson-Keasey, & K. Widaman (Eds.), *Studying lives through time: Personality and development* (pp. 93–119). Washington, DC: American Psychological Association.

Jones, C. J., & Meredith, W. (1996). Patterns of personality change across the life span. *Psychology and Aging, 11*, 57–65.

Jung, C. G. (1933). *Modern man in search of a soul*. New York: Harcourt Brace.

Jung, C. G. (1959). Conscious, unconscious, and individuation. In C. G. Jung, *Collected works* (Vol. 9, Part 1). Princeton, NJ: Princeton University Press. (Original work published 1939)

Labouvie-Vief, G. (1977). Adult cognitive development: In search of alternative interpretations. *Merrill-Palmer Quarterly, 23*, 227–263.

Lewin, K. (1935). *A dynamic theory of personality*. New York: McGraw-Hill.

McAdams, D. P. (2001). *The person: An integrated introduction to personality psychology* (3rd ed.). Fort Worth, TX: Harcourt Brace.

McCartney, K., Harris, M. J., & Bernieri, F. (1990). Growing up and growing apart: A developmental meta-analysis of twin studies. *Psychological Bulletin, 107*, 226–237.

McCrae, R. C., & Costa, P. T., Jr. (1999). A five-factor theory of personality. In L. A. Pervin & O. P. John (Eds.), *Handbook of personality: Theory and research* (2nd ed., pp. 139–153). New York: Guilford.

Mischel, W., & Shoda, Y. (1999). Integrating dispositions and processing dynamics within a unified theory of personality: The cognitive-affective personality system. In L. A. Pervin & O. P. John (Eds.), *Handbook of personality: Theory and research* (2nd ed., pp. 197–218). New York: Guilford.

Murray, H. A. (1938). *Explorations in personality.* New York: Oxford University Press.

Plomin, R., DeFries, J. C., McClearn, G. E., & Rutter, M. (1997). *Behavioral genetics* (3rd ed.). New York: Freeman.

Stern, W. (1924). *Die menschliche Persönlichkeit* [The human personality]. Leipzig, Germany: J. A. Barth.

Troll, L. E., & Skaff, M. M. (1997). Continuity of self in very old age. *Psychology and Aging, 12,* 162–169.

Whitbourne, S. K. (1999). Identity and adaptation to the aging process. In C. D. Ryff & V. W. Marshall (Eds.), *The self and society in aging processes* (pp. 122–149). New York: Springer.

ANNOTATED BIBLIOGRAPHY

Albom, M. (1997). *Tuesdays with Morrie: An old man, a young man and life's great lessons.* New York: Doubleday. Describes the relationship between a young newspaper reporter who meets regularly with one of his former college professors to chronicle his process of dying and to talk about life's great lessons. *Tuesdays with Morrie* is not only an emotionally touching book, but it also is a lasting document of human strength in the face of adversity. This book can serve as a literary companion to the more abstract contents related to adult development and aging.

Baltes, P. B., & Baltes, M. M. (1990). Psychological perspectives on successful aging: The model of selective optimization with compensation. In P. B. Baltes & M. M. Baltes (Eds.), *Successful aging: Perspectives from the behavioral sciences* (pp. 1–34). New York: Cambridge University Press. Summarizes Paul and Margaret Baltes' theory of successful aging, which focuses on the processes of selection, optimization, and compensation. Baltes and Baltes argue that throughout life, development involves maximization of gains over losses or increasing desirable states over undesirable ones. In old age, however, when physical changes may place new limits on individuals' range of functioning, individuals tend to select and optimize those behaviors that are rewarding to them and instrumental for independent living. In addition, older adults engage in behaviors that compensate for experienced or impending losses. Students very likely need some guidance with this chapter because the arguments are complex.

Bowlby, J. (1988). *A secure base: Parent-child attachment and healthy human development.* New York: Basic Books. Summarizes the major portions of Bowlby's work on attachment theory in a very readable format. In addition, it presents Bowlby's main ideas on what role attachment should play during the adult years. Students may need some assistance with some of the psychoanalytic terminology; otherwise, this book is easy to read.

Costa, P. T., Jr., & McCrae, R. R. (1997). Longitudinal stability of adult personality. In R. Hogan, J. Johnson, & S. Briggs (Eds.), *Handbook of personality psychology* (pp. 269–290). San Diego: Academic Press. Summarizes the research findings from the past 2 decades documenting the advances in trait-theoretical approaches to personality and in particular the support in favor of the stability of adult personality. The authors are ardent advocates of the Five-Factor-Model (FFM) of personality that has recently become a dominant force in personality psychology.

Erikson, E. H., Erikson, J. M., & Kivnick, H. Q. (1996). *Vital involvement in old age*. New York: Norton. Gives a succinct overview of Erik Erikson's life span theory of psychosocial development and its implications for late life development. The second part of the book presents the voices of older individuals who were followed over a long period as part of the Berkeley Guidance Study. These individuals were interviewed with regard to Erikson's eight psychosocial themes, and the book describes what they had to say with regard to their lifelong experiences, observations, and insights.

Jones, C. J., & Meredith, W. (1996). Patterns of personality change across the life span. *Psychology and Aging, 11,* 57–65. Presents data from the Berkeley Guidance and Oakland Growth Studies, two famous longitudinal studies that followed their participants over a 40-year period. The article employs sophisticated statistical methods and shows that both stability and change can be documented across the adult life span for six different personality characteristics. Instructors who look for a single piece of evidence related to the stability versus change controversy find a good example in this article and some figures that they can incorporate in their teaching.

Rowe, J. W., & Kahn, R. L. (1998). *Successful aging: The MacArthur Foundation Study*. New York: Pantheon Books. Describes the concept of "successful aging" and reports findings from the MacArthur Study on Successful Aging. The foreword of the volume states, "This book deals with three fundamental questions about human aging: What does it mean to age successfully? What can each of us do to be successful at this most important life task? What changes in American society will enable more men and women to age successfully?" This book can be recommended to instructors who have no background in aging and who look for a quick and efficient way of getting an overview.

8

INCORPORATING AGING INTO UNDERGRADUATE SOCIAL PSYCHOLOGY COURSES

KAREN KOPERA-FRYE, RICHARD WISCOTT, DEAN BLEVINS, AND ANA BEGOVIC

A brief review of contemporary undergraduate textbooks currently used in social psychology and gerontology courses demonstrates areas of considerable overlap. The incorporation of the rapidly expanding field of gerontology within the curriculum of traditional social psychology can be easily accomplished without the requirement of instructors becoming gerontologists themselves. Students and instructors usually find it "natural" in understanding social psychological issues within the context of later life, as most have had at least some personal experience with adult development whether through neighbors, grandparents, aging parents, or their own aging experiences. The present chapter highlights examples of topics that intersect

Please direct correspondence to Karen Kopera-Frye, University of Nevada–Reno, Department of Human Development and Family Studies & Sanford Center for Aging, Mail Stop 140, 1664 North Virginia, Reno, NV 89557; e-mail: kfrye@unr.edu. The authors would like to express their gratitude to Ms. Barb Bucur for her assistance in manuscript preparation.

social psychology and gerontology, particularly those in which research has demonstrated age group similarities and differences between younger and older adults.

The population of older adults is growing in absolute and relative terms. In 1900, 4% of the United States population was more than 65 years of age; that figure increased to approximately 13% in 2000 (U.S. Bureau of the Census, 2000). By 2030, it is projected that 20% of the population will be older than age 65, with 5% older than age 85 by the year 2050 (U.S. Bureau of the Census, 2000).

Consequently, older adults are certainly more visible, and particularly more influential than in the past. The very nature of the changing needs of an increasingly technological society has called for the involvement of experienced adults, including those who can offer the kinds of expertise that can only be accumulated over a lifetime. These trends are relevant to the instruction of social psychology for several reasons.

A critical concern involves the need to extend traditional social psychological research to later phases of the life span. Evidence has suggested that some areas of social psychology may be differentially experienced by older adults as both the social and cognitive changes that accompany aging produce circumstances that are qualitatively unlike those of the traditionally researched younger adults (Dixon & Hultsch, 1999). Second, new applications of constructs once predominantly studied among younger adults (e.g., identity development) may produce exciting new opportunities for research on social psychological issues among older adults. The discussions offered in this chapter demonstrate a few of the areas where gerontology may enhance the rich research base established by social psychologists. Encouraging both educational professionals to inspire colleagues and students to broaden their horizons by focusing on this growing population will create the foundation for a lasting bridge between the two disciplines.

The chapter provides practical recommendations on how to incorporate aging into instruction of undergraduate social psychology courses. Specifically, this chapter has the following objectives: (1) allow for an understanding of how social psychological topics overlap with those studied in the psychology of aging; (2) gain basic theoretical knowledge necessary to introduce instructional topics including the self, prosocial behaviors, intergroup relations, and health and policy issues; and (3) provide class exercises and resources that can be undertaken to illustrate areas of overlap between social psychology and aging.

Typical content covered in popular undergraduate social psychology textbooks includes methodology, social cognition, self theory, attribution and interpersonal processes, attitudes, social relationships, group processes, prosocial behavior, aggression, prejudice or stereotyping, and health. Commonly addressed content in the psychology of aging course includes research methods, physiological change, information processing, intelligence/

creativity, mature thought/wisdom, social relationships, education/work/ retirement/leisure, personality, coping/mental health/adaptation, and death and dying. At first glance, the interface of these two curricula may not be readily apparent purely because of differences in terminology. For example, is caregiving behavior, which is often studied in aging, an example of the social psychological phenomena called *prosocial behavior*? The main point is that all of these content areas do indeed overlap, especially if a life course perspective is promoted. By exposing students to a broader study of traditional social psychology concepts, instructors can prepare them for careers in an aging society.

Although limited space precludes parallels between aging and coverage of all traditionally studied social psychology topics, four topics are illustrated here: self processes, prosocial behaviors, intergroup processes, and health and politics. These topics were selected because they represent different levels of psychological analysis: individual, relational, group, and social, respectively. A brief description of these topics is provided here; more detailed explanations follow.

At the individual level of analysis, social identity processes (e.g., self) are key to understanding the placement of a person within the larger group. How we conceptualize and evaluate ourselves is a critical area in social psychology. However, prior studies of this concept have often been restricted to younger adults, without much focus on how social identity processes change with age, as is suggested by recent studies (Whitbourne, 1996).

Caregiving behavior, studied by aging researchers, is one example of prosocial/altruistic behavior in social psychology. Although many reasons underlie the exchange of care, several traditional social theories can apply to this situation (e.g., social exchange theory, Foa & Foa, 1975; kinship protection, Barash, 1979).

Stereotyping and discrimination are often studied within the context of an outgroup/ingroup distinction in social theory. However, the concept of ageism allows for a unique dimension of this phenomenon in that with increasing age, individuals may experience both sides of this distinction. This example allows for exciting exploration of whether group characteristics traditionally studied (e.g., ethnicity) can be generalized to ageism.

Because of the greater likelihood of health problems with age, attitudes and behaviors relevant to the course, treatment, and prevention of disease become a critical concern. Particularly because of increased longevity, declining health coverage, and greater concern for reducing health care costs, public policy implications are many.

Self

In the past few decades, the increased interest in self and its development across the life span has resulted in numerous theories and studies

(Brandtstädter & Greve, 1994; Cross & Markus, 1991; Labouvie-Vief, Chiodo, Goguen, Diehl, & Orwoll, 1995), reflecting a change from the belief that self is a unitary, conscious, and integrated entity toward the view that self is a complex, changing, multidimensional structure that may be influenced by a variety of contexts such as physiological changes (Whitbourne, 2003), history, culture, and interpersonal relationships (Brandtstädter & Greve, 1994). Brandtstädter and Greve further highlighted the self as instrumental in the representation, evaluation, and active control of the individual's development over the life span. It has been suggested that the developmental relevance of the self is in self-organization, self-reproduction, and self-stabilization (Markus & Kunda, 1986), which in turn are important to the stability, resilience, and resourcefulness of the aging self.

An aspect of the self that has received considerable attention is self-complexity. This involves organizing self-knowledge into relatively independent entities; the greater the degree of independence among self-aspects, the greater the self-complexity. Linville (1987) noted a significant relationship between self-complexity and stress-related illnesses and depression. Baltes and Carstensen (1991) asserted that those with greater self-complexity are able to adjust more easily their self-representation in response to the loss of competencies, opportunities, or interests with age. Therefore, the more well-defined and complex are the self-schemas older adults have acquired over the life span, the more versatile and flexible they will become in adapting to adversity. Although evidence has suggested a decline in complexity with age (Labouvie-Vief et al., 1995), older adults tend to exhibit more behaviors focused on the realization of desired self-states (Cross & Markus, 1991), seeking out experiences "before it's too late."

Assessment of such age differences can be used in classroom activities or as homework assignments through instruments such as the SELE, a self-referencing task consisting of 28 items (e.g., I am best at...), which is described in detail in Katzko, Stevernik, Dittmann-Kohli, and Herrera (1998). Each sentence should be completed as if it is true for the particular individual (i.e., student, parent, or grandparent). The responses are grouped into a manageable number of categories such as family (children, spouse), activities, socialization (nonfamilial), personality, maintenance, autonomy, and habitation. This exercise may include participation of students, parents, and grandparents, and the scores on the completed self-referencing instrument of the three age groups can be compared.

Another measure of self-complexity was developed by Linville (1985, 1987). The students are given a packet of 33 randomly ordered index cards, each containing the name of a positive or negative trait (e.g., outgoing, intelligent, lazy). Students are asked to think about themselves and to sort these traits into groups that are representative of them; not all traits have to be used, and some can be used more than once. Blank index cards can be provided for additional traits. The participants may choose a wide range of traits to describe themselves, and a self-complexity score can be calculated for each individual, based on each person's grouped traits. Discussion can then focus on commonly chosen or unique traits across the group.

Another good way to measure self-complexity is an adaptation of Labouvie-Vief et al.'s (1995) method. Students are given a paper with "I ..." in the upper left corner and instructed to spend approximately 5 minutes writing a brief paragraph about themselves, their likes and dislikes, and any thoughts about themselves. Although the scoring is a complex procedure and may not be easily completed in the classroom setting, the exercise could be assigned as homework and a modified scoring procedure could then be used to allow students to share themes evident in self-descriptions and affective tone.

Finally, students can explore "multiple selves" by employing the Cross and Markus (1991) method of possible selves. Students are asked to generate hoped-for selves (e.g., being a grandparent, traveling around the world, winning the lottery) or feared selves (i.e., being in poor health). This exercise takes 10 to 15 minutes to complete and can be conducted at home by students, their parents, and possibly by grandparents. Scoring can focus on the number and type of selves generated, such as parent, friend, student, and tennis player.

In summary, the most recent literature has indicated that the self-concept is active, forceful, and capable of change across the life span (Cross & Markus, 1991) and that an important ingredient to successful aging is a complex, positive view of the self, which is maintained more easily when a person has several selves to draw on and engage in during the aging process. The previously described instruments of self-assessment are by no means exhaustive; however, they can be amenable to demonstrating changing self-processes with increasing age.

Prosocial Behaviors

Given the improved health practices in today's society, individuals can expect to live longer than at any other time in the past. With this current trend comes the increased likelihood that people will find themselves in a caregiving role; either as recipient or provider of care. Much research on the psychology of aging has focused on this phenomenon (e.g., Zarit & Zarit, 1998) regarding the varieties of caregiving situations such as caring for older parents, custodial grandparenting, and caregiving in long-term care settings. Factors that influence why and how caregiving occurs have also been studied (Burton, 1995; Cavanaugh, 1998). In light of the importance of this increasing trend, the question becomes what social psychology might offer in terms of insight into the caregiving process.

A logical link to how caregiving can be illustrated in social psychological theory resides in the notion of prosocial/altruistic behavior. This is an important area in social psychology that has theoretical models focusing on why people help. Traditional definitions of prosocial/altruistic behavior in social psychology define this type of behavior as motives and behaviors directed toward increasing another's welfare without regard for one's self-interests. Much empirical attention on this type of behavior, whether it involves aiding strangers or related individuals, has concentrated on the motives and reasons for why aid is given and under what circumstances it is more likely to occur. Such social psychological theories include social exchange theory (Foa & Foa, 1975), kinship protection (Barash, 1979), and norms of reciprocity (Gouldner, 1960). Caregiving behavior, which may be a specific example of such helping behavior, can be understood in light of these theories.

Caregiving research in gerontology has suggested that people are more likely to offer help in situations where they believe that the favor will be returned (Parris Stephens & Franks, 1999). The work of Antonucci, Sherman, and Akiyama (1996) with younger and older adults suggested that there is a norm of reciprocity—that is, providing and exchanging emotional and tangible social support or aid is like a bank deposit where aid can be obtained from these individuals at a later date. Antonucci et al.'s research indicated that older adults often receive more aid than they provide, with women preferring support from friends and men preferring support from their spouses. The two most common forms of support include provisions of emotional reassurance and care when ill.

Additional support for the operation of prosocial motives is provided by research from another type of caregiving situation, custodial grandparenting. In this situation, grandparents assume the parental role over grandchildren when their parents are unable or unwilling to care for their children. The motive in this type of caregiving seems to be one of generational stake (Bengtson, Schaie, & Burton, 1995) or kin protection. The basic idea in this theory is that evolution has selected altruism toward one's close relatives (i.e., shared gene pool) to enhance survival of mutually shared genes. Research has documented the great lengths that older adults go through to provide surrogate parenting to grandchildren, including financial, emotional, and caretaking aspects (Burton, 1992; Hayslip & Goldberg-Glen, 2000; Minkler & Roe, 1993).

Students can understand the interface between aging and the social/psychological concept of prosocial behavior through several exercises. Having students interview caretakers who are custodial grandparents, professionals involved in long-term care settings (e.g., nursing homes), or adults caring for older adult parents can elucidate the different possible motives underlying prosocial behavior (such as norms of reciprocity versus kin protection). In some cases, the caregiving is undertaken purely for financial reasons because the families are not able to afford alternative means of caregiving. Therefore, altruism as a caregiving motive is rather minimal. Interviews with individuals in two different caregiving contexts can be completed and a discussion in class can focus on which social psychological theories best support the motives of the respondents. Furthermore, students can analyze the caregiving contexts to understand which forms of caregiving may be altruistically driven or otherwise.

Another helpful exercise involves understanding the costs and benefits of prosocial caregiving behavior—that is, what is the expense of caregiving in terms of physical, financial, emotional costs? Students can locate custodial grandparents recruited through the local community senior centers or custodial grandparent support groups (if available) to assess the type of assistance given, needs of the caregiver (e.g., financial), and reports of the positive (e.g., supporting the future generation) and negative aspects (e.g., greater life stress for self) of caregiving. These dimensions can be contrasted across caregiving individuals who differ in gender, ethnicity, and age. Overall, the research with diverse groups has suggested that despite great costs to the mental and physical health of caregivers, caregivers perceive their situations as rewarding.

Intergroup Relations

Research on intergroup relations has traditionally concentrated on ethnocultural and gender groups. Because an increasingly larger number and percentage of people are living into old age, concerns are being raised about how this growing number of older adults will interact with other age groups. The brief space available to this rather diverse and prolific area of research precludes a full examination of interpersonal relations. Thus, the following section focuses on the prevalence and effect of stereotypes, which may or may not constitute prejudice and discrimination.

Age-based stereotypes and discrimination are unique in that although an outgroup homogeneity effect is evident just as with other forms of group bias, eventually age "outgroups" become "ingroups" as one grows older. This type of universal personal relevance is not evident with other stigmatized groups. No work has explored how developmental changes influence the transitions between these statuses within a single individual. However, the theoretical positions of contemporary researchers (Brandtstädter & Greve, 1994; Whitbourne, 2003) suggest that attempts to adapt to the many physiological and social changes that accompany aging may lead to a gradual adoption of age stereotypes simply to reduce the intrapsychic threat that can arise because of these changes. Therefore, to reduce the dissonance that results from the realization that one is becoming a part of this stigmatized group, people may begin to apply age stereotypes to themselves.

Developmentally, then, one may introduce discussions in the classroom of the middle-age man who suddenly purchases a sports car and begins associating with groups that are primarily composed of people in their twenties.

This existence of a mid-life crisis is actually not as common as believed, but can serve as an example of how Tajfel and Turner's social identity theory (see Brown, Tajfel, & Turner, 1980) illustrates how one adjusts to becoming "middle-aged," fighting the reclassification as a part of this age-stigmatized group. In an attempt to maintain positive self-esteem, this man may be attempting to continue a personal identity as a younger adult by socially affiliating with groups composed of younger adults.

Research has shown that younger adults often endorse misperceptions about aging and older adults (Palmore, 1990). Consistent with the theories noted previously, growing older does not, however, diminish the prevalence of such misperceptions. In fact, several lines of converging evidence have suggested that older adults tend to endorse more stereotypes of their own age group than any of the younger age groups (Hummert, Garstka, Shanes, & Strahm, 1994). In addition to the negative stereotypes people of younger ages endorse, it has been suggested that this increase among older adults is the result of a greater acceptance among older adults of positive stereotypes. Critics have argued that this finding illustrates a possible cohort effect resulting from the cross-sectional design of many of these studies (e.g., Westerhof & Dittmann-Kohli, 2000). Nevertheless, additional evidence has suggested that overtly older adults expressing these views do not view themselves as being characteristic of the rest of their ingroup (i.e., older adults), which may indicate a new application of how subcategorization may occur or could be a form of stereotype threat.

Several exercises illustrate the pervasiveness of ageist stereotypes in the community. For example, instructors can have students collect greeting cards (especially birthday cards) depicting stereotypical images of older adults such as older adults playing bingo or notations in cards about being "chronologically challenged" and discuss the types of stereotypes found (e.g., image-oriented, activity-oriented). Furthermore, television shows such as reruns of *Golden Girls* or *Murder She Wrote* plus others can prompt a discussion of the role of stereotypes in media. Finally, instructors can have students observe the demeanor and verbal behavior of mall shoppers when an older adult is at the counter having difficulty during the holidays. The observations can prompt in-class discussions focusing on occurrence of impatience, negative comments, and the like among the customers waiting in line behind the older person.

This notion of stereotype threat among older adults, based on the existence of many stereotypes, has been extensively researched by such individuals as Becca Levy, Mary Lee Hummert, and Erdman Palmore (Levy, 1996, 1999, 2000; Hausdorff, Levy, & Wei, 1999; Hummert, 1999; Hummert et al., 1994; Palmore, 1998, 2000). Their work indicates that numerous negatively and positively valenced stereotypes of aging can either hinder or facilitate performance depending on which type is activated; effects that have similarly been demonstrated among ethnic and gender groups (Shih,

Pittinsky, & Ambady, 1999). However, in a later study, adults were primed with an image of an older adult to examine the effects stereotypes have on sense of self. Those people with more accurate knowledge of aging demonstrated self-portrayals that were more similar to controls than to the rest of the primed participants (i.e., those that were less knowledgeable). Thus, accurate knowledge of aging may mediate the effects of age-based stereotypes, qualifying evidence that stereotypes automatically and inevitably influence perceptions and behavior (Blevins & Kopera-Frye, 2001).

In the context of classroom instruction, the inclusion of age in the discussions of interpersonal relations can easily be piggybacked onto discussions of the traditionally examined groups. Several gerontologists have begun discussing the multiplicative effect age can have in interpersonal relations, especially among the most rapidly growing segment of older adults—women and nonwhite ethnic groups. A concept of triple jeopardy has been proposed for older women who are African American, Latino, or Asian. Similarly, the processes that have been proposed to operate to maintain esteem between groups may allow aging adults to begin gradually to accept (or deny) their own maturation into the older adult category.

Health and Public Policy

A recent interest among faculty and students has focused upon the practical applications of social psychological knowledge. This change in orientation creates many opportunities for social psychologists to build on prior research to explore and expand applied areas of study. Because of longer life expectancies, the older population explosion, and new insight into the capabilities of older individuals, instructors can draw from many real-world examples. In the following sections, we offer suggestions for integrating aging into two such areas: health and public policy.

Health

The study of health is an important dimension in many undergraduate social psychology classes. In this part of the course, students are asked to apply previously learned concepts and theories. For example, a startling and disturbing statistic is that the risk for all of the 10 leading causes of death in the United States today can be lowered by behavior modification and lifestyle changes (U.S. Department of Health and Human Services, Centers for Disease Control and Prevention, 2000). Thus, an understanding of attitude formation, attitude change, and the relationship between attitudes and behavior becomes paramount. Although health issues are important across the life span, examples from the aging literature can help students to link theory with practice. Older people are far more likely to die from chronic health conditions such as heart disease, stroke, suicide, diabetes, and atherosclerosis. Thus, it becomes important to explore ways to effect change in health attitudes, beliefs, and behavior among older adults. By using elders as examples in the classroom, students are not only exposed to important gerontological information but also have the opportunity to brainstorm possible ways to promote lifestyle changes in this group. An additional benefit is that students may take their combined knowledge of aging health risks and social psychological theory to family and friends who may benefit from their zeal.

An applied example helps illustrate this important point. Mary Jane has just learned from her social psychology professor that smoking is a leading cause of health disability among the old. Mary Jane's grandfather smokes. She also remembers the previous week when the professor spoke about the use of persuasion and attitude change. Later, in an attempt to change her grandfather's smoking patterns, Mary Jane relies on several known persuasive techniques (Kosslyn & Rosenberg, 2001). She provides information from the American Cancer Society (expert testimony), brings up the topic at various times throughout the next week (mere exposure effect), and tells him that she really wants him to live long enough to enrich the lives of her own children (use of strong emotion). This example highlights both the potentially powerful classroom (i.e., remember material) and practical (i.e., applied) benefits that introducing aging-related material into social psychology courses can bring.

Another important area of health covered by many social psychologists includes the relationship between stress and illness. The influence of stress on illness is important at all ages (Taylor, 1999). However, it is also essential to emphasize to students that older people may be subject to unique stressors later in life and may deal with those stressors differently than adults of younger ages (Aldwin, 1994). Many of the items contained on common stress inventories (Sarason, Johnson, & Siegel, 1978) may not be applicable to older adults and may not include potential stressors that are late-life–specific (e.g., the loss of friends and relatives because of death). For example, the majority of older people are no longer employed, do not have children living at home, and are not engaged in formal education. Because many stress measures ask a disproportionate number of questions in these domains, a false impression is created of reduced stress when these scales are used with older adults.

It is important for instructors to include possible late-life–specific experiences that may be sources of stress for older individuals (e.g., routine doctor visits or medical tests, changing medications, senior center activities, intergenerational conflict, ageism, and changes in physical appearance and ability). This analysis may additionally foster critical thinking about possible exclusions on stress inventories for other populations. Critical thought discussions can center on unique stressors experienced by younger adults (e.g., peer pressure to use alcohol and drugs), minority individuals (e.g., racism, family structure, values), and other stigmatized or marginalized groups (e.g., the unique challenges faced by individuals with severe physical or mental challenges). By encouraging students to apply these concepts to real-life situations, retention may be enhanced.

Public Policy

There are natural relationships between aging, social psychology, and public policy. More than 90% of people age 50 years and older are registered to vote. Older adults are more likely to cast a ballot in all levels of governmental elections than any other age group (Binstock & Day, 1996). In the United States today, more than 35% of the federal budget is allocated to programs that directly affect the health and well-being of older citizens (e.g., Social Security, Medicare; Siegler, 2000). These trends will continue as our government is certain to be significantly affected by the aging of the nation's 60-plus million Baby Boomers. Thus, it becomes imperative to include aging into discussions of the social psychology of politics.

Students can draw on previously learned material to understand this area in more depth. Some examples of particular concepts that could be discussed include person perception, conflict, cognitive dissonance, leadership, attitude formation, and persuasion. An applied example like the one that follows can help illustrate ways to incorporate gerontology into the social psychology of political behavior.

John is 75 years old. He is the president of his local senior citizens group. His parents were Democrats, and he has always voted for Democrats (attitude formation and consistency). However, in an upcoming election, the Democratic candidate for state senator has a platform that John perceives as unfriendly to older citizens (person perception and cognitive dissonance). He is torn because the Republican candidate is in favor of policies that are important to him such as prescription drug benefits for older adults and an increase in the state's funding of Medicare. Not only is John worried about how he will vote, but also others in his senior group are looking to him for guidance (leadership principles). Many people in his group are unhappy that he is considering a change in his lifetime voting patterns, and there has been talk about John not being president of the group in the future (conflict). To help ease his concerns, John has invited both candidates to an upcoming senior group meeting so they can present their positions on the issues (persuasion). Until then, John will consider to weigh the issues in the hopes of finding a solution to his problem.

As students discuss these types of scenarios, there are great opportunities for integration of class material. Applied examples also foster critical thought on the part of professors and students to find solutions to commonly encountered real world problems. By bridging the gap between theoretical concepts and applying these concepts to everyday issues and concerns, professors are more likely to pique student interest and facilitate learning.

REFERENCES

Aldwin, C. M. (1994). *Stress, coping, and development: An integrative perspective*. New York: Guilford Press.

Antonucci, T. C., Sherman, A. M., & Akiyama, H. (1996). Social networks, support, and integration. In J. E. Birren (Vol. Ed.), *Encyclopedia of gerontology: Age, aging, and the aged: Vol. 2 L-Z index* (pp. 505–515). Orlando: Academic Press.

Baltes, M. M., & Carstensen, L. L. (1991). Commentary. *Human Development, 34,* 256–260.

Barash, D. (1979). *The whisperings within*. New York: Harper & Row.

Bengtson, V. L., Schaie, K. W., & Burton, L. M. (1995). *Adult intergenerational relations: Effects of societal change*. New York: Springer.

Binstock, R. H., & Day, C. L. (1996). Aging and politics. In R. H. Binstock & L. K. George (Eds.), *Handbook of aging and the social sciences* (4th ed., pp. 362–387). San Diego, CA: Academic.

Blevins, D., & Kopera-Frye, K. (2001). *Impact of ageist stereotypes on the perception of self among older adults*. Unpublished manuscript.

Brandtstädter, J., & Greve, W. (1994). The aging self: Stabilizing and protective processes. *Developmental Review, 14,* 52–80.

Brown, R. J., Tajfel, H., & Turner, J. C. (1980). Minimal group situation and intergroup discrimination: Comment on the paper by Aschbrenner and Schaefer. *European Journal of Social Psychology, 10,* 399–414.

Burton, L. (1992). Black grandparents rearing children of drug-addicted parents: Stressors, outcomes and social service needs. *Gerontologist, 32,* 744–751.

Burton, L. (1995). Intergenerational patterns of providing care in African-American families with teenage childbearers: Emergent patterns in an ethnographic study. In V. L. Bengtson, K. Warner Schaie, & L. Burton (Eds.), *Adult intergenerational relations: Effects of societal change* (pp. 79–96). New York: Springer.

Cavanaugh, J. C. (1998). Caregiving to adults: A life event challenge. In I. H. Nordhus, G. R. VandenBos, S. Berg, & P. Fromholt (Eds.), *Clinical geropsychology* (pp. 131–136). Washington, DC: American Psychological Association.

Cross, S., & Markus, H. (1991). Possible selves across the life span. *Human Development, 34,* 230–255.

Dixon, R. A., & Hultsch, D. F. (1999). Intelligence and cognitive potential in later life. In J. C. Cavanaugh & S. K. Whitbourne (Eds.), *Gerontology: An interdisciplinary perspective* (pp. 213–237). New York: Oxford University Press.

Foa, U. G., & Foa, E. B. (1975). *Resource theory of social exchange*. Morristown, NJ: General Learning Press.

Gouldner, A. W. (1960). The norm of reciprocity: A preliminary statement. *American Sociological Review, 25,* 161–178.

Hausdorff, J. M., Levy, B. R., & Wei, J. Y. (1999). The power of ageism on physical function of older persons: Reversibility of age-related gait changes. *Journal of the Geriatrics Society, 47*(11), 1346–1349.

Hayslip, B., Jr., & Goldberg-Glen, R. (Eds.). (2000). *Grandparents raising grandchildren: Theoretical, empirical, and clinical perspectives*. New York: Springer.

Hummert, M. L. (1999). A social cognitive perspective on age stereotypes. In T. M. Hess & F. Blanchard-Fields (Eds.), *Social cognition and aging* (pp. 175–196). San Diego, CA: Academic Press.

Hummert, M. L., Garstka, T. A., Shanes, J. L., & Strahm, S. (1994). Stereotypes of the elderly held by young, middle-aged, and elderly adults. *Journal of Gerontology: Psychological Sciences, 49*(5), P240–P249.

Katzko, M. W., Stevernik, N., Dittmann-Kohli, F., & Herrera, R. R. (1998). The self-concept of the elderly: A cross-cultural comparison. *International Journal of Aging and Human Development, 46,* 171–187.

Kosslyn, S. M., & Rosenberg, R. S. (2001). *Psychology: The brain, the person, the world*. Needham Heights, MA: Allyn and Bacon.

Labouvie-Vief, G., Chiodo, L. M., Goguen, L. A., Diehl, M., & Orwoll, L. (1995). Representation of self across the life span. *Psychology and Aging, 10,* 404–415.

Levy, B. (1996). Improving memory in old age through implicit self-stereotyping. *Journal of Personality and Social Psychology, 71*(6), 1092–1107.

Levy, B. (1999). The inner self of the Japanese elderly: A defense against negative stereotypes of aging. *International Journal of Aging and Human Development, 48*(2), 131–144.

Levy, B. (2000). Handwriting as a reflection of aging self-stereotypes. *Journal of Geriatric Psychiatry, 33*(1), 81–94.

Linville, P. W. (1985). Self-complexity and affective extremity: Don't put all of your eggs in one cognitive basket. *Social Cognition, 3,* 94–120.

Linville, P. W. (1987). Self-complexity as a cognitive buffer against stress-related illness and depression. *Journal of Personality and Social Psychology, 52,* 663–676.

Markus, H., & Kunda, Z. (1986). Stability and malleability of the self-concept. *Journal of Personality and Social Psychology, 51,* 858–866.

Minkler, M., & Roe, M. (1993). *Grandmothers as caregivers: Raising children of the crack cocaine epidemic*. Newbury Park, CA: Sage.

Palmore, E. B. (1990). *Ageism: Negative and positive*. New York: Springer.

Palmore, E. B. (1998). *The facts on aging quiz* (2nd ed.). New York: Springer.

Palmore, E. B. (2000). *The facts on aging quiz* (3rd ed.). New York: Springer.

Parris Stephens, M. A., & Franks, M. M. (1999). Intergenerational relationships in later-life families: Adult daughters and sons as caregivers to aging parents. In J. C. Cavanaugh & S. K. Whitbourne (Eds.), *Gerontology: An interdisciplinary perspective* (pp. 329–354). New York: Oxford University Press.

Sarason, I. G., Johnson, J. H., & Siegel, J. M. (1978). Assessing the impact of life changes: Development of the Life Experiences Survey. *Journal of Consulting and Clinical Psychology, 46,* 932–946.

Shih, M., Pittinsky, T. L., & Ambady, N. (1999). Stereotype susceptibility: Identity salience and shifts in quantitative performance. *Psychological Science, 10*(1), 80–83.

Siegler, I. C. (2000). Aging research and health: A status report. In S. H. Qualls &
N. Abeles (Eds.), *Psychology and the aging revolution: How we adapt to longer life*
(pp. 207–222). Washington, DC: American Psychological Association.

Taylor, S. (1999). *Health psychology* (4th ed.). New York: McGraw-Hill.

U. S. Bureau of the Census. (2000). *Decennial census data and population projections,
2000*. Washington, DC: U. S. Government Printing Office.

U. S. Department of Health and Human Services. Centers for Disease Control and
Prevention. (2000). *CDC Fact Book 2000/2001*. Atlanta, GA.

Westerhof, G. J., & Dittmann-Kohli, F. (2000). Work status and the construction of
work-related selves. In K. W. Schaie & J. Hendricks (Eds.), *The evolution of the
aging self* (pp. 123–157). New York: Springer.

Whitbourne, S. K. (2003). *The aging individual: Physical and psychological perspectives*
(2nd ed.). New York: Springer.

Zarit, S. H., & Zarit, J. M. (1998). Family caregiving. In S. H. Zarit & J. M. Zarit (Eds.), *Mental disorders in older adults* (pp. 290–319). New York: Guilford
Press.

ANNOTATED BIBLIOGRAPHY

Self

Baltes, M. M., & Carstensen, L. L. (1991). Commentary. *Human Development, 34*,
256–260. Contains commentary on Cross and Markus (1991) article. The
authors agree with most concepts of possible selves and two proposed models
of successful aging. However, they express some reservations and offer some
cautionary notes regarding the degree of convergence and impact.

Cross, S., & Markus, H. (1991). Possible selves across the life span. *Human Development, 34*, 230–255. Discusses the study of individuals ages 18 and 86 describing
their hoped-for and feared possible selves. The authors found differences across
age groups in the above-mentioned categories of possible selves. The individuals scoring low in life satisfaction had different possible selves than those scoring high in life satisfaction.

Linville, P. W. (1985). Self-complexity and affective extremity: Don't put all of your
eggs in one cognitive basket. *Social Cognition, 3*, 94–120. Examines the buffering effects of complexity of self-representation on the life's stressful events. The
author found that level of self-complexity might provide a promising cognitive
vulnerability to depression.

Whitbourne, S. K. (2003). *The aging individual: Physical and psychological perspectives*
(2nd ed.). New York: Springer. Provides an in-depth review of the physiological
and cognitive changes that accompany aging; considers how an individual's self
adapts to these changes, coping with the realization of getting older.

Prosocial Behavior/Caregiving

Bengtson, V. L., Schaie, K. W., & Burton, L. M. (Eds.). (1995). *Adult intergenerational relations: Effects of societal change*. New York: Springer. Provides an excellent overview of the changing nature of intergenerational relationships, especially with respect to the intergenerational stake hypothesis as a possible motive for prosocial behavior and caregiving.

Hayslip, B., Jr., & Goldberg-Glen, R. (Eds.). (2000). *Grandparents raising grandchildren: Theoretical, empirical, and clinical perspectives*. New York: Springer. Edited volume that provides state-of-the-art research on the newly emerging phenomena, custodial grandparenting. It covers all aspects of the costs and benefits of this form of surrogate parenting among diverse ethnicities.

Parris Stephens, M. A., & Franks, M. M. (1999). Intergenerational relationships in later-life families: Adult daughters and sons as caregivers to aging parents. In J. C. Cavanaugh & S. K. Whitbourne (Eds.), *Gerontology: An interdisciplinary perspective* (pp. 329–354). New York: Oxford University Press. Provides a nice overview of current findings regarding adults who are caring for older parents, with an eye to the notion of a "sandwich generation" phenomenon.

Self and Intergroup Processes

Hess, T. H., & Blanchard-Fields, F. (Eds.). (1999). *Social cognition and aging*. San Diego, CA: Academic Press. Edited volume that provides a broad review of the contemporary gerontological theory and research in social cognition. Two of the four topics discussed in the present chapter (intergroup processes and self) are extensively reviewed.

Pratt, M. W., & Norris, J. E. (1994). *The social psychology of aging*. Cambridge, MA: Blackwell Science. Somewhat dated edited volume that provides insights within the many intersections of gerontological and social psychological topics ranging from the self, attitudes, group perceptions, and societal perceptions to communication and decision making.

Health and Public Policy

Caro, F. G., Morris, R., & Norton, J. R. (Eds.). (2000). *Advancing aging policy as the 21st century begins*. New York: Haworth Press. In discussing numerous areas of geropolicy, the contributing authors focus on how current gerontological research knowledge from psychology, nursing, sociology, and other areas can be included in public policy initiatives to improve the conditions of older adults.

Siegler, I. C. (2000). Aging research and health: A status report. In S. H. Qualls and N. Abeles (Eds.), *Psychology and the aging revolution: How we adapt to longer life* (pp. 207–222). Washington, DC: American Psychological Association. Provides a great global overview of how we measure disease and illness, what life span developmental health psychology is about, and what we know to date about the health status of older adults.

Stroebe, W., & Stroebe, M. S. (1995). *Social psychology and health*. New York: Brooks/ Cole. Provides a theoretical overview of the attitudes toward health prevention, determinants of health behavior, stress and health, and the role of social psychological theory in health.

U.S. Census Bureau. *Gender and Aging: Mortality and Health*, http://www.census.gov/ ipc/prod/ib98-2.pdf (successfully accessed 6/21/01). Web site that displays a report prepared by the International division of the U.S. Census Bureau.

OTHER SUGGESTED RESOURCES

The following Web sites cover a broad array of gerontological issues related to health, quality of life, attitudes, and self.

American Association of Retired Persons, http://www.aarp.org/indexes/about.html

American Society on Aging, http://www.info@asa.asaaging.org

Administration on Aging, http://www.aoa.dhhs.gov/aoa/resource.html

American Sociological Society, http://www.asanet.org

Duke University Claude D. Pepper Older Americans Independence Center, http://www.geri.duke.edu

9

INFUSING AGING CONTENT INTO HEALTH PSYCHOLOGY COURSES

AURORA M. SHERMAN

Siegler (1989; Siegler, Bastian, & Bosworth, 2001) conceptualized a "developmental health psychology" at "the intersection of health, behavior and aging" (Siegler et al., 2001, p. 469). Elias, Elias, and Elias (1990) proposed a "health psychology of aging" (p. 80) that focuses on including psychological constructs in the prevention and treatment of disease and in improving the quality of life for persons with illnesses or disabilities. Teaching health psychology from a perspective informed about the aging process and current gerontological research can both illuminate Siegler's intersection and improve our progress toward the goals outlined by Elias et al. as we educate future researchers, social workers, and health care practitioners.

Aging and a life span perspective can be naturally incorporated into health psychology courses because health and development are intimately related across the life course. For example, the expansion of life expectancy over the past century and the extended survival of older cohorts have influ-

Please direct correspondence to Aurora M. Sherman, Department of Psychology, Brandeis University MS062, Waltham, MA 02454; e-mail: asherman@brandeis.edu

enced much of our knowledge about coping with chronic illness. Changes in lifestyle and health care have resulted in a shift in the major causes of illness and death from acute (e.g., influenza, tuberculosis, pneumonia, and other infectious diseases) to chronic illnesses (e.g., heart disease, cancer, arthritis; see Ory, Abeles, & Lipman, 1992). The fields of epidemiology, behavioral medicine, and health psychology all consider age a significant factor in the incidence, prevalence, and progression of disease (Siegler et al., 2001). Thus, a thorough understanding of the relationship between aging and health is crucial.

OVERVIEW

Two general concerns should be addressed before turning to a review of specific topics. The first is the importance of diversity in the experience of health across the life course; the second is the definition of the relationship between aging and disease.

Health Across the Life Course

Using a systems model approach (see Taylor, 1999) in overall course organization is very helpful for including aging in the range of specific topics. Inherent in a systems model is the proposition that individuals have different experiences over their life span due to the influence of varying cultural, biologic, genetic, socioeconomic, and sociostructural systems (Driedger & Chappell, 1987), which can have positive and negative influences on well-being at all stages of the life course. The accumulation of differences over time influences adjustment to major life transitions (e.g., education, formation of significant relationships, adjustment to loss of a spouse or disability; Jackson, 1996). This perspective can explain, to some degree, the disparity in health over the life course as well as earlier mortality for African Americans and Hispanics in the United States, or any group that experiences high levels of negative life events and structural barriers to education, employment, and health care. No one monolithic aging experience occurs; rather, aging in general, and health over the life course specifically, has multiple determinants (Moen, 1998; Riley, 1987).

Most topics in a health psychology course can include discussion of diversity in the aging process and disparity in illness and treatment. Short assignments may ask students (individually or in small groups) to report back on morbidity and mortality statistics for different ethnic groups in the United States by age and gender. Discussion can then focus on the diversity in aging and the many reasons for that diversity, using readings from Riley (1987) and Jackson (1996) as a base.

Aging and Disease

Several views exist on the relationship between aging and health decline. One view (e.g., Evans, 1988) holds that disease and normal aging are not separate processes and that losses of function and treatment implications of inevitable decline are inextricably intertwined. For example, defects in immune functioning (T- and B-cell lymphocytes) may be responsible for the process of physiologic aging (Vogt, 1992). Other researchers (e.g., Hayflick, 1996; Mostofsky, 1998) have pointed out that some losses of function do not produce increased vulnerability to death, whereas some do (e.g., compare graying of hair to changes in immune system). Aging and illness are correlated, and both age and disease lead to increased vulnerability to morbidity and mortality; but the question of whether or how to consider them separate processes is complex.

Kohn (1985) offered a useful method of distinguishing aging from disease processes. He argued that some illnesses are universal, progressive, and irreversible with age (e.g., atherosclerosis), whereas some diseases are common with age but not universal or inevitable (e.g., cancer). In addition, some diseases are not necessarily age related, but have more negative impact on older adults (e.g., pneumonia, influenza). To be defined as normal aging, a change in a physical system should be universal, progressive, and irreversible, not secondary to some other process or modifiable with treatment. The change should contribute to the vulnerability of the person to disability and disease and not be adapted to or compensated for effectively.

Using Kohn's criteria, the narrowing of arteries as a result of plaque deposits (i.e., fatty substances, cholesterol, and other substances) in the inner arterial lining can be termed a condition of normal aging. The narrowing is observed in all populations, signs of plaque buildup are evident even in early adulthood, and the condition progressively worsens over time, although positive lifestyle factors over the life span (e.g., diet, exercise, stress) can prevent the condition from manifesting as arteriosclerosis or cardiovascular disease. Although theoretically distinct from the disease atherosclerosis, in which the arteries become narrowed through the accumulation of fat-based and other substances (Carr & Burke, 2000), a resemblance exists between some of the structural changes that occur normally with aging and those associated with diseases of the arteries.

Cancer, on the other hand, is not defined as part of normal aging. Age is a risk factor for some, but not for all, types of cancer, and cancer affects different subgroups differently. Lung cancer decreases in probability with age, while breast and colon cancer risk increase in older age groups. The distinction is important, because classifying a change in function as part of "normal" aging may lead to delays in seeking treatment (Kane & Kane, 1990), delays in starting treatment, or no treatment at all—even for a condition that could be easily reversed. This problem is especially true for stigmatized health conditions.

Several instructional methods can be used to illustrate the relationship between aging and disease. Students could apply Kohn's criteria to different "case studies" provided by the instructor to get a feel for the difference between disease and aging processes. Students may be invited to discuss their own experience with an older friend or relative. Students may describe situations in which they had assumed a behavior or illness was related to normal aging when it actually was not. Small groups can survey current media (e.g., television, radio, or print advertisements; greeting cards) for the popular perceptions of the aging–disease relationship. They can report back to the class informally or write an in-depth paper exploring these issues.

SPECIFIC TOPICS

A number of topics within health psychology can incorporate aging. The topics reviewed here either have important implications for the health and well-being of older adults or have a significant literature related to age differences or change over time.

Health Behavior

The area of health behavior, including theoretical perspectives on behavior change, is likely to make up a major portion of most courses on health psychology. Health behavior is a broad topic, and the concepts typically subsumed under it (e.g., illness prevention, health promotion, health risk, behavior change) often form the cornerstone for understanding other material in the course and current research and health-related news in the popular press.

Health behavior is a good illustration of the importance of taking a life span or developmental perspective. First, goals for health behaviors change over time. From childhood into early adulthood, health promotion and prevention of illness are the primary goals of health behaviors such as vaccinations, checkups, nutrition, and exercise. Health behaviors for older adults often include recovery from illness, rehabilitation after a health crisis, and physical and psychological adjustment to chronic illness, in addition to illness prevention.

Second, responsibility for health behaviors changes over time. During infancy and childhood, parents are responsible for the health of their children, but children assume more responsibility for their own health and health care through adolescence and into adulthood. Over the adult life course, those who choose to have children will take on the responsibility for the children's health. In addition, they may assume partial or complete responsibility for the health and health care of their own parents.

Third, health behaviors change over the life course in response to life events. For example, a woman may stop smoking during pregnancy but begin again after giving birth. Similarly, an older adult may be prompted to begin a program of regular mammograms by the death of her sister from breast cancer.

Fourth, good health behavior habits acquired early in life can have substantial benefit across the life course. This may be especially true of later adulthood, when positive health behaviors such as cancer screening, nutrition, physical activity, and refraining from smoking are linked to increased longevity and decreased morbidity. There are some age differences in health behaviors. For example, older adults are more likely to engage in some positive health behaviors than are younger adults (e.g., medical checkups, healthy diets, avoidance of smoking and alcohol; see Leventhal, Leventhal, & Cameron, 2001). Furthermore, older adults are less likely to drop out of treatment and more likely to adhere to medication programs than are younger adults. However, older adults are not more likely to exercise than are younger adults (Leventhal, Leventhal, & Schaefer, 1992). According to the 1996 U.S. Surgeon General's report on physical activity, only 19% of women ages 65 to 74 and 27% of men ages 65 to 74 reported regular sustained physical exercise (U.S. Department of Health and Human Services). Older adults may exaggerate the dangers of exercise, underestimate their physical capabilities, or feel embarrassed by their performance (King, 2001; Lachman et al., 1997). Lachman et al. theorized that part of older adults' lack of physical activity may also be the result of negative stereotypes about aging (e.g., good health is not under personal control). A life span developmental approach to studying health behaviors allows a better understanding of the differing social contexts within which older and younger adults make complex decisions about preventative and treatment-oriented behaviors.

Life span and aging issues can be discussed in the context of health behaviors using a class exercise on estimated personal longevity. Although not fully reflective of current findings on health and longevity, a table from Schultz (1978) is reprinted in several texts (Taylor, 1999); also several Web sites include "longevity calculators (http://www.life-expectancy.longtolive. com; http://www.beeson.org/livingto100/default.htm). Students can use the table or Web site to approximate their individual longevity based on current health behaviors and accumulated lifestyle factors. Many undergraduates have never considered putting a specific age to their own life span, which they may find intriguing. Furthermore, the exercise emphasizes personal control over many aspects of aging and mortality, in addition to inherited predispositions to disease.

Most theories of health behavior change (e.g., health belief model, theory of reasoned action, modeling, stages of change, relapse prevention) do not explicitly include age differences or age-related changes. However, many investigators have applied current models to intervention work with older adults, particularly in the areas of physical activity (e.g., King, Rejeski, & Buchner, 1998; Rejeski et al., 2001), diet and nutrition (e.g., Leermakers, Perri, Shigaki, & Fuller, 1999; Perri, 1998), and cancer screening (e.g., Brenes & Paskett, 2000; Paskett et al., 1999). Primary sources by these authors can be incorporated as readings or in lectures.

Systems of the Body

The overt physical effects of aging are perhaps the most familiar to students, but there are numerous changes to less obvious physical systems as well. Specific sources detail the state of the literature regarding the changes in hearing, vision, motor performance, muscle strength and endurance, cardiovascular and immune system functioning (Siegler et al., 2001; Whitbourne, 2001). It is important to keep in mind, however, that "descriptions of 'average' behavior for specific age groups grow less and less accurate for an individual's performance as the age of the group increases. . . . it is difficult to distinguish physiological changes due to aging per se from those due to declining physical activity, decreases in motivation, lower societal expectation, and . . . disease" (Spirduso & MacRae, 1990, p. 183). For example, the age-related decline in muscle strength is related to deterioration of muscle mass, which is smaller in physically active older adults compared to their sedentary counterparts, and can be reversed to a large extent with resistance training. The importance of lifelong physical fitness can be stressed, along with discussion of the aging stereotypes that can lead to artificial inflation of the scope of age-related physical changes.

Stress, Illness, and Coping

Vogt (1992) has provided an overview of the literature on links between stress and illness over the life span. The literature suggests that physical reactivity to stress may decline with age, indicating that the impact of stress may have a less negative effect on health at later ages. The cumulative effect of long-term psychological stress, however, along with the interaction of stress with different physical systems, is not well understood. Robinson-Whelen, Kiecolt-Glaser, and Glaser (2000) reviewed evidence on the link between stress and immune functioning and suggested that older adults may be especially vulnerable to the cumulative effects of stress on immune functioning, putting them more at risk for infectious diseases. Solomon and Benton (2000) described immunosenescence as "changes that occur in all older individuals . . . that are not the results of immunodeficiencies caused by genetic defects, malnutrition, infection, toxins, or malignancies" (p. 111). They concluded that immunosenescence has been considered part of normal aging, but studies of centenarians reveal that unusually psychologically resilient individuals may be protected from some changes. Further, Robinson-Whelen et al. pointed out that changes in immune function, especially small changes such as those seen with age in healthy individuals, do not directly translate into decreased physical functioning.

Psychosocial modifiers of the stress–illness relationship can be approached from the standpoint of aging to provide students with excellent examples of these processes. Several personality traits have been discussed as modifiers of the stress–illness relationship. Some (e.g., neuroticism, negative affectivity) are related to worse health outcomes, whereas others (e.g., optimism, hardiness, control) result in better health outcomes, apparently by buffering the effects of stress. Although major personality constructs (e.g., extroversion, neuroticism) appear to be stable across time after middle adulthood (McCrae et al., 1999), a few good studies of personality and health in older adults have been conducted (Marks & Lutgendorf, 1999).

Rodin and Timko's (1992) review of some of the findings from intervention studies on control, aging, and health indicated that a strong sense of personal control is indicative of positive adjustment to relocation (typically after a health crisis) and to better health outcomes for nursing home residents. More recent empirical and theoretical work (Chipperfield, Perry, & Menec, 1999; Fung, Abeles, & Carstensen, 1999; Wrosch, Heckhausen, & Lachman, 2000) has distinguished between primary and secondary control processes, providing a more detailed approach to the definition and examination of personal control over the life span. Current perspectives assert that older adults face increasing obstacles to exercising primary control (e.g., attempts to modify the environment to achieve a desired goal) and increasingly turn to the use of secondary control strategies (e.g., restructuring inner goals and beliefs) to gain a better fit with the environmental conditions, deal with failure, and retain a sense of personal control. Fung et al. argued that older adults use active strategies of selective optimization to maintain a sense of control throughout life. They also suggested that the meaning of control changes throughout life, so that some control beliefs are related to negative behavioral outcomes for young adults but to positive behavioral outcomes for older adults. In the domain of health, Chipperfield et al. reported that older adults who used primary control strategies were less healthy than younger adults who used primary control strategies, whereas the age pattern was reversed for the use of secondary control strategies. Wrosch et al. reported similar findings.

Another modifier of the stress–illness relationship is coping behavior. Leventhal et al. (1992) summarized some of the research on age differences and age changes in coping. They reported that the literature is generally lacking in both cross-sectional comparisons and longitudinal studies of age and coping behavior. However, some patterns can be discerned. Cross-sectional studies have shown that older adults, like younger ones, use an array of coping strategies to move successfully through stressful events. The few longitudinal studies have suggested that coping styles evolve over time, such that middle-age and older adults, compared with younger adults, place less emphasis on hostility, escapism, and self-blame and use more adaptive coping strategies, especially in relation to dealing with health problems. A large-scale cross-sectional study (Diehl, Coyle, & Labouvie-Vief, 1996) supported this view, showing that older adults (especially women) favored coping strategies related to strengthened impulse control, whereas younger adults were more likely to use directly aggressive strategies and report lower impulse control.

Adaptation to Chronic Illness

Adaptation to chronic illness can easily be addressed from many points along the life course. From an aging perspective, older adults are at increased risk for chronic illnesses such as heart disease, arthritis, cancer, and osteoporosis. In addition, because of early detection and better treatments, current cohorts of older adults are more likely to survive health crises that previously would have been fatal (e.g., heart attacks, cancers), but the survival may come at the cost of a long period of rehabilitation or disability. Therefore, many issues related to living with chronic illness are directly linked to the experience of aging. The topic is also a good example of the importance of health psychology, because adjustment to chronic disease is closely tied to resilience, coping, and other psychological resources. In addition, chronic physical illness adds to the risk for negative psychological outcomes (Penninx et al., 1997).

The statistics are stunning: More than 85% of adults older than age 65 experience at least one chronic illness (Helgeson & Mickelson, 2000). Thus, the scope of the problem of chronic illness has wide-ranging implications for health psychologists dealing with aging. These implications include multiple medications and medication adherence, pain management, changes in diet and physical activity (rehabilitation or preventative exercise and fitness), psychological and emotional coping responses, and increases in caregiving responsibilities for family members.

In addition, some, although not all, chronic illness will result in temporary or long-term disability. Physical disability is an indicator of quality of life, life expectancy, and the ability to remain independent. It is often defined as experiencing difficulty with one or more activities of daily living (ADLs) or instrumental activities of daily living (IADLs), although there is disagreement on definition and measurement. Disability can have acute (e.g., injury) or chronic onset (e.g., arthritis). Disability increases with age, with disability rates at 35% for those ages 65 and older, compared with 62% for those ages 85 and older (Prohaska, Mermelstein, Miller, & Jack, 1993).

Women are more likely to be disabled than men (Federal Interagency Forum on Aging-Related Statistics, 2000). Also substantial ethnic differences are evident in disability rates, with Caucasians at an advantage, compared with other ethnic groups (Jette, Crawford, & Tennstedt, 1996). Substantial literature is available on predictors of disease-specific and generic disablement, but disagreement exists regarding the balance of individual and social–environmental factors that influence the course of disability (Baltes & Wahl, 1992). Verbrugge and Jette (1994) provided a review of theoretical perspectives on disability and offered a model of disability as a process, rather than as a personal condition—an approach that easily includes a life span perspective.

Again, however, *treatable conditions* should not be defined as normal aging, and more longitudinal data on health changes are needed. Many students are amazed at the ability of older adults to adapt to even long-term disability without substantial decreases in self-esteem and self-rated health. Data from the Older Americans 2000 study showed that although positive health evaluations decline with age, the majority of older adults rate their health as good to excellent, with the exception of African American men over age 85 (Federal Interagency Forum on Aging-Related Statistics, 2000). Thoughtful discussion of these issues may result in fewer stereotypes about aging. Discussion can emphasize the cyclical nature of physical and psychological changes with age and opportunities for adaptation over time. It may be possible to supplement class time with a field trip to a physical rehabilitation program at a local clinic or hospital, or invite a guest lecturer (e.g., physical therapist or someone who works with cardiac or arthritis patients) to speak to the class about working in disability or rehabilitation.

Age Stereotypes and Stigmatization of Disease

Those interested in incorporating topics related to aging can find a growing literature on the consequences of inaccurate stereotypes about aging. In general, discrimination is based on drawing sharp distinctions between the self and other; in contrast, ageism involves negative ideas about a group to which everyone will eventually belong. Health care providers, as well as older adults and their family members, can hold age stereotypes, and the consequences can be severe. Discrimination that is based on inaccurate stereotypes in the context of health care can lead to inappropriate treatment, lack of care, misdiagnosis, unrealistically low expectations for treatment, or early termination of care (Crose, Leventhal, Haug, & Burns, 1997).

A secondary consequence of discrimination is the stigmatization of health issues, resulting in lack of discussion by patients and health care professionals, even when there are interventions or treatments available. For example, urinary incontinence is a primary reason for admittance of older adults to nursing homes (Crose et al., 1997). In addition, incontinence curtails social activities and overall quality of life, which can lead to inactivity and depression—further risk factors for other health conditions (Dugan et al., 2000). Cohen et al. (1999) reported that older adults are reluctant to discuss incontinence with their physicians for fear of embarrassing the physician. Similarly, physicians are reluctant to discuss incontinence with older adults to avoid embarrassing their patients.

Other stigmatized topics important to older adults are abuse and neglect, and sexuality. Disabled older adults are usually cared for by family members or through nursing home placement. Those most in need of extended care are also the most vulnerable to abuse and neglect. Older adults may also be targets of criminal fraud or stranger violence. Students considering medical careers should know that health care providers are often the only resource for an older adult experiencing abuse. Because of their rights to privacy and independence, assessment of suspected neglect or abuse must be made with sensitivity, and the potential for abandonment of the older adult must be considered (Crose et al., 1997). Zeiss (1998) argued that age-related changes in hormonal levels and sexual response do not necessarily mean the end of satisfying sexual activity for older adults, but she also noted that health-related problems experienced by either partner could cause couples to give up on sex. Furthermore, many people, especially those in older cohorts, find it difficult to discuss sexual issues openly. The importance of clear and sensitive communication between health care providers and older adults around issues of sexuality can be stressed.

SUMMARY

Aging is directly relevant to the teaching of many typical components of undergraduate health psychology courses. Appropriate materials are available to supplement current textbooks (many of which are unfortunately lacking in comprehensive gerontological information). It is preferable to integrate related information across as many topics as possible, rather than taking a segregated, "unit on aging" approach, as integration is likely to be more appropriate to the topic-based organization of many texts. However, teaching a separate unit may be preferable for some instructors; personal preference should be the guiding force. As eloquently expressed by Leventhal et al. (1992), "a greater understanding of health and illness behaviors across the life course will contribute to the health and functioning of people at all ages" (p. 135).

REFERENCES

Baltes, M. M., & Wahl, H. W. (1992). The behavior system of dependency in the elderly: Interaction with the social environment. In M. G. Ory, R. P. Abeles,

& P. D. Lipman (Eds.), *Aging, health and behavior* (pp. 83–106). Newbury Park: Sage.

Brenes, G. A., & Paskett, E. D. (2000). Predictors of stage of adoption for colorectal cancer screening. *Preventive Medicine, 31*, 410–416.

Carr, J. J., & Burke, G. L. (2000). Subclinical cardiovascular disease and atherosclerosis are not inevitable consequences of aging [editorial comment]. *Journal of the American Geriatrics Society, 48*(3), 342–343.

Chipperfield, J. G., Perry, R. P., & Menec, V. H. (1999). Primary and secondary control-enhancing strategies: Implications for health in later life. *Journal of Aging and Health, 11*, 517–539.

Cohen, S. J., Robinson, D., Dugan, E., Howard, G., Suggs, P. K., Pearce, K. F., et al. (1999). Communication between older adults and their physicians about urinary incontinence. *Journals of Gerontology: Biological Sciences and Medical Sciences, 54A*, M34–M37.

Crose, R., Leventhal, E. A., Haug, M. R., & Burns, E. A. (1997). The challenges of aging. In S. J. Gallant, G. P. Keita, & R. Royak-Schaler (Eds.), *Health care for women: Psychological, social, and behavioral influences* (pp. 221–234). Washington, DC: American Psychological Association.

Diehl, M., Coyle, N., & Labouvie-Vief, G. (1996). Age and sex differences in strategies of coping and defense across the life span. *Psychology and Aging, 11*, 127–139.

Driedger, L., & Chappell, N. (1987). *Aging and ethnicity: Toward an interface.* Toronto: Butterworth.

Dugan, E., Cohen, S. J., Bland, D. R., Preisser, J. S., Davis, C. C., Suggs, P. K., et al. (2000). The association of depressive symptoms and urinary incontinence among older adults. *Journal of the American Geriatrics Society, 48*, 413–416.

Elias, M. F., Elias, J. W., & Elias, P. K. (1990). Biological and health influences on behavior. In J. E. Birren & K. W. Schaie (Eds.), *The handbook of the psychology of aging* (3rd ed., pp. 79–102). San Diego: Academic Press.

Evans, J. G. (1988). Aging and disease. In D. Evered & J. Whelan (Eds.), *Experimental and clinical interventions in aging* (pp. 38–57). New York: Wiley.

Federal Interagency Forum on Aging-Related Statistics. (2000, August). *Older Americans 2000: Key indicators of well-being* (Federal Interagency Forum on Aging-Related Statistics). Washington, DC: U.S. Government Printing Office.

Fung, H. H., Abeles, R. P., & Carstensen, L. L. (1999). Psychological control in later life: Implications for life-span development. In J. Brandtsädter & R. M. Lerner (Eds.), *Action and self-development: Theory and research through the life span* (pp. 345–372). Thousand Oaks, CA: Sage.

Hayflick, L. (1996). *How and why we age.* New York: Ballantine Books.

Helgeson, V. S., & Mickelson, K. (2000). Coping with chronic illness among the elderly: Maintaining self-esteem. In S. B. Manuck, R. Jennings, B. S. Rabin, & A. Baum (Eds.), *Behavior, health, and aging* (pp. 153–178). Mahwah, NJ: Lawrence Erlbaum.

Jackson, J. S. (1996). A life-course perspective on physical and psychological health.

In R. J. Resnick & R. H. Rozensky (Eds.), *Health psychology through the life span: Practice and research opportunities* (pp. 39–57). Washington, DC: American Psychological Association.

Jette, A. M., Crawford, S. L., & Tennstedt, S. L. (1996). Toward understanding ethnic differences in late-life disability. *Research on Aging, 18,* 292–309.

Kane, R. L., & Kane, R. A. (1990). Health care for older people: Organizational and policy issues. In R. H. Binstock & L. K. George (Eds.), *The handbook of aging and the social sciences* (3rd ed., pp. 415–437). San Diego: Academic Press.

King, A. C. (2001). Interventions to promote physical activity by older adults [Special issue II]. *Journals of Gerontology, 56A,* 36–46.

King, A. C., Rejeski, W. J., & Buchner, D. M. (1998). Physical activity interventions targeting older adults: A critical review and recommendations. *American Journal of Preventive Medicine, 15,* 316–333.

Kohn, R. R. (1985). Aging and age-related diseases: Normal processes. In H. A. Johnson (Ed.), *Relations between normal aging and disease* (pp. 1–43). New York: Raven.

Lachman, M. E., Jette, A., Tennstedt, S., Howland, J., Harris, B. A., & Peterson, E. (1997). A cognitive-behavioural model for promoting regular physical activity in older adults. *Psychology, Health and Medicine, 2,* 251–261.

Leermakers, E. A., Perri, M. G., Shigaki, C. L., & Fuller, P. R. (1999). Effects of exercise-focused versus weight-focused maintenance programs on the management of obesity. *Addictive Behaviors, 24,* 219–227.

Leventhal, H., Leventhal, E. A., & Cameron, L. (2001). Representations, procedures, and affect in illness self-regulation: A perceptual-cognitive model. In A. Baum, T. A. Revenson, & J. E. Singer (Eds.), *Handbook of health psychology* (pp. 19–47). Mahwah, NJ: Lawrence Erlbaum.

Leventhal, H., Leventhal, E. A., & Schaefer, P. M. (1992). Vigilant coping and health behavior. In M. G. Ory, R. P. Abeles, & P. D. Lipman (Eds.), *Aging, health and behavior* (pp. 109–140). Newbury Park, CA: Sage.

Marks, G. R., & Lutgendorf, S. K. (1999). Perceived health competence and personality factors differentially predict health behaviors in older adults. *Journal of Aging and Health, 11,* 221–239.

McCrae, R. R., Costa, P. T., Jr., de Lima, M. P., Simoes, A., Ostendorf, F., Angleitner, A., et al. (1999). Age differences in personality across the adult life span: Parallels in five cultures. *Developmental Psychology, 35,* 466–477.

Moen, P. (1998). Aging and women's life course. In E. A. Blechman & K. D. Brownell (Eds.), *Behavioral medicine and women: A comprehensive handbook* (pp. 87–92). New York: Guilford Press.

Mostofsky, D. I. (1998). Aging and behavioral medicine: A triaxial model. In J. Lomranz (Ed.), *Handbook of aging and mental health: An integrative approach* (pp. 497–510). New York: Plenum Press.

Ory, M. G., Abeles, R. P., & Lipman, P. D. (1992). Introduction: An overview of research on aging, health, and behavior. In M. G. Ory, R. P. Abeles, & P. D. Lipman (Eds.), *Aging, health and behavior* (pp. 1–23). Newbury Park, CA: Sage.

Paskett, E. D., Tatum, C. M., D'Agostino, R., Rushing, J., Velez, R., Michielutte, R., et al. (1999). Community-based interventions to improve breast and cervical cancer screening: Results of the Forsyth County Cancer Screening (FoCaS) Project. *Cancer Epidemiology, Biomarkers and Prevention, 8*, 453–459.

Penninx, B. W. J. H., Van Tilburg, T., Deeg, D. J. H., Kriegsman, D. M. W., Boeke A. J. P., & Van Eijk, J. T. M. (1997). Direct and buffer effects of social support and personal coping resources in individuals with arthritis. *Social Science and Medicine, 44*, 393–402.

Perri, M. G. (1998). The maintenance of treatment effects in the long-term management of obesity. *Clinical Psychology: Science and Practice, 5*, 526–543.

Prohaska, T., Mermelstein, R., Miller, B., & Jack, S. (1993). Functional status and living arrangements. In J. F. Van Nostrand, S. E. Furner, & R. Suzman (Eds.), *Health data on older Americans: United States, 1992* (DHHS Publication No. PHS 93–1411, pp. 23–41). Washington, DC: U.S. Government Printing Office.

Rejeski, W. J., Shelton, B., Miller, M., Dunn, A. L., King, A. C., & Sallis, J. F. (2001). Mediators of increased physical activity and change in subjective well-being: Results from the activity counseling trial (ACT). *Journal of Health Psychology, 6*, 159–168.

Riley, M. W. (1987). Aging, health, and social change: An overview. In M. W. Riley, J. D. Matarazzo, & A. Baum (Eds.), *Perspectives in behavioral medicine: The aging dimension* (pp. 1–14). Hillsdale, NJ: Lawrence Erlbaum.

Robinson-Whelen, S., Kiecolt-Glaser, J. K., & Glaser, R. (2000). Effects of chronic stress on immune function and health in the elderly. In S. B Manuck, R. Jennings, B. S. Rabin, & A. Baum (Eds.), *Behavior, health, and aging* (pp. 69–82). Mahwah, NJ: Lawrence Erlbaum.

Rodin, J., & Timko, C. (1992). Sense of control, aging, and health. In M. G. Ory, R. P. Abeles, & P. D. Lipman (Eds.), *Aging, health and behavior* (pp. 174–206). Newbury Park, CA: Sage.

Schultz, R. (1978). *The psychology of death, dying, and bereavement.* Reading, MA: Addison-Wesley.

Siegler, I. C. (1989). Developmental health psychology. In M. Storandt & G. R. VandenBos (Eds.), *The adult years: Continuity and change* (pp. 119–142). Washington, DC: American Psychological Association.

Siegler, I. C., Bastian, L. A., & Bosworth, H. B. (2001). Health, behavior, and aging. In A. Baum, T. A. Revenson, & J. E. Singer (Eds.), *Handbook of health psychology* (pp. 469–476). Mahwah, NJ: Lawrence Erlbaum.

Solomon, G. F., & Benton, D. (2000). Immune functions, their psychological correlates, and health. In S. B Manuck, R. Jennings, B. S. Rabin, & A. Baum (Eds.), *Behavior, health, and aging* (pp. 109–117). Mahwah, NJ: Lawrence Erlbaum.

Spirduso, W. W., & MacRae, P. G. (1990). Motor performance and aging. In J. E. Birren & K. W. Schaie (Eds.), *The handbook of the psychology of aging* (3rd ed., pp. 183–200). San Diego: Academic Press.

Taylor, S. E. (1999). *Health psychology* (4th ed.). Boston: McGraw-Hill.

U.S. Department of Health and Human Services. (1996). *Physical activity and health: A report of the Surgeon General*. Centers for Disease Control and Prevention, National Center for Chronic Disease Prevention and Health Promotion. Atlanta, GA: International Medical Publishing.

Verbrugge, L. M., & Jette, A. M. (1994). The disablement process. *Social Science and Medicine, 38*, 1–14.

Vogt, T. M. (1992). Aging, stress, and illness: Psychobiological linkages. In M. G. Ory, R. P. Abeles, & P. D. Lipman (Eds.), *Aging, health and behavior* (pp. 207–236). Newbury Park, CA: Sage.

Whitbourne, S. K. (2001). *Adult development and aging: Biopsychosocial perspectives*. New York: John Wiley & Sons.

Wrosch, C., Heckhausen, J., & Lachman, M. E. (2000). Primary and secondary control strategies for managing health and financial stress across adulthood. *Psychology and Aging, 14*, 387–399.

Zeiss, A. M. (1998). Sexuality and aging. In A. Blechman & K. D. Brownell (Eds.), *Behavioral medicine and women: A comprehensive handbook* (pp. 87–92). New York: Guilford Press.

ANNOTATED BIBLIOGRAPHY

Films

On Our Own Terms: Moyers on Dying in America, a four-part video series, aired on PBS in 2000. Available at Films for the Humanities and Sciences: http://www.films.com. Moyers interviews dying patients, their families, doctors, nurses, medical students, hospice workers, and clergy. Reserve time for discussion and debriefing; episodes are deeply moving and some students may find them controversial. Each episode can stand alone; it is not necessary to show all four if time is limited. Available at: http://www.pbs.org/wnet/onourownterms/index.html.

Wit, a Home Box Office (HBO) production, aired on HBO in March 2001. Available at http://www.amazon.com and other commercial outlets. Starring Emma Thompson and directed by Mike Nichols, the film was released in theaters in Europe and aired on HBO in March 2001. It follows Thompson's character, a former English professor dying of ovarian cancer, to show different aspects of hospital interactions and attitudes about death. Reserve time for discussion.

Web Sites[1]

http://www.cdc.gov/nchs/agingact.htm: From the Centers for Disease Control, this site reports from Trends in Aging database, the Longitudinal Studies of Aging,

---

[1]Note: All Web sites were active when this chapter went to press, but Web content does change rapidly.

and the Federal Interagency Forum on Aging-Related Statistics (no advertisements).

http://www.life-expectancy.longtolive.com/: This site calculates life expectancy, estimated date and time of death, and "life meter" from input to calculator with pull-down options. Gives suggestions on how to live longer (advertisement supported).

http://www.northwesternmutual.com: With fun graphics, this site calculates estimated longevity, has useful health-related information about each element of the calculator; supported by Northwestern Mutual Insurance (no advertisements).

http://www.beeson.org/livingto100/default.htm: This site is based on information from the centenarian study and supported by the Alliance for Aging Research; has pictures of centenarians and includes detailed information on the reasoning behind each element.

Written Resources

Binstock, R. H., George, L. K., Marshall, V. W., Meyers, G. C., & Schultz, J. H. (Eds.). (1996). *Handbook of aging and the social sciences* (4th ed.). San Diego: Academic Press. An excellent source for readings and/or lecture material. See Disability Trends and Transitions (chapter 6) and Social Factors and Illness (chapter 13). Also useful from the third edition are Mortality and Morbidity (chapter 4), Illness Behavior in Later Life (chapter 12), and Aging and Dying (chapter 13).

Birren, J. E., & Schaie, K. W. (Eds.). (2001). *Handbook of the psychology of aging* (5th ed.). San Diego: Academic Press. An excellent source for readings or lecture material. Also useful from the 4th edition is Health, Behavior, and Aging (chapter 7); Personality and Aging (chapter 13); and Activity, Exercise, and Behavior (chapter 19). Useful from the third edition is Biological and Health Influences on Behavior (chapter 5).

Blechman, E. A., & Brownell, K. D. (Eds.). (1998). *Behavioral medicine and women: A comprehensive handbook*. New York: Guilford Press. An excellent source for variety of information on women's health, an increasingly important area because of gender differences in longevity and in patterns of illness and disability. Chapters on midlife and aging and major sections on stress and coping, illness prevention, health care, links between psychosocial functioning and physical illness, and culture and health.

Eisler, R. M., & Hersen, M. (Eds.). (2000). *Handbook of gender, culture, and health*. Mahwah, NJ: Lawrence Erlbaum. Contains useful chapters for readings or lecture material, especially Behavioral and Sociocultural Aspects of Aging, Ethnicity, and Health (chapter 7).

Gallant, S. J., Keita, G. P., & Royak-Schaler, R. (Eds.). (1997). *Health care for women: Psychological, social, and behavioral influences.* Washington, DC: American Psychological Association. A second good source for information specific to women's health, especially Premenstrual Syndrome and Menopause (chapter 14) and The Challenges of Aging (chapter 15). Obesity (chapter 8) and Physical Activity (chapter 9) also include some information related to life stage.

Lachman, M. E. (Ed.). (2001). *Handbook of midlife development.* New York: John Wiley and Sons. An excellent reference for information on physical, psychological, and social aspects of middle adulthood, consistent with a life span developmental approach.

Manuck, S. B., Jennings, R., Rabin, B. S., & Baum, A. (Eds.). (2000). *Behavior, health, and aging.* Mahwah, NJ: Lawrence Erlbaum. Contains excellent chapters on genetics and aging, gender and quality-adjusted life years, women and aging, immune system functioning and age, disability, chronic illness and coping, psychological factors in health and disease, and issues in heart disease.

Orth-Gomer, K., Chesney, M. A., & Wenger, N. K. (Eds.). (1998). *Women, stress, and heart disease.* Mahwah, NJ: Lawrence Erlbaum. Chapter 8 is a good treatment of the life span approach focused on women's risk for heart disease and social isolation/integration.

Ory, M. G., Abeles, R. P., & Lipman, P. D. (Eds.). (1992). *Aging, health and behavior.* Newbury Park, CA: Sage. Excellent chapters on coping, disability, sense of control, health behaviors, disease prevention and health promotion for older adults.

Resnick, R. J., & Rozensky, R. H. (Eds.). (1996). *Health Psychology through the life span: Practice and research opportunities.* Washington, DC: American Psychological Association. Chapter 4 provides a helpful overview of life span aging issues related to health, particularly for populations of color or those who face economic disadvantage.

Riley, M. W., Matarazzo, J. D., & Baum, A. (Eds.). (1987). *Perspectives in behavioral medicine: The aging dimension.* Hillsdale, NJ: Lawrence Erlbaum. Although somewhat dated, a groundbreaking book that is still a good source for lecture material or supplemental course readings.

Sarafino, E. P. (2001). *Health psychology: Biopsychosocial interactions* (4th ed.). New York: John Wiley & Sons. A good introductory text for undergraduates. Aging is not a strong focus. Information on chronic illness is included in chapters 13 and 14.

Shumaker, S. A., Schron, E., Ockene, J., & McBee, W. L. (Eds.). (1998). *The handbook of health behavior change* (2nd ed.). New York: Springer. Aging is not a focus, but see Problems With Adherence in the Elderly (chapter 15).

Taylor, S. E. (1999). *Health psychology* (4th ed.). Boston: McGraw-Hill. A good introductory text for undergraduates. Aging is not a main focus; however, information on life span development and aging is integrated throughout, especially in Health Behaviors (chapter 3); Psychological Issues in Advancing and Terminal Illness (chapter 12); and Psychoneuroimmunology, AIDS, Cancer, and Arthritis (chapter 14). Reprints the table from Schultz (1978) for class exercise on personal longevity.

10

ABNORMAL PSYCHOLOGY

DANIEL L. SEGAL

Of all the self-fulfilling prophecies in our culture, the assumption that aging means decline and poor health is probably the deadliest.

—Marilyn Ferguson, *The Aquarian Conspiracy* (1980)

The topics covered in abnormal psychology classes are fascinating to a broad range of people. Indeed, mental health and mental illness are relevant constructs to every one of us. Students in abnormal psychology classes are typically intrigued about the different types of psychological disorders that afflict some people, the causes of those disorders, and the kinds of ameliorative strategies or interventions that can be applied to those disorders. Discussions about mental health and aging can be particularly provoking because most of us are expected to live to an old age and most of us have close contact with family members or friends who are elderly. On reflection about aging and mental health, many people may wonder whether their "Golden Years" will be a time of relaxation, productivity, and joy or a period of inevitable impairment both psychologically and physically.

Please direct correspondence to Daniel L. Segal, Department of Psychology, 1420 Austin Bluffs Parkway, University of Colorado at Colorado Springs, Colorado Springs, CO 80933-7150; e-mail: dlsegal@mail.uccs.edu.

Unfortunately, the integration of aging into abnormal psychology classes can be a challenge, especially if the instructor does not have a strong background or specialty in aging issues. The purpose of this chapter is to provide some practical advice regarding how to effectively integrate concepts about aging into undergraduate abnormal psychology classes. The chapter begins with an overview of the typical abnormal psychology course, followed by a description of coverage of aging in current abnormal psychology textbooks. A discussion of potential age-related topics is then provided. Suggestions for class activities and films are provided. The chapter concludes with a listing of several professional resources in aging and mental health.

OVERVIEW OF THE ABNORMAL PSYCHOLOGY COURSE

It is fair to say that abnormal psychology courses are popular with undergraduate students across the nation. At a typical university, Abnormal Psychology is usually taught several times each year, and the enrollments are usually large. Most students who take this course are psychology majors, although a significant minority of students typically have other majors (e.g., sociology, nursing, communications) and select the class because of their interest in the subject. The class is usually composed of sophomores, juniors, and seniors because it is an upper-level class with the prerequisite of Introduction to Psychology. A typical course description for an abnormal psychology class states that it is an introduction to the various approaches to the definition and study of abnormal behavior and mental illness. In the class, the major diagnostic categories of the *Diagnostic and Statistical Manual of Mental Disorders*, fourth edition (*DSM–IV*; American Psychiatric Association, 1994) are reviewed with emphasis on descriptive features, theories of etiology, and treatment models. As a result of the growing interest and importance of multiculturalism and diversity issues in teaching, it may be helpful to emphasize a critical thinking approach about the roles that age, gender, and race play in our conceptions of abnormal behavior. This emphasis will likely lead to some lively class discussions.

Many diverse topics are typically covered in an abnormal psychology class. The historical and broad conceptual foundations for the study of abnormal psychology are usually emphasized with chapters addressing topics such as: definitions of abnormal behavior, history of mental illness, the major theoretical models or paradigms in understanding mental illness, treatment planning, diagnosis and classification of mental illness, assessment strategies and instruments, and research methods. Next, the official categories and specific types of mental disorders are analyzed. These include mood disorders, substance-related disorders, schizophrenia and psychotic disorders, anxiety disorders, somatoform disorders, dissociative disorders, factitious disorders, impulse control disorders, eating disorders, sexual and gender identity disorders, personality disorders, sleep disorders, childhood disorders, cognitive disorders, and adjustment disorders. Note that considerable class time is usually spent covering the disorders, and this is where interest peaks for many students. During discussions of the different mental disorders, it is helpful to address information about epidemiology, signs and symptoms, theories about causes, treatment strategies, and current controversies in the area. Case presentations are encouraged to bring the material to life and enliven class discussion. As is discussed later, there will be numerous opportunities for instructors to incorporate information about aging into each area.

In addition to the engaging subject matter, the abnormal psychology course typically has strong personal relevance to students who often recognize signs and symptoms of diverse disorders in themselves, in their friends, and family members. Almost all students who have career aspirations as a mental health professional take this class. Because it is important that information about aging theory and research be included in undergraduate classes, this class provides a good opportunity to educate a broad group of students about the main facts of mental health and aging.

TEXTBOOK COVERAGE OF AGING:
THE CURRENT STATE OF AFFAIRS

Numerous abnormal psychology textbooks from major publishers are available in a crowded abnormal psychology textbook market. In fact, at least 22 different texts are available, and most have been around long enough to have undergone several revisions. To what extent is aging covered in these texts? Inspection of the tables of contents in these texts revealed that 5 (22.7%) included a specific chapter on aging, whereas 17 (77.3%) did not. Examples of chapter titles relevant to aging included "Aging and Psychological Disorders," "Problems of Aging," "Disorders of Childhood and Old Age," "Cognitive Disorders and Disorders Related to Aging," and "Late-Onset Disorders."

What about coverage of specific aging-related topics in these texts? All texts devoted at least some attention to aging. The average number of pages including aging-related content was 17 in texts that averaged about 600 total pages. Dementia was the aging-related topic covered most often (81%), followed by depression and aging (50%), anxiety and aging (32%), suicide and aging (27%), and substance abuse and aging (14%). Important topics that were noticeably neglected or covered minimally included sexual disorders and aging, personality disorders and aging, and assessment and psychotherapy with older people.

Notably, the first textbook to include a full chapter on aging was Davison and Neale's *Abnormal Psychology*, third edition, published in 1982. Sadly, 20 years later, only a handful of other texts have devoted a chapter to aging issues. Overall, it appears that the integration of aging into abnormal psychology books has improved over time but coverage remains insufficient in the majority of cases. Most of the textbooks do not have a specific chapter on aging and psychological disorders. Moreover, the texts that do have a chapter on aging typically do not integrate aging into the rest of the book.

THE IMPORTANCE OF INTEGRATION OF AGING

Why is it important to integrate aging into an abnormal psychology class? Several significant factors point to the relevance of aging-related material in an abnormal psychology class, and instructors are encouraged to share some of this information with students to provide a context for further discussion. The discussion that follows details the major factors involved.

Public Education

A dire need exists to increase public education about the main facts and biases regarding mental health and aging. Clearly, this is an area filled with stigmatization, myths, and inappropriate stereotypes. In class, instructors should try to provide a forum for open and frank discussion about the realities (positive and negative) of mental health and aging. Educational efforts in class may serve to increase awareness of the types of mental disorders experienced by older adults, and as such, the chances of appropriate identification and intervention may be increased (see Exhibit 10.1 for class activity).

Older Adults and Psychological Disorders

Sources project a dramatic increase in the number of older people who experience psychological disorders. National data on the mental health needs of older adults in the United States suggest that approximately 20% of community-dwelling older people have a diagnosable mental disorder (Jeste et al., 1999). An even higher number, up to 30% of older people, have subclinical but significant symptoms of a mental disorder. The prevalence rates for mental disorders in nursing home residents have always been high, about 80%. Approximately 50% of such residents have dementia, and another 33% experience major depression. Notably, the occurrence of mental illness is expected to increase as the baby boomers age because of their extant base rates (Gatz, 1995).

Older Adults and Mental Health Services

Older adults have a long history of underuse of mental health services (Gatz & Smyer, 2001). A survey of the general health sector serving older

EXHIBIT 10.1
Class Activity

Instructors may consider using or creating a brief vignette of a person with a mental illness such as depression (see sample in chapter). Two forms of the vignette are needed, and both are identical with the exception that age is manipulated: One vignette describes a 22-year-old, and the other describes an 82-year-old. Distribute each vignette to half the class and ask students to rate the vignette (using a 1 to 10 scale, anchored at extremely negative or extremely positive) on several dimensions. Some options include the following:

- "Rate this individual's overall level of functioning."
- "If you were a mental health professional, what is your attitude towards taking on this person as a client?"
- "What would you consider the prognosis to be for this individual?"
- "Rate this individual's likelihood of success in psychotherapy."
- "How hopeless is this individual (extremely hopeless/not at all hopeless)?"
- "Rate the extent to which this individual has a memory impairment, such as Alzheimer's disease (extremely impaired/not at all impaired)."

Next, the instructor can share the age-manipulation "secret" with the class and should divide students into small groups for discussion. The instructor can ask for volunteers to share their reactions with the full class. Typically, many students will rate the older person differently (usually as less healthy, more hopeless, and more demented) than the younger person, and the instructor can lead the class in discussion about ageism, and positive and negative stereotypes about aging and older people.

Example

Susan, age 22/82, is a library attendant. Lately, she feels down in the dumps, as if a dark cloud is hanging over. Her energy level is in the pits. She regularly starts tasks and then ends up forgetting what she had begun; she wonders if she has a memory problem. She does not enjoy playing cards or shopping like she used to. She used to have a nice social network, but lately, she seems to be staying home alone, crying in bed. Sometimes, she thinks about "ending it all" because she sees no other way to deal with her emotional pain.

---

adults revealed that only 56% of older adults with mental disorders used the mental health system (Gatz & Smyer, 1992). The remainder used primary care physicians (Gatz & Smyer, 1992) who often poorly identify the mental health needs of older adults and do not provide appropriate referrals. Estimates have suggested that only 2% of clients seen in private practice are older adults, and about 10% of community mental health center clients are older adults (Knight & Kaskie, 1995), which is below the percentage of older people in the population (about 13%).

Mental Health Professionals and the Aging Population

There is a current and projected lack of mental health professionals who specialize in aging. Presently, it is clear that older adults are underserved by psychologists. In part, this reflects a lack of psychologists proficient in clinical geropsychology to provide appropriate treatment (Qualls, 1998). Astonishingly, a projection of need for mental health services among older adults (Gatz & Finkel, 1995) suggested that about 7,500 full-time psychologists would be needed by the present day. A recent large survey of psychologists indicated that the equivalent of only about 3,000 full-time psychologists are currently providing such services (Qualls, Segal, Norman, Niederehe, & Gallagher-Thompson, in press). In 1990, federal legislation has created reimbursement incentives for the provision of psychological services to older people, making geriatric mental health a potential growth industry for psychologists. Unfortunately, less than 50% of those psychologists serving older adults have specialized formal training in clinical geropsychology (Qualls et al., in press). Only 10% of clinical or counseling psychology doctoral programs offer a concentration focusing on issues and treatment of older adults (Gatz & Finkel, 1995). Only 15 training programs offer intensive postdoctoral training in clinical geropsychology (Karel, Molinari, Gallagher-Thompson, & Hillman, 1999). Currently, there are only about 300 members of the American Psychological Association (APA) Division 12, Section II (Clinical Geropsychology). Incorporating information about aging and the need for trained professionals in an abnormal psychology class may serve to stimulate new professionals to enter the pipeline to become specialists in clinical geropsychology. Indeed, good opportunities await such professionals of the future, based on the need for geropsychologists and the booming older population.

POTENTIAL TOPICS

If a professor wanted to increase coverage of aging in an abnormal psychology class, many important areas are available from which one might pick and choose. Several areas that could potentially be informative and important to cover are highlighted next.

Prevalence of Mental Disorders Among Older Adults

As noted previously, community studies have suggested that approximately 20% of older people meet official criteria for diagnosis of mental disorder. Interestingly, this overall rate is actually similar to or lower in people age 65 years and older when compared with other age groups (APA Working Group on the Older Adult, 1998) and highlights the facts that mental illness is not a part of normal aging and that older adults appear to cope quite well with the challenges of aging. Older adults are known to have low rates of major depression (1%) and dysthymic disorder (2%), although significant but subsyndromal rates of mood disorder symptoms are typically much higher.

Younger adults have higher rates of all specific disorders, with the exception of cognitive impairment (e.g., dementia), which affects about 5% to 7% of those older than age 65 and nearly 30% of those older than age 85 (APA Working Group on the Older Adult, 1998).

Presentation of prevalence data may be useful in combating the myth that it is normal to become demented or depressed with advancing age. In fact, most older adults are in good mental health. An instructor may take such an opportunity to discuss ageism and reasons why people may have negative and prejudicial attitudes toward aging and older adults.

Common Geropsychological Disorders

Instructors should highlight the fact that older adults can experience the full spectrum of mental disorders, not just the cognitive disorders. A sole focus on the cognitive disorders may give a slanted presentation about aging and mental health. It is important that students do not think only of dementia when they think of geriatric mental health problems. Instructors should give a brief overview of how aging relates to several conditions, including depression, anxiety disorders, substance abuse, personality disorders, sexual disorders, schizophrenia, and dementia. If the textbook does not include an adequate chapter on aging, the instructor might consider assigning a reading that provides a broad overview of the common disorders, and several excellent sources are available (Zarit & Haynie, 2000; Qualls, 1999). Other options can be found in the Annotated Bibliography. Several useful films and journals are also listed as additional resources.

Analysis of Myths About Mental Health and Aging

It is imperative to combat misinformation, negative myths, and stereotypes about mental health and aging and to provide factual data about aging so as to provide students with critical thinking skills and knowledge about an aging and diverse world population (see Exhibit 10.2 for class activity). Students often appear surprised (and sometimes pleased) to learn that some of their notions are based in myth. Several potential myths and facts are described.

1. *Myth:* Schizophrenia only afflicts young people. In fact, schizophrenia can occur in later life as a continuation of a chronic lifelong illness, or it may appear for the first time in middle age or old age (called *late-onset schizophrenia*). Of all people with schizophrenia, 23% have an onset after age 40.
2. *Myth:* Depression is the most common mental disorder in old age. In fact, anxiety disorders appear to be a more common form of psychopathology across all age ranges, including old

EXHIBIT 10.2
Class Activity

An instructor may take the myths described in this section and create a true/false questionnaire to be distributed to the class before discussion. For each myth, ask the class to vote whether the statement is true or false and then tally the response. Then, the instructor should present the facts and encourage class discussion. How do such myths develop? Are some myths more widely held than others? What could be the reasons for that?

age (approximately 6%). Generalized anxiety disorder is the most common specific anxiety disorder among older people. The rate of diagnosable depression among older people is quite low (about 1%), and younger adults have much higher rates of depression.

3. *Myth*: Old age is a period of decline and pathology. In contrast, wisdom and maturity are known to be age-related positive changes in psychological functioning. Many older people also show resilience and adaptability in the face of serious stressful challenges associated with aging, such as chronic health problems and the loss of friends and family members.

4. *Myth*: Most older adults are frail and are doomed to live out their final years confined in a nursing home. The reality is that only a small percentage (less than 5%) of older people are living in a nursing home at any one time, and most older people live independently or with family.

5. *Myth*: Older adults are unlikely to benefit from psychotherapy. A variant on this theme is the famous saying, "You can't teach old dogs new tricks." When it comes to progress in psychotherapy, the old adage is simply not true. More than 20 years of research on depressed older adults points to some interesting conclusions about the effectiveness of psychotherapy with older people. The overall conclusion is that depressed older adults respond quite well to psychotherapy. Scogin and McElreath (1994), in their meta-analysis of 17 studies that compared a psychosocial treatment for depression with a control group, reported a large effect size (a portion of a standard deviation, by which means of treatment and control groups differ, independent of sample size) of 0.79. This is similar to psychotherapy effectiveness for depressed adults of all ages (0.85) and slightly better than pharmacological interventions (0.60) but without the risk of side effects. The major treatment outcome studies in the area report success rates in approximately 50% to 70% of older people with major depression, with a consistent finding

that no single "brand" of therapy performs better than others. Other studies have indicated that psychotherapy is effective for other late-life mental disorders (APA Working Group on the Older Adult, 1998). Should older people experience psychological problems, chances are they will benefit from intervention. Negative attitudes about psychological treatment from family members, physicians, and some older people themselves should be challenged and replaced with a good measure of hope and the reasonable expectation that meaningful improvement is possible.

6. *Myth:* Suicide is more common among younger than older adults. It is true that as a society, we tend to view suicides of young adults as far more prevalent than those of older adults. This may result from the fact that dramatic youth suicides attract considerably more media attention than late-life suicides. In fact, suicide rates are higher among older age groups than younger age groups. Older adults account for about 20% of the suicides yet comprise about 13% of the U.S. population. In contrast, young people (ages 15 to 24) comprise about 14% of the population yet account for 15% of the suicides (Bharucha & Satlin, 1997). Depression is a major risk factor for suicide, and the biggest risk group is white men who are 85-years-old and older. Older adults who attempt suicide die from the attempt more often than any other age group, suggesting more lethal and determined suicide attempts among older people. Another disconcerting fact is that older adults tend to be less likely to seek relief from suicide prevention centers, crisis hotlines, or other types of mental health services compared with younger adults. Older adults also have relatively poor knowledge about suicide facts and myths (Segal, 2000), suggesting that they are not receiving adequate educational efforts and open dialogue about suicide (see Exhibit 10.3 for class activity).

EXHIBIT 10.3
Class Activity

As an activity, the instructor may divide the students into small groups to discuss the reasons why older adults are an at-risk group for suicide. Have them list their hypotheses on a sheet so they may share with the larger group. What do these reasons say about the way our society treats older people? The instructor can challenge students to analyze cultural and social factors that may be causing or exacerbating the problem. What can be done to prevent elderly suicide? Should ill older people have the right to die?

7. *Myth:* Older adults are sexless and prone to sexual dysfunction. Actually, the majority of older adults report that they are satisfied with their sexual experiences despite a normal decline in the frequency of sexual activity (Pedersen, 1998). The best predictor of the level of sexual behavior among older people is the level of sexual behavior when they were younger. The main barrier to healthy sexual functioning in later life is not an inability to perform but rather the lack of an available partner, especially for older women who have outlived their partner or who have a partner with serious health problems.

Unique Symptom Presentation of Mental Disorders of Later Life

The issue in this section is the extent to which some common disorders manifest differently among older adults compared with younger adults. It may be important to point out that the *DSM–IV* does not do an adequate job of incorporating age-related characteristics in the diagnostic criteria for mental disorders. Indeed, some disorders are known to have an unusual manifestation in later life making some criteria inadequate. For example, an older adult with major depression may not show the "classic" sign of a subjective sad or depressed mood but rather may describe memory problems and a multitude of somatic complaints (e.g., loss of appetite, weight loss or gain, sleep disturbances, loss of interest in sex, apathy, muscle aches and pains).

Some personality disorders characterized by intense emotionality and erratic behavior (e.g., borderline, histrionic, narcissistic, antisocial personality disorders) may appear in muted form in older adults, although the underlying psychological processes remain unchanged (Segal, Coolidge, & Rosowsky, 2000). The diagnosis of substance-related disorders is also problematic for older adults. The criteria do not reflect the fact that older adults are less likely to abuse illegal substances compared with younger adults but are more likely to abuse prescribed medications and over-the-counter (OTC) drugs (King, Van Hasselt, Segal, & Hersen, 1994). Also, older substance abusers may not be identified as having a problem because they drive less often and are more likely to be retired, thus avoiding detection of a substance problem through the typical means of a drunken driving offense or blatant problems at work. Finally, anxiety disorders may be especially difficult to detect and diagnose among older people because the symptoms of many anxiety disorders denote physical sensations that actually may be caused by a physical (not mental) problem, by drug interactions, or by side effects of medications—all of which are more common among older adults compared to younger adults (see Exhibit 10.4 for class activity).

EXHIBIT 10.4
Class Activity

Distribute the Beck Depression Inventory (BDI) and the Geriatric Depression Scale (GDS) to the class. Ask each student to review both questionnaires and list three ways in which the measures are similar and three ways in which they are different. Then, the instructor may break up students into small groups for discussion or discuss as a larger group. How do the measures differ? Which one is more appropriate for older people and why? Why was it necessary to develop the GDS (and other age-specific instruments)? The instructor should highlight the fact that the GDS was developed because the BDI did poorly in identifying depression in older persons because it includes many somatic symptoms that older adults endorse with high frequency even if the symptoms result from age-related changes or physical illness and not depression. The GDS is known to be more reliable and valid for use with older people.

Other Topics

Besides assigning a text chapter on aging (or a suitable reading) and covering aging and mental health as a distinct module, another strategy is to integrate concepts of aging into nonaging chapters where appropriate. Following are some suggestions of potential topics for integration. For example, in the classification and assessment chapters, the instructor may discuss how certain psychological assessment instruments may not be appropriate (i.e., reliable and valid) for older adults, and how a slew of specific instruments have been developed over the last decade (Segal, Coolidge, & Hersen, 1998) including the GDS, the Senior Apperception Test, and the Older Adults Pleasant Events Schedule. This type of discussion can occur during a general critique of the questionable reliability and validity of some tests with minority populations (e.g., African Americans, older adults). During presentations of the symptoms of mental disorders in a particular module, the instructor may describe how the symptoms of the disorders may manifest differently among younger and older people (discussed previously). The instructor is encouraged to use case examples of older clients as a pedagogical tool, and an excellent case book is available (Knight, 1992) if the instructor does not have cases from his or her own clinical work.

During a presentation of research methods, the instructor may discuss the problems with generalization of research findings on younger adults to older adults (or other diverse groups not represented adequately in the research sample). In the psychotherapy module, the instructor can consider discussing the adaptations to psychotherapy that are needed for clinical work with older adults, including the greater need to address feelings of embarrassment and shame about seeking mental health help among older adults, the greater need to explain and educate older people about the process of psychotherapy because they may not be as familiar with psychotherapy as younger people, and the greater need to assess and understand the role that medical problems and medications may play in the development or maintenance of psychological symptoms (APA Working Group on the Older Adult, 1998). Finally, during discussion of ethical issues, the instructor can highlight the important challenges and national debate about assisted suicide among older adults.

This chapter focused on how to integrate aging into undergraduate abnormal psychology classes. The typical abnormal psychology course was discussed, followed by a description of the coverage of aging in abnormal psychology textbooks and a discussion of the main facts about aging and mental health. Throughout, techniques and strategies for integrating aging were described. I hope the information and ideas presented here will provide a firm foundation from which to build as the "aging dimension" is added to your abnormal psychology class.

REFERENCES

American Psychiatric Association. (1994). *Diagnostic and statistical manual of mental disorders* (4th ed.). Washington, DC: Author.

APA Working Group on the Older Adult. (1998). What practitioners should know about working with older adults. *Professional Psychology: Research and Practice, 29,* 413–427.

Bharucha, A., & Satlin, A. (1997, July–August). Late-life suicide: A review. *Harvard Review of Psychiatry,* 55–65.

Gatz, M. (Ed.). (1995). *Emerging issues in mental health and aging.* Washington, DC: American Psychological Association.

Gatz, M., & Finkel, S. I. (1995). Education and training of mental health service providers. In M. Gatz (Ed.), *Emerging issues in mental health and aging* (pp. 282–302). Washington, DC: American Psychological Association.

Gatz, M., & Smyer, M. (1992). The mental health system and older adults in the 1990s. *American Psychologist, 47,* 741–751.

Gatz, M., & Smyer, M. (2001). Mental health and aging at the outset of the 21st century. In J. E. Birren & K. W. Schaie (Eds.), *Handbook of the psychology of aging* (5th ed., pp. 523–544). San Diego, CA: Academic Press.

Jeste, D. V., Alexopoulos, G. S., Bartels, S. J., Cummings, J. L., Gallo, J. J., Gottlieb, G. L., et al. (1999). Consensus statement on the upcoming crisis in geriatric mental health: Research agenda for the next 2 decades. *Archives of General Psychiatry, 56,* 848–853.

Karel, M. J., Molinari, V., Gallagher-Thompson, D., & Hillman, S. L. (1999). Post-doctoral training in professional psychology: A survey of fellowship graduates. *Professional Psychology: Research and Practice, 30,* 617–622.

King, C., Van Hasselt, V. B., Segal, D. L., & Hersen, M. (1994). Diagnosis and assessment of substance abuse in older adults: Current strategies and issues. *Addictive Behaviors, 19,* 41–55.

Knight, B. G. (1992). *Older adults in psychotherapy: Case histories.* Newbury Park, CA: Sage.

Knight, B. G., & Kaskie, B. (1995). Models of mental health service delivery to older adults. In M. Gatz (Ed.), *Emerging issues in mental health and aging* (pp. 231– 255). Washington, DC: American Psychological Association.

Pedersen, J. B. (1998). Sexuality and aging. In I. H. Nordhus, G. R. VandenBos, S. Berg, & P. Fromholt (Eds.), *Clinical geropsychology* (pp. 141–145). Washington, DC: American Psychological Association.

Qualls, S. H. (1998). Training in geropsychology: Preparing to meet the demand. *Professional Psychology: Research and Practice, 29,* 23–28.

Qualls, S. H. (1999). Mental health and mental disorders in older adults. In J. C. Cavanaugh & S. K. Whitbourne (Eds.), *Gerontology: An interdisciplinary perspective* (pp. 305–328). Oxford: Oxford University Press.

Qualls, S. H., Segal, D. L., Norman, S., Niederehe, G., & Gallagher-Thompson, D. (in press). Psychologists in practice with older adults: Current patterns, sources of training, and need for continuing education. *Professional Psychology: Research and Practice.*

Scogin, F., & McElreath, L. (1994). Efficacy of psychosocial treatments for geriatric depression: A quantitative review. *Journal of Consulting and Clinical Psychology, 62,* 69–74.

Segal, D. L. (2000). Levels of knowledge about suicide facts and myths among younger and older adults. *Clinical Gerontologist, 22,* 71–80.

Segal, D. L., Coolidge, F. L., & Hersen, M. (1998). Psychological testing of older people. In I. H. Nordhus, G. R. VandenBos, S. Berg, & P. Fromholt (Eds.), *Clinical geropsychology* (pp. 231–257). Washington, DC: American Psychological Association.

Segal, D. L., Coolidge, F. L., & Rosowsky, E. (2000). Personality disorders. In S. K. Whitbourne (Ed.), *Psychopathology in later adulthood* (pp. 89–115). New York: Wiley.

Zarit, S. H., & Haynie, D. A. (2000). Introduction to clinical issues. In S. K. Whitbourne (Ed.), *Psychopathology in later adulthood* (pp. 1–25). New York: Wiley.

ANNOTATED BIBLIOGRAPHY

APA Working Group on the Older Adult. (1998). What practitioners should know about working with older adults. *Professional Psychology: Research and Practice, 29,* 413–427. This article for practitioners is an excellent overview of many areas of aging including demographics, realities of aging, psychological problems, psychological assessment and interventions, and professional issues.

Hersen, M., & Van Hasselt, V. B. (Eds.). (1996). *Psychological treatment of older adults: An introductory text*. New York: Plenum Press. This undergraduate text focuses primarily on the assessment of older adults and treatment strategies for diverse psychological disorders, and it includes many case examples.

Hersen, M., & Van Hasselt, V. B. (Eds.). (1998). *Handbook of clinical geropsychology*. New York: Plenum Press. This graduate-level text provides literature reviews on diverse topics. It is divided into sections on general issues (e.g., government policy and clinical geropsychology, moral and ethical issues), psychopathology, assessment and treatment (for all major classes of disorders), and special issues (e.g., bereavement, marriage and divorce, minority issues, elder abuse).

Knight, B. G. (1996). *Psychotherapy with older adults* (2nd ed.). Thousand Oaks, CA: Sage. This is a sophisticated, practical, and coherent introduction to psychotherapy with older adults. It provides a theoretical model for understanding the social context and specific developmental challenges faced by older people.

LaRue, A., & Watson, J. (1998). Psychological assessment of older adults. *Professional Psychology: Research and Practice, 29*, 5–14. This article covers the basic principles in the assessment of older adults. It provides sound practical advice regarding the assessment and describes how such assessment differs from work with younger people.

Molinari, V. (Ed.). (2000). *Professional psychology in long-term care*. New York: Hatherleigh Press. This is a helpful resource book for clinicians who are interested in clinical work in nursing home settings. It is divided into sections on assessment, treatment, and professional issues.

Nordhus, I. H., VandenBos, G. R., Berg, S., & Fromholt, P. (Eds.). (1998). *Clinical geropsychology*. Washington, DC: American Psychological Association. This broad graduate level edited volume covers theoretical views, practical issues (e.g., friendships, sexuality, elder abuse, dementia, anxiety, depression), and assessment and psychotherapy with older adults.

Qualls, S. H., & Abeles, N. (Eds.). (2000). *Psychology and the aging revolution: How we adapt to longer life*. Washington, DC: American Psychological Association. This book focuses on the latest theories and research on how aging affects many important domains of life, including cognition, social functioning, emotion, physical and mental health, and reactions to psychotherapy.

Smyer, M. A., & Qualls, S. H. (1999). *Mental health and aging*. London: Blackwell Publishers. This book provides a thorough introduction and overview of aging and mental health, including information about basic gerontology, the common mental disorders, and pragmatics of geropsychological practice. A unique feature of this book is the thorough explication and description of 4 theoretical models to understand mental health in later life. Rich case material is provided.

Whitbourne, S. K. (Ed.).(2000). *Psychopathology in later adulthood*. New York: Wiley. A rich and current overview of the major classes of psychological disorders experienced by older persons, with a focus on assessment, diagnosis, and treatment issues. Each chapter includes an integrated case study. Chapters also cover the normal aging process, assessment of older adults, and general principles of psychotherapy.

Zarit, S. H., & Zarit, J. M. (1998). *Mental disorders in older adults*. New York: Guilford Press. This excellent and comprehensive graduate-level text focuses primarily on thorough literature reviews of the major classes of psychological disorders experienced by older persons. Chapters also address psychotherapy and caregiving issues.

OTHER SUGGESTED RESOURCES

Readings

Carstensen, L. L., Edelstein, B. A., & Dornbrand, L. (Eds.). (1996). *The practical handbook of clinical gerontology*. Thousand Oaks, CA: Sage.

Knight, B. G., Teri, L., Wohlford, P., & Santos, J. (Eds.). (1995). *Mental health services for older adults. Implications for training and practice in geropsychology*. Washington, DC: American Psychological Association.

Storandt, M., & VandenBos, G. R. (Eds.). (1994). *Neuropsychological assessment of dementia and depression in older adults: A clinician's guide*. Washington, DC: American Psychological Association.

Zarit, S. H., & Knight, B. G. (Eds.). (1996). *A guide to psychotherapy and aging: Effective clinical interventions in a life-stage context*. Washington, DC: American Psychological Association.

Films: Mental Health and Aging

A Safer Place (about elder abuse), Fanlight Productions, (800) 937-4113

Alzheimer's: A True Story, Films for the Humanities and Sciences, (800) 257-5126

Alzheimer's Disease, Fanlight Productions, (800) 937-4113

Alzheimer's Disease: How Families Cope, Films for the Humanities and Sciences, (800) 257-5126

Alzheimer's: The Tangled Mind, Films for the Humanities and Sciences, (800) 257-5126

Caring . . . Sharing: The Alzheimer's Caregiver, Fanlight Productions, (800) 937-4113

Chronic Anxiety in the Elderly, Films for the Humanities and Sciences, (800) 257-5126

Depression in Older Adults, Fanlight Productions, (800) 937-4113

Elder Abuse: Five Case Studies, Fanlight Productions, (800) 937-4113

Help Me Die (about assisted suicide), Fanlight Productions, (800) 937-4113

Living Longer . . . Aging Well, Films for the Humanities and Sciences, (800) 257-5126

Lost in the Mind (about Alzheimer's disease), Aquarius Health Care Videos, (888) 440-2963

Sexuality and Aging, Fanlight Productions, (800) 937-4113

Signs and Symptoms of Alzheimer's Disease, Videopress, (800) 328-7450

Something Should Be Done about Grandma Ruthie, Fanlight Productions, (800) 937-4113

Substance Abuse in the Elderly, Films for the Humanities and Sciences, (800) 257-5126

The Alzheimer's Mystery, Films for the Humanities and Sciences, (800) 257-5126

The Oldest Victims: Elder Abuse, Films for the Humanities and Sciences, (800) 257-5126

Groups, Organizations, and Professional Resources: Mental Health and Aging

Alzheimer's Association

> 919 North Michigan Avenue, Suite 1100
> Chicago, IL 60611-1676
> (800) 272-3900
> Available at: http://www.alz.org

Alzheimer's Disease Education and Referral Center

> P.O. Box 8250
> Silver Spring, MD 20907-8250
> (800) 438-4380
> Available at: http://www.alzheimers.org

American Association for Geriatric Psychiatry

> 7910 Woodmont Avenue
> Bethesda, MD 20814-3004
> (301) 654-7850
> Available at: http//www.aagpgpa.org

American Psychological Association (APA)

> Public Interest Directorate–Committee on Aging
> Public Interest Directorate
> 750 First Street, NE

Washington, DC 20002-4242
(202) 336-6135
Available at: http://www.apa.org/pi/aging/homepage.html

APA *Division 12 (Society for Clinical Psychology)*

Section II (Clinical Geropsychology)
Available at: http://bama.ua.edu/~appgero/apa12_2/

APA *Division 20 (Adult Development and Aging)*

Available at: http://aging.ufl.edu/apadiv20/apadiv20.htm

American Society on Aging

Mental Health and Aging Network
833 Market Street, Suite 511
San Francisco, CA 94103-1824
(415) 974-9600
Available at: http://www.asaging.org

Gerontological Society of America

Mental Health Practice and Aging Interest Group
1030 15th Street NW, Suite 250
Washington, DC 20005
(202) 842-1275
Available at: http://www.geron.org

Psychologists in Long Term Care

Coordinator: Victor Molinari, PhD
Houston Veterans Affairs Medical Center (HVAMC)
Mental Health Care Line 116A
2002 Holcombe Boulevard
Houston, TX 77030
(713) 791-1414 ext. 5669
E-mail: molinari.victor@houston.va.gov
Available at: http://www.wvu.edu/~pltc/

Selected Journals: Mental Health and Aging[1]

American Journal of Geriatric Psychiatry (American Psychiatric Publishing)

---

[1]This is not an exclusive list. Rather, it is a listing of journals that regularly publish articles related to mental health and aging.

Clinical Gerontologist (Haworth Press)

Journal of Aging and Mental Health (Carfax Publishing, Taylor & Francis)

Journal of Clinical Geropsychology (Kluwer Academic/Plenum)

Journal of Mental Health and Aging (Springer)

Journal of Geriatric Psychiatry and Neurology (BC Decker)

International Journal of Geriatric Psychiatry (John Wiley and Sons)

International Psychogeriatrics (Springer)

Psychology and Aging (American Psychological Association)

Journal of Gerontology: Psychological Sciences (The Gerontological Society of America)

11

MEN AND WOMEN IN OLD AGE: INCORPORATING AGING INTO PSYCHOLOGY OF GENDER COURSES

VICTORIA HILKEVITCH BEDFORD

Development continues throughout the life span. This basic precept of the life-span perspective apparently has not penetrated the discipline judging from the undergraduate psychology curriculum. In consequence of this missing concept, what often passes for a knowledge base on human behavior is, in actuality, an age-specific representation. Courses on the psychology of gender (or the psychology of women and men) are no exception. Most textbooks designed for these courses rarely consider how gender issues are played out in later life. Issues typically targeted are gender development, gender stereotypes, social relationships, sexuality, school, work and careers, health, and psychopathology and its treatment (Brannon, 1999). Most of these topics are relevant to older adults. Without consideration of gender, a distorted

Please direct correspondence to Victoria Hilkevitch Bedford, School of Psychological Sciences, University of Indianapolis, 1400 East Hanna Avenue, Indianapolis, IN 46227; e-mail: bedfordv@indiana.edu or bedford@uindy.edu.

picture of aging results. Because of gender differences in life expectancy and morbidity, for instance, statistics combining men and women describe neither. Furthermore, the stakes of ignoring gender in older women's health and financial well-being are extremely high. For example, the feminization of aging, namely, the preponderance of women, particularly among those who are very old is rarely mentioned in the debates on Capitol Hill concerning Social Security, prescription drug coverage, Medicare, and Medicaid. These entitlements are essential primarily to women (and minority men), but the future and shape of them are determined mostly by men. In this chapter, several illustrations are provided in the field of the psychology of aging that should help students appreciate the importance of considering older adults in their understanding of the psychology of gender.

OVERVIEW OF COURSE SUPPLEMENT ON AGING AND THE PSYCHOLOGY OF GENDER

The first objective of the aging supplement to a course on the psychology of gender is to "demarginalize" old age. It is essential to make students aware of age as one of the many diversities of human experience. It is relatively easy to convey the marginalization of women in a mixed-gender class by simply addressing the students as "you gals" instead of "you guys." Even the female students in the class may feel uncomfortable on behalf of the male students. The instructor should point out, however, that everyone tends to accept being addressed as "you guys." Older people are similarly marginalized, as conveyed in assumptions about, for instance, family structure, employment status, and sensory functioning (e.g., size of print on the dashboard of an automobile).

The next objective of this aging supplement is to concretize the role gender plays in old age by examining topics in which gender differences are dramatic. These concrete examples can serve as templates for students to use when considering other topics, including those that may touch their personal and professional lives. As such, it is hoped that students will apply critical thinking skills to discern gender issues, which will inform decision making with respect to their personal lives and the larger community. The topics discussed in this chapter include gender identity, gender mortality and morbidity gaps, suicide, income, household composition, and social relationships.

Another objective is to understand the complex interaction of factors that account for the gender differences in old age. Again, this goal is not expected to be met in its entirety, but the process involved in analyzing causes of gender differences will be demonstrated.

SPECIFIC TOPICS IN THE PSYCHOLOGY OF GENDER AND AGING AND CORRESPONDING SUGGESTIONS FOR TEACHING ASSIGNMENTS AND ACTIVITIES

Gender Identity and Stereotypes

Gender identity and stereotypes are examples of topics that are central to the psychology of gender but have received little attention with respect to middle age and old age. These areas can be explored through informal research projects within the course structure.

Changes in gender identity may be compared using various formulations. Three formulations to compare, for instance, are (a) the gender-crossover phenomenon that coincides with the end of active parenting (Gutmann, 1997), (b) changes in the criteria one uses to feel gender congruent (Huyck, Zucker, & Angellaccio, 2000), and (c) traditional concepts of gender identity (Bem, 1974). Students will be familiar with Bem's popular formulation. Gutmann ties traditional gender identity with traditional roles and their cessation. By applying critical-thinking skills, students should be able to identify sexist assumptions and outmoded conceptions of social reality in this model. Huyck et al.'s view presents a complex and refreshing take on gender identity that relies on informants to define gender identity as they experience it.

Gender stereotypes in old age can be studied to illustrate the intersection between age and gender. One might assume that the stereotypes of old women are more negative than are those of old men (Rainey, 1998). This view is supported by the finding that men label women as middle aged and old earlier than men label men. Yet, as discussed later, the suicide rate for older men is at least tenfold the rate for older women, implying that men do not benefit from their more positive stereotype. This discussion could help understand the meaning of women's appearance to men and women's alienation from appearance in later life (Healey, 2000). After acknowledging these trends, it would be interesting to consider alternative models of aging men and women that neither devalue women nor create unrealistic expectations of men. This discussion can be followed with the question of why such positive models are so much less visible in American culture.

Gender Mortality and Morbidity Gaps

Gender gaps (i.e., differences) in life expectancy and illness or disability provide some intriguing examples of the possible outcome of a wide variety of gendered behaviors throughout life. Students may develop sensitivity to the lifelong consequences of their decisions for their well-being as an older adult. It is equally important, however, that they understand that the link between these decisions and health outcomes are not inherent but a result of deliberate legislative actions (Quadagno & Harrington Meyer, 1994). The instructor can use these figures to illustrate the large gender gap in mortality in the United States. The data were compiled from the Internet releases of the U.S. Bureau of the Census (1999) and the U.S. National Center for Health Statistics (2001):

- There are 83 men to every 100 women between ages 65 and 69.
- There are 42 men to every 100 women after age 84.

A discussion of possible reasons for this gender mortality gap should consider (a) the higher death rate of males in infancy and childhood resulting from many genetic abnormalities that are more prevalent in males than in females; (b) more deaths in adulthood of males resulting from occupational hazards, lifestyle choices (e.g., alcohol and tobacco use), and violence; and (c) men dying earlier than women because they tend to contract fatal diseases earlier and more often (Rainey, 1998). The actual reason for the mortality gap eludes scientists because it is likely to result from a complex interaction of biological, social, and behavioral conditions. Men's behaviors alone do not explain the gap because as women participate more in these behaviors, the gap does not change consistently across nations (Kinsella, 2000). In the United States, however, the mortality gap may be narrowing (U.S. Bureau of the Census, 1999). The following are some facts that may contribute to this trend (U.S. National Center for Health Statistics, 2001).

- The leading causes of death are decreasing, particularly heart disease, which men contract earlier than women.
- Death from lung cancer, breast cancer, and hypertension are increasing in women and not men (except in the case of hypertension for African American men).

The issue of women's higher rate of morbidity offers the opportunity to put their life expectancy advantage in perspective. Women are more likely to have chronic illnesses than men, which, together with their financial disadvantage, results in a higher rate of institutionalization than for men at all ages (Shyoun, Pratt, Lentzner, Dey, & Robinson, 2001). A somewhat greater proportion of women are disabled than men at all levels of disability in old age. However, the actual number of disabled women far outstrips the number of older men because there are so many more older women than there are men. For instance, of people age 80 and older with severe disability, 51% are men and 61% are women, yet in actual numbers, more than twice as many women are severely disabled in this age category than are men (2,823,000 women versus 1,247,000 men; U.S. Bureau of the Census, 1997). Because of the higher numbers of disabled women (physically and cognitively), the gender mortality advantage of women does not appear to apply to active life expectancy for large numbers of women. Their excess years are spent disabled

(Ginn & Arber, 1991). It may be pointed out to students that disseminating knowledge about risk factors for disability may result in a higher quality of life for women in old age in more recent and future cohorts.

Suicide

Suicide rates offer a dramatic lesson in gender differences in old age. Gender differences in suicide rates illustrate how meaningless statistics can be when gender is ignored. For instance, the following is based on 1998 data for Whites only (Murphy, 2000):

- The rate of suicide (per 100,000) for persons age 65 and older was 16.9.
- The rate for women in this age category was 5.
- The rate for men in this age category was 36.6.

Furthermore, these differences increase steadily from age 55 so that in the age 85 and older category, White men have the highest suicide rate of all. Without this gender analysis, then, the highly disproportionate suicide risk for White men could not have been identified. Apparently this finding is replicated across most developed countries (U.S. Department of Health and Human Services, 1996).

These dramatic figures can be used to engage students into exploring the underlying reasons. Gender socialization early in life and its consequences later should be discussed. Susan Faludi's thesis in her book, *Stiffed* (1999), analyzed the cohort of WWII veterans and the messages of invincibility conveyed to their sons. The instructor may want to consider how these messages may be antithetical to coping with the losses likely to occur during the aging process.

Income

Women are at greater risk of poverty as older adults than are men. Instructors can make this fact come to life with the following quote from Older Women's League (OWL; 2001):

> More than half of women age 65 and over have personal incomes of less than $10,000 a year; three out of four women have incomes under $15,000. . . . [These] severe economic disadvantages limit the quality of their lives, including their ability to access health care, pay for prescription drugs, and afford assistance with their daily living needs and other long-term care. (p. 1)

The instructor should discuss some of the factors accounting for this greater risk, such as Social Security inequality, lower pensions for widows, male–female salary inequalities, lifelong financial dependency on husbands

(Rainey, 1998), and gender-assigned work patterns (e.g., part time, leaves of absence; OWL, 2001).

Statistics are available for each risk factor. For instance, widowed and divorced women receive one third of the income they would have had as a couple from Social Security because a woman receives half her spouse's Social Security benefit. Women's erratic work history as a result of unpaid caregiving leads even wage-earning women to take the spousal benefit rather than the lesser benefit based on their own earnings. Traditionally "female work" is the greatest source of women's financial disadvantage. The instructor can engage students in this concept with the statement that motherhood is the single largest cause of poverty for women (Crittenden, 2001).

Social Relationships

Gender differences in social relationships can be discussed with respect to both negative and positive consequences. For women, one burden to discuss is the stress women experience from too much involvement in the lives of others (Antonucci, 1994), whereas men experience severe loss when widowed as a result of their lack of investment in other intimate relationships. Pointing out this contrast between men and women provides an opportunity to link gender socialization as caring beings with women's impoverishment in later life. The instructor should point out that even today traditional family values support women staying home at least to care for young children and older parents. The value system also supports that women volunteer in local schools, community events and institutions, and charitable organizations. The loss of wage-earning years leaves women at risk in an entitlement system based on income and a health care system that requires supplemental insurance for preventive care, prescription drugs, and long-term care, which typify health care needs in old age (Lamphere-Thorp & Blendon, 1993).

It should also be pointed out that the very qualities that result in such disadvantages to women also give them advantages over men despite women's inferior finances and health. For instance, homemakers do not experience the transition from the wage-earner role with which men must cope. In very old age, women's homemaking tasks can be carried out with less difficulty than men's wage-earning tasks. The physical constraints women cope with throughout their adult lives (e.g., pregnancy, lactation, menstruation, menopause) may make it easier to adapt to the physical changes involved in aging that men may be encountering for the first time in old age. Finally, women's social roles also contribute to strong family bonds and friendships that provide social and material support in later life (Rainey, 1998). An area to explore in terms of its consequences in older age is the different relationship style men and women seem to demonstrate; women's relationship style tends to be intimate and disclosing, whereas men's tends to be activity-based. Do these differences have different consequences in old age? Are the differences sustained in old age or do gender constraints on relationship styles relax?

Household Composition

Gender differences in household composition present another dramatic example for instructors to use to integrate aging into courses on gender. One tactic to use in presenting these data is to link them with gender differences in marital status, widowhood, and differences in the consequences of widowhood for men and women. For instance, in 1998, two thirds of women lived alone at age 85 and older, but only one third of men did so (U.S. Bureau of the Census, 1998). The primary cause of this difference is related to marriage status. In 1999, 49% of men at this age were married, whereas only 12% of women were married (U.S. Bureau of the Census, 1999).

Instructors can challenge students to consider the differential consequences of widowhood for men and women. The consequence for men can be devastating for reasons described previously; in the cohorts studied, men's restricted social relationships have left them bereft of social involvement in widowhood (Ginn & Arber, 1991). The consequences for women were also severe, but different from those of men. Women suffered a sharp drop in income, became "home poor" and experienced status loss, role loss, and loss of possessions (Rainey, 1998).

ACTIVITIES AND SUPPLEMENTAL MATERIALS

In this section, ideas are offered on how to engage students in topics suggested in this chapter. These activities are designed to put the student in the driver's seat to seek information and become involved through inductive methods. The activities suggested engage students by relating issues to themselves and to older people they know, by allowing them to gather data and draw their own conclusions, by exposing them to contradictions in the data, and by directing them to other sources of information. Ideas are presented in relation to the topics discussed.

Gender Identity

Instructors can have students administer Huyck et al.'s interview questions to themselves, or have them conduct interviews on older people such as family members. If both sources are used, cross-sectional comparisons can be made. If results differ, discuss the possible cohort and developmental differences. Huyck et al.'s questions are as follows:

1. Do you think of yourself as masculine or feminine?
   In what ways?
   In what ways does being masculine or feminine affect the things you do or the things you do not do?
2. In what ways do you think you are not so masculine or feminine?
   How do you account for that?
   How do you feel about it?

For an alternative view of gender identity and aging, refer students to Gutmann (1997) or to his earlier books on the topic of the parental imperative and its influence on personality.

Gender and Aging Stereotypes

For gender stereotypes, instructors can have students watch television advertisements for 1 hour or select a magazine and record (a) the proportion of older adults appearing compared with total number of adult actors, (b) the proportion of older women in relation to older men, and (c) the differences between older men and women in terms of their activity level, emphasis on sexuality, importance of appearance and any particular aspect of their appearance. This assignment works especially well for fashion magazines and most television shows.

Another activity is for the instructor to distribute an excellent, very short essay on gender and ageism, Shevy Healey's *Growing to Be an Old Woman: Aging and Ageism* (Healy, 2000). Help students visualize an older man and woman where age is not the central dimension.

An instructor may also send students to various stores that sell birthday cards and have them classify the cards according to the stereotypes portrayed. Compare cards designed for men versus those designed for women. Ask students to code the cards in terms of shared stereotypes on aging and on gender-specific stereotypes. Have students compare their findings in class. Were students surprised by their findings? Did men or women seem to be advantaged in the depictions? Why might this be?

Gender Differences in Mortality, Morbidity, and Income in Old Age

Students should be encouraged to visit some Web sites that contain updated information on gender differences. Explain that someone had to excerpt the information from large data sets such as census data, and, therefore, human error is always a possibility. Encourage students to compare statistics from different Web sites in service of reliability. Instruct students to make note of whether references and citation information are available on the Web site. Without such information, it may be better to search for a Web site with better documentation.

General Web sites that provide some statistics on aging by gender are as follows:

- Administration on Aging; available at: http://www.aoa.gov/
- U.S. Bureau of the Census; available at: http://www.census.gov/
- Center for Disease Control; available at: http://www.cdc.gov/nchs/
- Older Women's League (OWL); available at: http://www.owl-national.org
- National Institute on Aging; available at: http://www.nih.gov/nia/

Comparing statistics on different Web sites is also a way to trace current trends in the data that have not yet been reported. Because data are constantly changing, groups of students could be assigned different Web sites to compare statistics based on different data sets and different years of data collection. Again, they should attend to the documentation provided on the Web site.

Examples of readings that present and interpret statistics on gender differences are Ginn and Arber (1991), Barer (1994), Kinsella (2000), Rainey (1998), and Lamphere-Thorp & Blendon (1993). Again, students could be encouraged to brainstorm or research what events (e.g., legislation, economic conditions) and what geographical or cultural factors may account for the changes and differences in the data.

More specific cites are available, but they tend to become obsolete quickly. A few are presented here, alphabetically, by topics covered in this chapter, but students should be prepared to find they have changed and to embark on new searches:

Cause of Death

- http://www.cdc.gov/NCHS/about/otheract/aging/trendsoverview.htm#New Series
- http://www.cdc.gov/NCHS/releases/01news/declindea
- http://www.cdc.gov/nchs/fastats/lcod

Disability Rate

- http://www.census.gov/population/www/pop-profile/disabil
- http://www.census.gov/hhes/www/disable/sipp/disab97/ds97t1

Life Expectancy Data

- http://www.infoplease.com/ipa/A0005148

Nursing Home Residents

- http://www.cdc.gov/nchs/releases/00facts/nurshome.htm

Suicide

- http://www.suicidology.org/index
- http://www.fortnet.org/WidowNet/demographics/cdcstudy
  provides the rate of change in the incidence of suicide for
  men and women in the United States
- http://www.trinity.edu/~mkearl/death-su gives suicide rates for
  men and women grouped by age in 16 developed countries

As a classroom activity, instructors can organize students into breakout groups for the purpose of brainstorming possible explanations for the dramatic gender differences in suicide rates. Each group can present one possible explanation for the differences such as specific gender socialization practices or specific cohort differences. A designated scribe in each group takes notes. A representative from each group presents the group's conclusion to the class.

Social Relationships

Show the Canadian documentary video *Living With Dying*, which describes how a dying man with multiple fatal illnesses goes into remission because of the efforts of his wife who is supported by excellent formal health services, neighbors, friends, and family members. After viewing the movie, ask students to write in what ways the wife's dying process is likely to be similar and in what ways different from her husband's. Students are graphically confronted with the hurdles the wife will face as a widow at the end of life.

GENERAL ASSIGNMENTS

Use of Videos in Learning About Gender and Aging

A number of full-length films are available in video format that could be used as a basis for a writing assignment. These videos should be made available for students to see in their dormitories or the media department of the library. A useful exercise is to require that students imagine the gender of the protagonist(s) reversed and to answer a series of questions, or select an in-depth topic. For example, one series of questions to consider is as follows:

1. Is the reversal realistic in the United States?
2. Which characteristics are unlikely and why? Consider marital status, finances, household composition, and so on.
3. Are such characteristics likely or unlikely due to gender alone or gender in relation to age?

Alternatively, students could be asked to identify gender and aging issues in the films that have been discussed in class (e.g., relationship style differences, population statistics, income differentials, differences in household composition, differences in suicide rate, and so on). Small groups could be assigned to each movie. A class project would be for students to compile an annotated bibliography of films with respect to gender and aging on the basis of each group's analysis of its film. Some well-known films on aging are as follows: *Age-Old Friends, Cocoon, Driving Miss Daisy, Fried Green Tomatoes, Grumpy Old Men, On Golden Pond, Steel Magnolias, Terms of Endearment,* and *Trip to Bountiful* (e.g., Scheidt, 2002).

Writing Assignments

Frequent writing assignments are ideal teaching tools. Only a few require the instructor to grade them. Most of the assignments can be informal opportunities for students to put ideas into words within a format that they can review. A number of informal suggestions have been made in the previous discussion. One kind of writing exercise takes place in class. Students are required to engage in free writes on a particular topic before it is even discussed so they can identify common misconceptions as well as to help motivate them to attend actively to the discussions and lectures on the topic that follow. Finally, shy students can be asked to read their entries during the discussion.

Journaling is a popular form of informal writing outside of the classroom. Ask students to keep an "Aging and Gender Journal" or to include such an entry each day while maintaining a more general journal on the "Psychology of Gender." Ask students to keep track of whether they encountered (in person, by phone, in the media) anyone older than age 65. Request that students make note of the person's gender and the context of the encounter. At the end of each week, have students summarize their encounters in terms of gender (e.g., media personnel are overwhelmingly male at all ages) or context (e.g., activity level, service-related, family vs. non-family context). Compare summaries in class and consider such topics as invisibility of older women versus men in daily life or gender segregation (or lack thereof) in various aspects of daily life. Have students write papers or free writes in class that summarize the findings, critique the findings in terms of advantages and costs of these patterns, and offer solutions for a more inclusive society. Have students share their insights with the class.

Formal writing could be related to an experience, library research (term papers), or both. Because emotional engagement makes writing most interesting for students, it is a good idea to assign an experiential paper first from which topics for the research paper will naturally follow. Experiential papers that are highly successful derive from interviewing older adults. Recommend that students submit questions ahead of the interview on specific topics targeted in the class, and they will quickly learn that the more prepared they are the more likely they are to elicit information on the topic of interest. Another source of experiential papers derives from field observations such as those just described in relation to the media and journaling. Often, these experiences easily arouse students' curiosity and can generate interesting topics for term papers.

REFERENCES

Antonucci, T. C. (1994). A life-span view of women's social relations. In B. F. Turner & L. E. Troll (Eds.), *Women growing older: Psychological perspectives* (pp. 239–269). Thousand Oaks, CA: Sage.

Barer, B. M. (1994). Men and women aging differently. *Journal of Aging and Human Development, 38,* 29–40.

Bem, J. L. (1974). The measurement of psychological androgyny. *Journal of Consulting and Clinical Psychology, 42,* 155–162.

Brannon, L. (1999). *Gender: Psychological perspectives* (2nd ed.). Boston: Allyn & Bacon.

Crittenden, A. (2001). *The price of motherhood: Why the most important job in the world is still the least valued.* New York: Henry Holt.

Faludi, S. (1999). *Stiffed: The betrayal of the American man.* New York: William Morrow.

Ginn, J., & Arber, S. (1991). Gender, class and income inequalities in later life. *British Journal of Sociology, 42*(3), 369–396.

Gutmann, D. (1997). *The human elder in nature, culture, and society.* New York: Westview Press.

Healey, S. (2000). Growing to be an old woman: Aging and ageism. In E. P. Stoller & R. C. Gibson (Eds.), *Worlds of difference: Inequality in the aging experience* (3rd ed., pp. 81–83). Thousand Oaks, CA: Pine Forge Press.

Huyck, M. H., Zucker, P., & Angellaccio, C. (2000). Gender across generations. In E. Markson & L. Hollis-Sawyer (Eds.), *Intersections of aging: Readings in social gerontology* (pp. 87–103). Los Angeles: Roxbury.

Kinsella, K. (2000). Demographic dimensions of global aging. *Journal of Family Issues, 21,* 541–558.

Lamphere-Thorpe, J., & Blendon, R. J. (1993). Years gained and opportunities lost: Women and healthcare in the aging America. In J. Allen & A. Pifer (Eds.), *Women on the front lines* (pp. 75–104). Washington, DC: Urban Institute Press.

Murphy, S. L. (2000). Deaths: Final data for 1998. *National Vital Statistics Report, 48*(11), DHHS Publication No. (PHS) 2000-1120, 100.

Older Women's League (2001). *The state of older women in America.* Retrieved May 27, 2002, from http://www.owl-national.org/reports.htm

Rainey, N. (1998). Old age. In K. Trew & J. Kremer (Eds.), *Gender and psychology* (pp. 153–163). New York: Arnold.

Quadagno, J., & Harrington Meyer, M. (1994). Gender and public policy. In E. P. Stoller & R. C. Gibson (Eds.), *Worlds of difference: Inequality in the aging experience* (3rd ed., pp. 134–138). Thousand Oaks, CA: Pine Forge Press.

Scheidt, R. J. (2002). *Aging and the cinema.* Retrieved May 27, 2002, from http://aging.ufl.edu/apadiv20/cinema.htm

Shyoun, N. R., Pratt, L. A., Lentzner, H., Dey, A., & Robinson, K. N. (2001). *The changing profile of nursing home residents: 1085–1997. Aging Trends: No. 4.* Hyattsville, MD: National Center for Health Statistics.

U.S. Bureau of the Census. (1997). *Americans with disabilities: Table 1.* Retrieved May 27, 2002, from http://www.census.gov/hhes/www/disable/sipp/disab97/ds97t1.html

U.S. Bureau of the Census (1998, March). Household and family characteristics. *Current Population Reports*, P20-515. Cited in The Administration on Aging's "Statistical Information on Older Persons." Retrieved May 27, 2002, from http://www.aoa.gov/aoa/stats/statpage.html

U.S. Bureau of the Census (1999). *New CDC report on U.S. mortality patterns.* Retrieved May 27, 2002, from http://www.cdc.gov/NCHS/releases/01facts/99mortality

U.S. Department of Health and Human Services. (1996, January 12). Suicide among older persons, United States, 1980–1992. *Morbidity and Mortality Weekly Report.*

U.S. National Center for Health Statistics, National Vital Statistics Reports. (2001, September 21). *Deaths final data for 1999.* Vol. 48, No. 8. Retrieved May 27, 2002, from http://www.cdc.gov/nchs/about/major/dvs/mortdata.htm

ANNOTATED BIBLIOGRAPHY

Barer, B. M. (1994). Men and women aging differently. *Journal of Aging and Human Development*, 38, 29–40. This article is an excellent overview of gender issues in very old age. It is readable and relatively brief, ideal for undergraduates. After an introduction on increased life expectancy, a San Francisco study of the oldest old (age 85 and older) is described. The men and women are compared in terms of demographics, economic status, perceived health status, functional limitations, social supports, and their ability to manage daily routines. A unique contribution of this article is a section comparing the life trajectories of older men and women that reveal how very old men are at a disadvantage because their transitions occur later, at a time when adjustment to transitions is complicated by infirmities of very old age and lack of anticipatory socialization. Case studies are provided to illustrate these differences.

Healey, S. (2000). Growing to be an old woman: Aging and ageism. In E. P. Stoller & R. C. Gibson (Eds.), *Worlds of difference: Inequality in the aging experience*

(3rd ed., pp. 81–83). Thousand Oaks, CA: Pine Forge Press. This brief essay is a compelling description of the author's personal encounters with and exploration of sexism and ageism. When she considers having a facelift, she realizes how she has internalized self-hatred. Ultimately, she comes to terms with her own aging.

Huyck, M. H., Zucker, P., & Angellaccio, C. (2000). Gender across generations. In E. W. Markson & L. A. Hollis-Sawyer (Eds.), *Intersections of aging* (pp. 87–102). Los Angeles: Roxbury. This fairly complex article reports on findings of an intergenerational study of gender identity. Findings are discussed in terms of variability of gender identity, which is coded into the styles within the categories of gender-congruent, gender-expanded, and gender-compromised for both men and women, but the content of these styles differs for men and women and for younger and older generations of adults. Generational differences are interpreted tentatively as developmental rather than cohort effects. The chapter also includes implications for theory and practice, further research, and five discussion questions.

Rainey, N. (1998). Old age. In K. Trew & J. Kremer (Eds.), *Gender and psychology* (pp. 153–163). New York: Arnold. This volume on gender and psychology is one of the few that includes a chapter on old age. As such, it gives an excellent overview of many of the gender issues in old age in broad strokes. The chapter focuses on gender differences in socioeconomic class, life experiences, and social networks. Four excellent discussion questions are included.

Turner, B. F., & Troll, L. E. (Eds.). (1994). *Women growing older: Psychological perspectives*. Thousand Oaks, CA: Sage. This edited volume is for advanced students. It provides an understanding of women as they grow older from a strong research base. One chapter addresses gender differences in family relationships and is more accessible than the others. In "Family Connectedness of Old Women: Attachments in Later Life," L. E. Troll begins with a theoretical discussion of the concept of human connectedness and some key issues that have been studied. Next, she turns to family data on three generations of adult family members consisting entirely of men or women. Combining quantitative analyses and case studies, men and women are compared on salience of family bonds and at different ages.

12

COMPLETING THE LIFE CYCLE: INCORPORATING ADULT DEVELOPMENT AND AGING INTO LIFE SPAN PSYCHOLOGY COURSES

KAREN L. FINGERMAN

The cliché "Life is short" may not feel that way to instructors who are charged with teaching its entire contents in a single academic term. The demands of teaching a life span psychology course are multifold. Instructors must divide a plethora of course material across only 10 to 15 weeks. In this process, they must decide what material to include each term and address difficulties in creating a sense of cohesion across units in the course. There are also challenges in generating activities for the latter half of the life span, which may be less interesting to students who have not yet experienced these stages of life. Furthermore, most instructors of developmental psychology courses have acquired expertise in one area of the life span, such as early

Please direct correspondence to Karen L. Fingerman, Department of Human Development and Family Studies, 135 E. Nittany Ave, Suite 405, Pennsylvania State University, State College, PA 16801; e-mail: kxf18@psu.edu.

childhood or late life, rendering the majority of the course material outside the instructor's expertise.

It is tempting to deal with these issues by simply focusing life span development courses on issues that interest the instructor most or on topics that readily engage undergraduate students, such as adolescent dating. This approach to teaching life span development leaves students with a sense that little change occurs in adulthood, however, because they learn most about issues that are familiar to them. By giving adequate attention to adult development, instructors can enhance students' overall sense of the shape of the life span, how development progresses, and where there are continuities and where there are discontinuities.

COURSE OBJECTIVES, TOPICS COVERED, AND ORGANIZATIONAL STRUCTURE

In teaching any course, the first demand involves the organization and sequence of material. Courses that cover life span development may seem luxurious in that regard; such courses can be organized in a prescribed manner, from birth to death. An alternate approach to organization involves covering different domains of development. For example, physical development might be covered in one unit, and cognitive development from birth to old age in another unit. Most introductory developmental psychology textbooks use a combination of these approaches; the book first covers infant physical development, then infant social development, then infant cognitive development. Next, physical development in early childhood is highlighted, followed by social development in early childhood, then early cognitive development, and so forth through the life span. The overarching design of the course lies under the rubric of time, and life progresses from infancy to old age. Such an organization makes the structure of the course transparent to students, but it obscures the bigger picture as each domain of development (i.e., physical, cognitive, social) is parsed up into small chunks of the life span.

In more advanced courses where instructors rely on primary materials, they may wish to use a thematic approach. Indeed, the thematic approach is the best solution to covering adult development issues in the context of life span courses. Specific units cover the entire life span with regard to a given topic. For example, students learn how infant temperament emerges into personality and how personality changes and stabilizes across adulthood (Caspi & Silva, 1995; Costa, Metter, & McCrae, 1994). Nonetheless, given the dominance of the "chunks of the life span" approach found in introductory textbooks, this approach to organizing a life span psychology course is covered in this chapter.

ORGANIZING THE COURSE TO INCLUDE ADULT
DEVELOPMENT AND AGING

With the sequential organization of life span courses, adult development and aging always falls in the second part of the course. Textbook writers sometimes joke that it is all right to slough off writing the end of the book because nobody covers those chapters anyway! Indeed, life span development textbooks often condense 50 years of life into single chapters that cover "midlife and aging." Furthermore, scholars who study child and adolescent development conceive of adulthood as the end state of development, rather than as a period characterized by development. These conceptualizations render many life span development courses as child development courses with a smattering of adulthood in the final 2 weeks. To deal with these issues, instructors need to allocate adequate time to cover material pertaining to adulthood. Instructors often consider units of the early part of the life span: prenatal development, infancy, early childhood, middle childhood, and adolescence. Likewise, instructors should consider the next 80 years as discrete units such as early adulthood, midlife (the largest segment of adulthood), young old age, oldest old age, and death. Thus, childhood consumes half the term, and adulthood consumes half the term. Given that adulthood lasts up to four times longer than the preadulthood period, spending half the course on adulthood seems like a bare minimum.

This organization of the a life span development course as "chunks" of adulthood emphasizes that changes in adulthood are as large and important as changes in childhood. Furthermore, instructors can illustrate how different aspects of development fit together. For example, in infancy, changes in cognition such as object permanence coincide with changes in social behaviors underlying attachment. Likewise, in later life, changes in emotion regulation occur contemporaneously with a selection of social ties that are most rewarding (Carstensen, Gross, & Fung, 1998). When the course is organized around such units, the central challenge facing the instructor then becomes tying the adult part of the life span to childhood and adolescence.

LIFE SPAN THEMES AND THEORIES TO UNIFY THE COURSE

The most direct way to unify a life span development course involves introducing common themes early in the course and referring to these themes during the childhood and adulthood units. Many themes can lend a unified sense of child and adult development, such as the following: (1) development involves complexity; (2) development occurs in a larger social context; (3) genetic, biological, psychological, and sociological factors interact to drive development; (4) discontinuities and continuities characterize development; and (5) individual differences in developmental patterns are evident at all stages of life. Each of these themes might be used to more adequately cover adult development in life span development courses.

As an example, instructors should emphasize that development has a complex shape throughout life. Common misperceptions portray the early part of the life span as characterized by gains and the latter part as characterized by losses. In actuality, there are gains and losses throughout life (Uttal & Perlmutter, 1989). Furthermore, different domains involve different trajectories throughout life. There are losses with regard to reaction speeds in late life, yet older adults who have played tennis throughout their lives may beat younger game partners based on their expertise with the game (Salthouse, 1999). To better integrate child and adult development, in each unit of the course, instructors should emphasize areas of gains, loss, and stability.

Additionally, instructors might consider theories that deal with gains and loss across periods of development. For example, Paul Baltes' (1987, 1997) theory of selection, optimization, and compensation applies to the entire life span. In reaching a goal, individuals face limits on capacities, time, and resources. Therefore, organisms select as they develop. As an example, infants are predisposed to learn any language, but by 1 year, they show clear preferences for sounds of their own language. Selective processes are greater at the end of life, as energy and health wane. By relying on such theories, teachers can treat different parts of the life span as illustrations, leaving students with a unified sense of the themes of the course.

In recent years, the field of life span psychology has placed a strong emphasis on social contextual influences on development. Uri Bronfenbrenner's ecological theory of development is often introduced to illustrate these concepts in childhood (Bronfenbrenner & Morris, 1997). However, a careful examination of the details of Bronfenbrenner's theory reveals that it has little application to adults' lives. For example, Bronfenbrenner emphasizes *proximal processes* in which social interactions must be repeated over time to have an effect on the individual. Although repetition may be necessary in social ties in childhood, recent research has revealed that older adults find meaning from social contacts whom they have not seen for more than 50 years (Fingerman & Griffiths, 1999). Bronfenbrenner's microsystem includes parents, teachers, mentors, and coworkers (Bronfenbrenner & Morris, 1997); older adults are unlikely to have these social ties. Instead, instructors might introduce ecological theories more applicable to adulthood. Glenn Elder's (1998a, 1998b) work on the life course emphasizes the ways in which historical events interact with other social factors in individuals' lives. For example, Elder and Liker (1982) found that older women reacted to the losses involved in aging based on their experiences as young adults during the Great Depression.

Furthermore, Neugarten (1979) argued that adult development should not be conceptualized in the same terms as child development. Whereas patterns of events are sequential in childhood (e.g., rolling over, then crawling, then walking), events do not unfold in such sequences in adulthood. Rather, different issues arise repeatedly across adulthood and vary by individual and context. Neugarten's theoretical work further addressed the issue of whether adults view events in their lives as being "on time" or "off time." By introducing work like Neugarten's, instructors can raise questions about where and when discontinuities may occur in the life span. Is adult development driven by the same forces that drive child development? Even introductory level students can grapple with this question and in doing so extend their critical thinking abilities.

Finally, in considering issues of continuity and discontinuity, instructors might introduce evidence from longitudinal studies that have covered the life span. For example, the Berkeley Growth Study (Caspi, Elder, & Bem, 1987), the Children of Kaui Study (Werner, 1989), and the Seattle Longitudinal Study (Schaie, 1998) are useful resources. In recent years, instructors have tended to veer away from covering empirical studies in introductory courses as students' ratings of their enjoyment of the course have gained increasing importance in university evaluations of instructors. By encouraging student discussion and activities around interesting questions, such as the disconnection between childhood and adulthood, instructors can introduce longitudinal data in exciting ways.

SPECIFIC TOPICS IN A LIFE SPAN COURSE

In addition to the larger themes that instructors might use to anchor the course, they can introduce the same topics in the same order with regard to each stage of life. Common topics in life span psychology courses include physical, social, emotional, cognitive, and personality areas of development. Clearly, instructors cannot give adequate attention to each of these topics at each stage of life. Instructors must make choices about the topics they cover. In part, these choices are guided by the chunk of the life span currently considered. Different issues are salient at different stages of life. For example, it is almost essential to cover genetics in a unit on prenatal development, attachment in a unit on infancy, and cognitive changes in a unit on early childhood. By contrast, genetics and cognitive development may receive short shrift in midlife, when women's hormonal changes may garner more attention.

In considering specific topics that instructors will emphasize, they should reconsider the larger themes of the course. Rather than simply teaching genetics, followed by attachment, followed by language development, instructors might think about ways in which each of these smaller topics illustrates larger principles of life span development. For example, a unit on cognitive changes can illustrate the larger principles of continuity and discontinuity, individual variation, and social context. Instructors can point out how cognitive functioning varies with age across childhood but is associated with education level in midlife.

In general, the course will seem more cohesive if instructors work to use a similar rubric for the topics they cover in each unit. For example, instructors might cover physical, social, and cognitive issues at each stage of life. Physical development might include genetics, health issues, hormonal changes, brain, or sensory development in different units of the course. With regard to social ties, the course might focus on relationships with peers during the teenage years, but more specifically on relationships with children and grandchildren for adults over age 80. Likewise, instructors might cover language development in early life, schooling in childhood, and fluid and crystalized intelligence in late life. The key to using these subtopics successfully involves providing students with an explicit framework and referring back to prior units of the course. It is also important to remind students that each issue is relevant at each stage of life (e.g., hormones exist from prenatal stage to death) and that the instructor is highlighting different examples at different stages of life.

INCORPORATING ADULT DEVELOPMENT AND AGING INTO LIFE SPAN COURSES

Although the general issues described thus far allow integration across units, adulthood and aging may still receive short shrift in a life span course. In addition to textbook biases, various intellectual and societal biases contribute to the ways in which adult development is presented. This next section describes ways of making the adult development units as relevant and exciting as material pertaining to child development.

PRESENTING ISSUES IN ADULT DEVELOPMENT

Instructors must be particularly sensitive to the fact that our society is ridden with fears of aging. Indeed, instructors of life span development courses face their own prejudices against old age (Fingerman, 2000). As was already mentioned, these fears can infiltrate a life span development course through instructors' failure to spend adequate time on the gains of late life development. To make the premise of gains and losses a central theme throughout the course, instructors might ask themselves "Have I pointed out what students have to look forward to when they reach this stage of life?" as they write each lecture pertaining to adult development.

From an intellectual perspective, instructors face an additional hurdle in presenting adult development. Paradoxically, the field of adult development and aging is considerably younger than the field of child development.

Whereas researchers have studied children for over a hundred years, the Gerontological Society of America recently celebrated its fiftieth birthday. From a history of science perspective, this gap in maturity of the fields renders research on child development more sophisticated and detailed at certain levels. For example, whereas researchers who study adolescent development have examined how parents and children treat one another with regard to different areas of conflict (e.g., homework, personal style; Smetana, Yau, & Hanson, 1991), researchers who study adults are still mapping out areas of parent–child conflict (Fingerman, 1996, 2001). Middle-age adults, like adolescents, may react with different behaviors in the face of different types of problems with their aging parents. Unfortunately, researchers in the field of gerontology have not yet determined the nature of those behaviors or the contexts that elicit different behaviors.

Different topics have received research attention at different stages of life. For example, researchers who study adolescence have focused primarily on social development, with little attention to cognitive changes. By contrast, development psychologists have looked closely at cognitive development in early childhood and late life. This variable attention to different phenomena shapes our sense of the life span. Such nuances are beyond the level of complexity that introductory students should master, but instructors should be aware of these issues for their own understanding of the material.

ACTIVITIES FOR THE SECOND HALF OF LIFE

Finally, it is important to acknowledge that students enrolled in college courses in the 21st century expect each lecture to include a fair amount of pizzazz. With multimedia available for presenting material, instructors must "keep up with the Joneses" to retain students' attention and enthusiasm for the course. In life span psychology courses, instructors face the task of making adult development as interesting and exciting as child development. Child development is inherently interesting to many undergraduate students for two reasons. First, students relate to periods of life they have already experienced. Students who have returned to college in midlife may be captivated by the adult development units, but undergraduates who are young adults usually gravitate towards the child and adolescent development units. Second, it is easier to find activities and videotapes that capture childhood experiences in entertaining ways. When presenting Piaget, instructors can have students act out the tasks with young children they know or bring in videotapes of the tasks; students are riveted. Nonetheless, it is possible to generate activities and materials that illustrate principles of adult development and capture student interest. Mass media lend various materials that can engage students. For example, commercials during the national news tend to be targeted at older adults. Asking students to watch these commercials and consider either health implications (many commercials target older adults' health) or societal stereotypes can generate lively discussion in class. Further discussion of societal stereotypes might arise from having students visit card shops and systematically count the number of cards that denigrate aging in different ways. Magazines, sitcoms, and movies can also be used to look at the presence or absence of different messages about old age.

Many movies and television shows are also available to illustrate different topics of adult development. Identity formation is a common theme in movies and sitcoms with young adults (e.g., the television series *Friends* or the feature film *The Breakfast Club*). Likewise, it is possible to find this theme in movies that include older adults (e.g., *Driving Miss Daisy*). Instructors can use short 5- to 10-minute segments of movies to back up different parts of their lectures. A complete list of such videotapes is available on the American Psychological Association (APA) Division 20 Web site.

Some of the most memorable activities may involve having students interact with older adults. Although students themselves may not have lived through the entire life span, they can draw vicariously on the experiences of individuals who have. Several ways are available for using such an activity. Students could read a journal article on a topic of interest and then interview an older adult about that topic. A subsequent paper might focus on individual differences in development by asking students to compare and contrast the research findings to the life of the person they interviewed. Alternately, groups of students might interview several older adults about their experiences during a specific historical or social event to show how social context shapes life span development. A key issue in these assignments involves linking students with older adults. Most college students do have a grandparent or other older adult to interview, but instructors should also have a list of volunteers on standby when they use such exercises.

Community service-based activities have also gained in popularity on many college campuses in recent years. These activities allow students to receive academic credit for participating in volunteer activities in their local communities (Fingerman, 2000). Students in life span psychology courses might spend part of the term volunteering in a setting with children in some capacity and part of the term volunteering in a setting with older adults. A pitfall of this approach in a life span course involves a lack of comparability between groups, however. Whereas students might interact with healthy, normal children in a school setting, they might see only the most debilitated older adults in a nursing home or hospital setting. Instructors must work hard to make the volunteer experiences comparable. Furthermore, these exercises introduce the contrast between early life and old age, obscuring changes in young and middle adulthood. Nonetheless, given the increase in such community-based activities on campuses, instructors might think about ways to integrate such service into life span psychology courses. Possible advantages of service-learning activities include better understanding of course concepts, dispelling myths about aging, and reinforcing career choices (Blieszner & Artle, 2001).

Finally, some instructors have used activities that simulate the effects of aging to help students understand the latter years of life (Fingerman & Bertrand, 1999; Whitbourne & Cassidy, 1994). In such exercises, students might don earplugs to experience hearing loss, smear petroleum jelly on glasses to simulate cataracts, and wear gloves with some of the fingers sewn shut to understand the effects of arthritis. It is important to use these exercises in a relevant manner, however, and not allow students to come away with a sense that they have experienced "old age." Not all older adults experience multiple impairments. Instead, instructors might randomly assign impairments by having students draw note cards from a bag. Some cards might indicate many impairments, whereas other cards might indicate few impairments. After putting on their assigned impairments, students might engage in an activity for 5 to 10 minutes. Class discussion could then focus on why some adults "age successfully," and other adults do not. Such discussion is useful in showing how behaviors in early life (e.g., smoking, diet) might have an impact on later life and bringing home messages about healthy choices early on.

Alternately, physical simulation exercises might be used in conjunction with simulations of social behaviors. For example, we asked students to work in groups and had one student per group assigned as the person who would experience physical changes of aging (Fingerman & Bertrand, 1999). These group leaders did not know that their groups were instructed to treat them differently when they took on the characteristics of old age. The leaders received respect from group members when they were "middle age" but their groups belittled and derided them when they were "old." Discussion following this exercise focused on how the social effects of aging can be considerably worse than the physical impairments that accompany late life. In any case, instructors should beware that simply mimicking physical impairments and calling the exercise "old age" may convey stereotypes about declines of old age rather than accurately educating students about this stage of life. Of course, simulation activities can be exciting and engaging; when used appropriately, these may be the most memorable activities that students experience.

SUMMARY

In summary, life is not short when it is a topic of attention in a psychology course. Instructors face several challenges with regard to material pertaining to adult development and aging in these courses. They must organize the course to provide adequate attention to the adult years. They must unify the material across the life span while still recognizing that certain issues are not comparable at different stages of life. Finally, instructors must find creative ways to make the later years exciting and engaging for students who have not yet personally experienced these stages of life. All of these tasks can be accomplished by giving as much attention to the latter 80% of life as the first 20% of life.

REFERENCES

Baltes, P. B. (1987). Theoretical propositions of life-span developmental psychology: On the dynamics between growth and decline. *Developmental Psychology, 23*, 611–626.

Baltes, P. B. (1997). On the incomplete architecture of human ontogeny: Selection, optimization, and compensation as foundation of developmental theory. *American Psychologist, 52*, 366–380.

Blieszner, R., & Artle, R. M. (2001). Benefits of intergenerational service learning to human services majors. *Educational Gerontology, 27*, 71–87.

Bronfenbrenner, U., & Morris, P. A. (1997). The ecology of developmental processes. In W. Damon (Ed.) *Handbook of child psychology* (5th ed., pp. 993–1028). New York: Wiley.

Carstensen, L. L., Gross, J. J., & Fung, H. H. (1998). The social context of emotional experience. In K. W. Schaie & M. P. Lawton (Eds.), *Annual review of gerontology and geriatrics* (Vol. 17, pp. 325–352). New York: Springer.

Caspi, A., Elder, G. H., & Bem, D. J. (1987). Moving against the world: Life-course patterns of explosive children. *Developmental Psychology, 23*, 308–313.

Caspi, A., & Silva, P. (1995). Temperamental qualities at age three predict personality traits in young adulthood: Longitudinal evidence from a birth cohort. *Child Development, 66*, 486–498.

Costa, P. T., Metter, E. J., & McCrae, R. R. (1994). Personality stability and its contribution to successful aging. *Journal of Geriatric Psychiatry, 27*, 41–59.

Elder, G. H. (1998a). The life course and human development. In R. M. Lerner (Ed.), *Handbook of child psychology (Vol. 1). Theoretical models of human development* (pp. 939–991). New York: Wiley.

Elder, G. H. (1998b). The life course as developmental theory. *Child Development, 69*, 1–12.

Elder, G. H., Jr., & Liker, J. K. (1982). Hard times in women's lives: Historical influences across forty years. *American Journal of Sociology, 88*, 241–269.

Fingerman, K. L. (1996). Sources of tension in the aging mother and adult daughter relationship. *Psychology and Aging, 11*, 591–606.

Fingerman, K. L. (2000). Enhancing student interest in the psychology of aging: An interview with Susan Whitbourne. *Teaching of Psychology, 27*, 224–229.

Fingerman, K. L. (2001). *Aging mothers and their adult daughters: A study in mixed emotions.* New York: Springer.

Fingerman, K. L., & Bertrand, R. (1999). Approaches to teaching adult development within a lifespan development course. *Teaching of Psychology, 26,* 55–57.

Fingerman, K. L., & Griffiths, P. C. (1999). Season's greetings: Adults' social contact at the holiday season. *Psychology and Aging, 14,* 192–205.

Neugarten, B. L. (1979). Time, age, and the life cycle. *American Journal of Psychiatry, 136,* 887–894.

Salthouse, T. (1999). Theories of cognition. In V. Bengston & K. W. Schaie (Eds.), *Handbook of theories of aging* (pp. 196–208). New York: Springer.

Schaie, K. W. (1998). The Seattle Longitudinal Studies of adult intelligence. In M. P. Lawton & T. A. Salthouse (Eds.), *Essential papers on the psychology of aging* (pp. 263–271). New York: New York University Press.

Smetana, J. G., Yau, J., & Hanson, S. (1991). Conflict resolution in families with adolescents. *Journal of Research on Adolescence, 1,* 189–206.

Uttal, D. H., & Perlmutter, M. A. (1989). Toward a broader conceptualization of development: The role of gains and losses across the life span. *Developmental Review, 9,* 101–132.

Werner, E. E. (1989). Children of the garden island. *Scientific American, 260,* 107–111.

Whitbourne, S. K., & Cassidy, E. L. (1994). Psychological implications of infantilization: A class exercise. *Teaching of Psychology, 21,* 167–168.

ANNOTATED BIBLIOGRAPHY

Baltes, P. B. (1997). On the incomplete architecture of human ontogeny: Selection, optimization, and compensation as foundation of developmental theory. *American Psychologist, 52,* 366–380. This paper updates Baltes's theory of successful aging. Baltes considers biological and social cultural influences on human development throughout life. He argues that evolutionary pressures are greatest in early life, but cultural supports are essential to adaptation in late life. Throughout life, successful development involves maximization of gains over losses or increasing desirable states over undesirable ones. In late life, as individuals face physical declines, they must develop coping strategies to successfully maintain their independence. By selectively narrowing their activities, older adults can optimize functioning and compensate for losses. Students could grasp the material in this article, but the arguments are complex and introductory students would need guidance in reading it.

Elder, G. H. (1998). The life course and human development. In R. M. Lerner (Ed.), *Handbook of child psychology, Vol. 1: Theoretical models of human development* (pp. 939–991). New York: Wiley. This chapter includes a recent update on Elder's ecological theory. This theory looks at how transformed environments influence individuals' lives and developmental trajectories. Elder argues that personal biographies are shaped by historical and social events. Furthermore, the developmental impact of a life event depends on when it occurs in a person's life (i.e., childhood, adolescence, late life). Elder reviews studies he has authored to examine such historical events as the Great Depression, military service, and recent downturns in the farming economy. This chapter is rich with detail and information, a must-read for scholars, but it is too complex for undergraduate students. Elder's early work is more accessible to undergraduate students (see Elder & Liker, 1982 for an example).

Lerner, R. M. (1986). The continuity–discontinuity issue. In R. M. Lerner (Ed.), *Concepts and theories of human development* (pp. 183–215). New York: Random House. This chapter provides an excellent overview of the "shape" of development. Particular attention is given to the issue of continuity and discontinuity in development. The author examines questions about descriptive continuity, such as does a given behavior look the same at two points in time? The author also considers explanatory continuity, such as does the law governing the behavior remain constant? In examining these issues, he provides attention to theoretical work by Hans Werner and Jerome Kagan. The author also describes qualitative versus quantitative changes in development, plasticity in development, and resilience. This chapter is helpful to instructors, but it is too advanced for most undergraduate students.

Uttal, D. H., & Perlmutter, M. A. (1989). Toward a broader conceptualization of development: The role of gains and losses across the life span. *Developmental Review*, 9, 101–132. This paper presents a theoretical overview of the field of life span psychology. The authors specifically focus on two aspects of gains and losses across the life span by arguing: (a) gains are not limited to early life nor losses to late life, and (b) gains and losses are not always causally related across the life span. Rather, development is multidirectional and multidimensional at all stages of life. The authors provide an example of their gain–loss model by discussing the development of the nervous system in neonates, problem-solving skills among school children, and expertise in adulthood. Each of these issues can be understood as being characterized by gains and losses that are not inherently related. This article will provide instructors with a greater understanding of life span psychology at a conceptual level, but it is too complex for students.

13

INCORPORATING AGING INTO INDUSTRIAL/ORGANIZATIONAL PSYCHOLOGY COURSES

HARVEY L. STERNS, ANA BEGOVIC, AND DIANE L. SOTNAK

Industrial/organizational psychology is a specialty area within the field of psychology that studies human behavior in work settings (Cleveland & Shore, 1996). Areas of study include the way workers are recruited and selected, training and development, and measurement of employee job performance. Other important areas include study of the psychological processes involved in work behavior such as motivation to work, worker attitudes and feelings, job satisfaction, and stress (Sterns, Alexander, Barrett, Schwartz, & Matheson, 1990). More than 4 decades ago industrial gerontology in Great Britain began to address issues in aging and work. This research was motivated by concern regarding technological change and automation and the effects on the older worker (Committee on Economic Development, 1999; Sterns & Gray, 1999; Warr, 1994). Today, industrial gerontological psychology is an interdisciplinary approach to the study of aging and work that draws

Please direct correspondence to Harvey L. Sterns, Department of Psychology, University of Akron, 326 Polsky Building, Akron, OH 44325-4307; e-mail: hsterns@uakron.edu.

from industrial and organizational, developmental, and counseling psychology, and it focuses on employment and retirement issues of middle-age and older workers. In addition, the conception of the life span is changing. One can no longer view adulthood as a time of career stability; rather, it is a time to explore new work alternatives and consider different retirement options (Sterns, Matheson, & Park, 1997). Therefore, in teaching an industrial/organizational course, the instructor needs to consider many different types of issues. These issues may include social policy and law, stereotypes of the older worker, selection, job performance, job appraisal, training and retraining, career progressions and development, motivational factors and organizational design, job design and redesign, obsolescence, reentry workers, alternative work patterns, plant designs and layoffs, and retirement decisions.

COURSE OBJECTIVES, TOPICS COVERED, AND ORGANIZATIONAL STRUCTURE

With the aging of America's work force, a natural link exists between industrial/organizational psychology and aging and work issues. The instructor needs to explain how industrial/organizational psychology relates to the profession of psychology so that the students acquire a good understanding of its theoretical and methodological aspects, along with developing a basic knowledge of selection and placement, training and development, performance management, organizational development, quality of work life, human factors, and other related issues. As just indicated, a large number of topics are related to older adults and work, and discussing all of them in one semester might become an impossible task. Therefore, an instructor might focus on major areas of industrial gerontology, which include changes in the nature of work, career development, training and retraining, human factors and workplace design, job performance, and retirement. In addition, to teach an industrial/organizational course more effectively, the instructor should be aware of demographic changes in the workplace and have a good understanding of different definitions of older workers. The organization of this chapter consists of three parts. The first part includes relevant literature and how it can be incorporated into class lectures. The second part provides instructors with relevant exercise and activities that can be performed in class or on the World Wide Web. The third part includes an annotated bibliography with major resource articles.

DEMOGRAPHIC CHANGES AND THE WORKPLACE

The U.S. Bureau of Labor Statistics (BLS) projected that the U.S. labor force will grow from 127 million workers in 1992 to 151 million in 2005, an increase of approximately 19%. Workers ages 55 and older represented 12.2% of the entire labor force in 1992 and will represent 14.2% in 2005. Over the 1998 to 2008 period, total employment is projected to increase by 14%. The labor force of people ages 45 to 64 will grow faster than the labor force of any other age group as the baby-boom generation (i.e., those born from 1946 to 1964) continues to age. Between 1998 and 2008, the participation rate of workers ages 55 and older is expected to increase by 47.8%, from 17 million to 25 million workers (Sterns & Sterns, 2001).

Research has indicated that as many as 5.4 million Americans ages 55 and older report that they are willing and able to work but do not have jobs, 14.3 million are working, 26.4 million are retired and prefer not to work, and 6.3 million prefer to work but are unable (Sterns & Sterns, 1995). Once older workers lose their jobs, they stay unemployed longer than do younger workers, suffer a greater earnings loss in subsequent jobs than do younger workers, and are more likely to give up looking for another job (Committee on Economic Development, 1999; Crown, 1996).

DEFINITIONS OF OLDER WORKER

A continuing dilemma for industrial gerontology is an agreement on definitions for adult and older adult workers, and for the instructor to teach most effectively, he or she must be aware that aging is a multidimensional process that is difficult to reflect adequately in a single definition. Sterns and Doverspike (1989) proposed the following five approaches for defining older workers: chronological/legal, functional, psychosocial, organizational, and life span approach. These definitions provide discrete but related ways to conceptualize various aspects of aging, addressing several important levels of analyses and providing an organizing framework to discuss issues of aging and work.

The distinction between older and younger workers rests mostly on a definition that is using chronological age. Although little theoretical justification is offered for the age ranges, an implicit justification is based on a legal definition of age. The Age Discrimination in Employment Act (ADEA) of 1967, amended in 1978 and 1986, protects workers over age 40. Another commonly used cutoff point comes from the Job Training Partnership Act and the Older Americans Act. Both acts recognize people ages 55 and older as older workers. Thus, for federal programs, people ages 55 and older have been included in the older worker category. The instructor might discuss other examples of chronological age based on legal markers such as driving licensure, voting age, and drinking age. How are these ages decided? One example is that in 1967 when the ADEA was being legislated, research showed that it was taking people older than 40 twice as long to be rehired after losing a job (Sterns & Doverspike, 1989).

The second approach to defining older workers is a functional approach (Sterns & Doverspike, 1989). This is a performance-based definition of age and recognizes that there is a great individual variation in abilities and functioning at all ages. As chronological age increases, individuals go through various biological and psychological changes, including declines and increased experience, wisdom, and judgment. The concept of functional age refers to a performance-based definition of age. Individuals can be identified as "younger" or "older" than their chronological age based on objective measures. However, the instructor should be aware that the concept of functional age has been criticized from a number of perspectives, including the definitional, research design, and statistical points of view. Major problems are the use of a single index and the assumption of decline. Alternative approaches propose a more traditional methodology drawn from industrial psychology that emphasizes appropriate assessment strategies and the design of measures that assess attributes directly related to job performance.

Psychosocial definitions of older workers are the third approach. Sterns and Doverspike (1989) studied and based these definitions on social perceptions, including age typing of occupations; perceptions of the older workers; and the aging of knowledge, skill, and ability sets. The individual's self-perception was also considered. The way individuals perceive themselves and their careers at a given age may be congruent or incongruent with societal image. However, the instructor should be aware that relatively little research has addressed the basic question of how we know when workers will perceive themselves to be old and when they are perceived by others as old. On the other hand, a significant amount of research has investigated the perceived attributes of older workers. Older workers may be perceived as harder to train, less able to keep up with technological change, more prone to accidents, and less motivated. They are also seen as dependable, cooperative, conscientious, consistent, and knowledgeable.

The fourth approach, an organizational view of older workers, recognizes that the effects of age and tenure are necessarily related and that individuals age in jobs and organizations (Sterns & Doverspike, 1989). An older worker who has spent a substantial amount of time in a job will have, as a result, spent more time in an organization. A definition of older workers based on the aging of individuals in organizational roles is more commonly discussed under the topics of seniority and tenure. The effects of tenure and vice versa may often confound the effects of aging. Organizations age as well. Indeed, an organization may be perceived as old because of the average age of its members. As the average age of an organization's members increases, new demands are placed on the organizational subsystems such as human resources.

In one semester, the instructor might not have enough time to cover all the relevant literature on this topic of older worker. Thus, he or she may want to consider covering briefly the earlier mentioned definitions and devote more of the class time to the life span approach definition of older worker. The life span approach borrows from a number of the previous approaches but adds its own unique emphasis (Sterns & Doverspike, 1989). It advances the possibility for behavioral change at any point in the life cycle. Substantial individual differences in aging are recognized as critical in examining adult career patterns. Three sets of factors are seen as affecting behavioral change during the life cycle. The first set includes normative, age-graded, biological, or environmental determinants. These bear a strong relationship to chronological age. The second set of factors is normative, history-graded influences that affect most members of a cohort in similar ways. The third set of events is nonnormative. This includes unique career and life changes and individual health and stress-inducing events. The unique status of the individual is the result of the joint impact of these factors. According to this approach, there are more individual differences, as people grow older. Therefore, for the instructor and students, these different definitions of older workers may indicate that the late careers are often more complex to study than early careers because less consistency is evident in the developmental tasks. For example, in early career, individuals must choose a career. In late career, a person may continue a career, start a new career, modify a career, or retire.

As indicated earlier, the instructor and students should be aware and have a basic knowledge and understanding of the demographic changes and definitions of older workers. However, for the students to acquire a good understanding of the field of industrial gerontology, the instructor might focus discussion on changes in the nature of work, career development, training and retraining, human factors and workplace design, job performance, and retirement.

CHANGES IN THE NATURE OF WORK

Changes in organizational systems have repercussions for individuals within these systems. As organizations undergo downsizing and restructuring, employees may experience job loss, job plateauing, skill obsolescence, and the need for career self-management (Sterns & Gray, 1998). One of the more important factors that the instructor should know is that older workers may be singled out in downsizing efforts on the basis of stereotypic traits such as being unsuitable for retraining opportunities. In addition, middle age and older workers are more likely to occupy the midlevel managerial positions that are often the focus of downsizing and restructuring strategies (Sterns & Huyck, 2001). These events may lead to changes in the nature of work, which may be perceived as threatening by middle-age and older workers (Sterns & Gray, 1998).

The instructor might also consider covering more extensively the concerns and issues of middle-age workers. A critical issue for midlife workers is whether they will continue to be able to do the kinds of work they want to do, now and in the future (Sterns & Huyck, 2001). Even in a period of full employment, the threat of downsizing, layoffs, and early buyouts still leaves ambiguity in the minds of midlife and older workers regarding future work opportunities or the need to seek new employment. Midlife may be a period of evaluation, reassessment, and reflection for many workers. These workers may consider such issues as recognizing the limits of career progress, deciding to change jobs or careers, rebalancing work and family, further investing or withdrawing from work, and planning for retirement. Self-management of one's career may play an important role. Career self-management places the workers in control, and allows them to be able to shape their own careers (Sterns & Huyck, 2001).

CAREER DEVELOPMENT

The instructor might already be aware of early linear models of career development, which assume that individuals move through predictable career stages, and that for older adults, maintaining skills for a period and then declining was the predicted pattern. This notion that career stages are linked to age will lead managers to incorrectly choose career development opportunities for their older workers. It is of utmost importance for the managers to be aware of individual differences and the contributions that older workers make to the work force and the overall economy (Sterns & Huyck, 2001).

The conventional conception of career has been limited to a single career. The individual is to decide early in adulthood on the career goals that will be pursued. The individual then moves through establishing himself or herself and moving up in the organization, through a period of stability and then into retirement. For students to get a better understanding of career development and how it relates to the aging worker, the instructor might consider reading the works of Hall and Mirvis (1996) and Sterns and Gray (1999). Hall and Mirvis (1996) have described this career development path as an organizational career. Most vocational counseling and literature has been conceived under this or similar assumptions. However, at the present, career theorists and counselors must grapple with the fact that many individuals will not be able to follow such a simple trajectory. Technological changes and massive layoffs in some employment sectors have forced large numbers of individuals out of preordained career paths.

Furthermore, organizational changes are also altering the nature of the relationships between organizations and employees (Hall & Mirvis, 1996). Employers' commitment to employees may last only as long as a need exists for their skills and performance. Similarly, employees' commitment to the employer may last only as long as their expectations are being met. These changes place greater emphasis on employees' adaptability and abilities in learning to learn (Hall & Mirvis, 1996).

Hall and Mirvis (1996) captured this theme in their discussion of the protean career, which stresses continuous learning and self-direction of one's life and career. Greater tenure in protean-type careers may lead to the increased value of older workers. It may be rather expensive to replace such knowledgeable, adaptable, and continuously learning employees with younger workers with less protean-type career experience (Sterns & Gray, 1999).

Older workers, however, may be at a disadvantage in terms of moving toward greater career self-management. Transitioning from a typical, organizational career to a protean career may be a difficult task for individuals who entered the work force with a one career–one employer ideal (Sterns & Gray, 1999). Additionally, stereotypic beliefs about older workers may lead to the underuse of this group within the new relationships between organizations and employees (Hall & Mirvis 1996; Sterns & Gray, 1999).

TRAINING AND RETRAINING

To teach industrial gerontology in an industrial/organizational class effectively, it is important for the instructor to emphasize that older workers can be trained and retrained and that older workers have much to offer the modern organization and should be considered for training opportunities. Any training program should be based on a careful task analysis to determine the sequence of training (Sterns, 1986; Sterns & Doverspike, 1989). The individual will benefit from training that breaks the task into its component parts and trains each to a criterion level, with mastery of basic skills preceding the more difficult ones (Sterns, Junkins, & Bayer, 2001).

According to Sterns (1986) and Sterns and Doverspike (1989), training should be relevant, should provide positive feedback in an attempt to encourage the self-confidence of the trainee, and should target the development of new knowledge and skills for successful job performance. Furthermore, training is facilitated when material is organized to enhance learning. Finally, the training program should allow the older worker to take time necessary to learn the new tasks. Well-designed training programs will give individuals at all ages an equal opportunity to complete the program successfully (Sterns & Doverspike, 1989).

HUMAN FACTORS AND WORKPLACE DESIGN

In teaching the industrial/organizational course, it is important to include content related to human factors. It is crucial that a workplace is designed in a way that supports older workers, which most likely will be beneficial for both older workers and organizations (Fisk & Rogers, 1997; Sterns, Sterns, & Hollis, 1996). From an organizational perspective, increased productivity can occur if proper design of training and job equipment is taken into account (Sterns et al., 1996).

The design of workstations and work environments that take into account age-related factors (e.g., declines in visual acuity) have many advantages for older workers and organizations. Sensitive workplace design will assist older workers in developing compensatory behaviors to adapt to the work demands of the task, such as monitoring oneself for safety (Sterns et al., 1996). Regarding general workplace design, several considerations become increasingly important to older workers (Sterns et al., 1996). First, levels of illumination should be adequate without risking glare. Second, transitions in the level of illumination between work areas should be avoided because of the decreasing dark adaptation abilities of older adults. The need to discriminate between colors of the same hue and especially between colors in the blue-green range of the spectrum should also be avoided. Also, the print size of text materials should be sufficiently large to accommodate age-related changes in visual acuity.

JOB PERFORMANCE

The accurate evaluation of each employee's job performance is of paramount importance to the individual worker and organization. Accurate appraisals of job performance help ensure a better match between the positions held by the employee, the wages awarded to the employee, and the employee's value to the organization (Sterns & Alexander, 1988; Warr, 1994). When evaluating the performance of the older worker, the manager must use actual job performance. The appraisal system cannot be based on popular beliefs that performance declines with age. Sterns and Alexander (1988) reminded us that performance appraisals must be reasonable, relevant, and reliable. Decisions that are based on performance appraisal information should consider only relevant job performance data, regardless of age. For instance, when the older worker is being evaluated for a promotion, the information to consider is the worker's ability to perform the job relative to other workers. Whether these ideas are followed, however, is a topic of considerable debate.

RETIREMENT

The instructor of an industrial/organizational course might devote some time to topics and issues related to retirement. Retirement can be defined in many ways. Whether an individual is perceived as retired will depend on which definition of retirement is adopted. The process of retirement has common dichotomies pertaining to retirement: voluntary versus involuntary, early versus on time, and partial versus complete. Voluntary versus involuntary retirement is most often assessed through an individual's perception of choice in the retirement process. Early versus on-time retirement is often gauged by using age. Finally, number of hours worked is used to quantify the partial versus complete retirement distinction (Sterns, Junkins, & Bayer, 2001; Sterns, Matheson, & Park, 1997).

Although mandatory retirement policies have been eliminated with rare exceptions (e.g., airline pilots), pension plans can also be used as incentives to regulate the timing of an employee's retirement (Sterns & Gray, 1999). Employers may offer complete pension coverage before age 65 and may therefore influence the structure of the work force, with many older workers removing themselves from the labor force.

Some organizations now offer varying degrees of retirement education to their workers, ranging from financial planning to individual counseling. The federal government has encouraged people to plan and develop retirement income by using formal approaches such as Individual Retirement Accounts (IRAs), Social Security, investment, or private pension income. Concomitant with the use of IRAs and pension funds is the trend toward long-term retirement financial planning, often beginning when the individual enters the labor force.

Finally, the acceptance rates for Social Security reflect a societal change in retirement age. The Social Security Act of 1935 regards age 65 as the normal age for retirement, with eventual changes to 66 and 67 by 2010. Despite the advantage of waiting until full retirement age under Social Security, a growing proportion of workers have been choosing to retire earlier and receive reduced benefits. This option was first made available to women in 1956 and to men in 1961 (Sterns & Gray, 1999). Retirement creates many life changes for older adults. For the vast majority of people, with retirement comes an increase in free time and a decrease in income. These are not the only changes that occur as the result of retirement, but they are the ones most likely to be dramatic.

In conclusion, the term *older worker* has taken on a new meaning in the workplace. Currently, there is a greater variability in the definitions of work and retirement. Student interest is high in these areas, especially dealing with career development, training, and workplace design. This chapter's discussion, along with the annotated bibliography that follows, is an initial introduction to topics related to older worker and industrial gerontology. However, it is hoped that it will provide a starting point for the instructor in his or her quest to inform the students on the new and rapidly growing field of industrial/gerontological psychology.

CLASS ACTIVITIES

The use of exercises and class discussion are highly recommended. There are many excellent case studies relating to older worker issues in Rosen and Jerdee's (1985) *Older Employees: New Roles for Valued Resources.* Another useful exercise is to discuss stereotypes of older workers. An excellent resource on this discussion is in Fyock's (1990) *America's Work Force Is Coming of Age.*

Another area of interesting discussion is around the issues of cohort differences in the workplace. Zemke, Raines, and Filipczak (2000) have looked at four generations of individuals who are currently in the workforce. Defining events historically, core values, visible members, and music are presented for each generation. Excellent comparisons are available of how each generation approaches the workplace and how there is the potential for conflict and misunderstanding. Instructors can draw from these resources in many ways.

INTERNET EXERCISES AND RESOURCES

Students can examine trends in populations aging in the United States by exploring available data in the Demographics section. Available at: http://www.aoa.dhhs.gov./aoa/stats/statlink.html#Demographics.

In addition, students can examine population pyramids of the United States and other countries. For the class exercise, students can compare a pyramid of one developed country such as the United States to one developing nation such as Afghanistan and discuss differences and possible reasons for those differences. Available at: http://www.census.gov/ipc/www/idbpyr.html.

Additionally, a number of Web sites relating to work, training, and retirement can be resources, including the following:

1. Policy Brief No. 9: From Burkhauser, R. V., & Quinn, J. F. (1997). Pro-work Policy Proposal for Older Americans in the 21st Century. Center for Policy Research. Available at: http://www-cpr.maxwell.syr.edu/pbriefs/pblist.htm.
2. Scan the results of the retirement confidence survey. Available at: http://www.ebri.org/rcs/1998_results.html.
3. American Association of Retired People (AARP). Available at: http://www.aarp.org/.
   - Baby boomers and retirement. Available at: http://research.aarp.org/econ/boomer_seg_toc.html.
   - Money and work. Available at: http://www.aarp.org/indexes/money.html.
   - Career opportunities of the future. Available at:

http://www.aarp.org/confacts/money/futureacareers.html.

- Age discrimination in employment. Available at:
  http://www.aarp.org/ontheissues/issueagedisc.html.
- Mandatory retirement. Available at: http://www.aarp.org/
  ontheissues/issuemandret.html.
- Overcome the barriers to employment. Available at:
  http://www.aarp.org/working _options/barriers/home.html.
- Pursue lifelong learning. Available at: http://www.aarp.org/
  working _options/learning/home.html.

4. National Academy on Aging Society. Available at:
   http://www.agingsociety.org/.
5. Who are young retirees and older workers? Available at:
   http://www.agingsociety.org/retiree.htm.

REFERENCES

Cleveland, J. N., & Shore, L. M. (1996). Work and employment. In J. E. Birren (Ed.), *The encyclopedia of gerontology* (pp. 627–640). New York: Academic Press.

Committee on Economic Development. (1999). *New opportunities for older workers*. Retrieved May 28, 2002, from http://www.ced.org/docs/older.pdf

Crown, W. H. (Ed.). (1996). *Handbook on employment and the elderly*. Westport, CT: Greenwood Publishing Group.

Fisk, A. D., & Rogers, W. A. (Eds.). (1997). *Handbook of human factors and the older adult*. San Diego, CA: Academic Press.

Fyock, C. D. (1990). *America's work force is coming of age: What every business needs to know to recruit, train, manage, and retain an aging work force*. Toronto, Canada: Lexington Books.

Hall, D. T., & Mirvis, P. H. (1996). The new protean career: Psychological success and the path with a heart. In D. T. Hall & associates (Eds.), *The career is dead—long live the career: A relational approach to careers* (pp. 15–45). San Francisco: Jossey-Bass.

Rosen, B., & Jerdee, T. H. (1985). *Older employees: New roles for valued resources*. Homewood, IL: Dow Jones-Irwin.

Sterns, H. L. (1986). Training and retraining adult and older adult workers. In J. E. Birren, P. K. Robinson, & J. E. Livingston (Eds.), *Age health and employment* (pp. 93–113). Englewood Cliffs, NJ: Prentice-Hall.

Sterns, H. L., & Alexander, R. A. (1988). Performance appraisal of the older worker. In H. Dennis (Ed.), *Fourteen steps in managing an aging workforce* (pp. 85–93). Lexington, MA: Lexington Books.

Sterns, H. L., Alexander, R. A., Barrett, G. V., Schwartz, L. S., & Matheson, N. K. (1990). Aging, work and retirement, module VIII. In I. Parham, L. Poon, & I. Siegler (Eds.), *Access: Aging curriculum content for education in the social-behavioral sciences* (pp. 8.1–8.40). New York: Springer.

Sterns, H. L., & Doverspike, D. (1989). Aging and the training and learning process in organizations. In I. Goldstein & R. Casual (Eds.), *Training and development in work organization* (pp. 299–332). San Francisco: Jossey-Bass.

Sterns, H. L., & Gray, J. H. (1998). Employment and potential midlife career crisis. In I. A. Nordhus, G. R. VandenBos, S. Berg, & P. Fromholt (Eds.), *Clinical geropsychology* (pp. 147–153). Washington, DC: American Psychological Association.

Sterns, H. L., & Gray, J. H. (1999). Work, leisure, and retirement. In J. Cavanaugh & S. Whitbourne (Eds.), *Gerontology: Interdisciplinary perspectives* (pp. 355–390). New York: Oxford University Press.

Sterns, H. L., & Huyck, M. H. (2001). Midlife and work. In M. E. Lachman (Ed.), *Handbook of midlife development* (pp. 447–486). New York: John Wiley & Sons.

Sterns, H. L., Junkins, M. P., & Bayer, J. G. (2001). Work and retirement. In B. R. Bonder & M. B. Wagner (Eds.), *Functional performance in older adults* (2nd ed., pp. 179–195). Philadelphia: F. A. Davis.

Sterns, H. L., Matheson, N. K., & Park, L. S. (1997). Work and retirement. In K. F. Ferraro (Ed.), *Gerontology: Perspectives and issues* (pp. 171–191). New York: Springer.

Sterns, A. A., Sterns, H. L., & Hollis, L. A. (1996). The productivity and functional limitations of older adult workers. In W. H. Crown (Ed.), *Handbook on employment and the elderly* (pp. 276–303). Westport, CT: Greenwood Publishing Group.

Sterns, H. L., & Sterns, A. A. (1995). Health and the employment capability of older Americans. In S. A. Bass (Ed.), *Older and active: How Americans over 55 are contributing to society* (pp. 10–34). New Haven, CT: Yale University Press.

Sterns, H. L., & Sterns, A. A. (2001). Industrial gerontology. In G. L. Maddox (Ed.), *The encyclopedia of aging* (3rd ed., Vol. 1, pp. 537–538). New York: Springer.

Warr, P. (1994). Age and employment. In M. Dunnette, L. Hough, & H. Triads (Eds.), *Handbook of industrial and organizational psychology* (Vol. 4, 2nd ed., pp. 487–550). Palo Alto, CA: Consulting Psychologists Press.

Zemke, R., Raines, C., & Filipczak, B. (2000). *Generations at work: Managing the clash of veterans, boomers, xers, and nexters in your workplace*. New York: American Management.

ANNOTATED BIBLIOGRAPHY

General References: Aging and Industrial/Organizational Psychology

Crown, W. H. (Ed.). (1996). *Handbook on employment and the elderly*. Westport, CT: Greenwood Publishing Group. In this book, the author presents a wide range of topics relevant to the development of employment policies and programs for older individuals. Some of the topics include descriptive profile of older worker, implications of aging population on future employment of older people, decline of older individuals in labor force, participation of older females in labor force, and international perspective on aging and labor force.

Schaie, K. W., & Schooler, C. (Eds.). (1998). *Impact of work on older adults.* New York: Springer. In this book, the emphasis is on the impact of the workplace on older workers and older workers' impact on workplace, along with examining mediating effects of cultural and social factors on that impact. In addition, because psychologists and sociologists share a common interest in area of aging, the editors include relevant literature from both disciplines. The topics cover aging and work, retirement norms and strategies, organizational structure of the workplace, careers for older workers, and health and work.

Sterns, H. L., & Gray, J. H. (1999). Work, leisure, and retirement. In J. Cavanaugh & S. Whitbourne (Eds.), *Gerontology: Interdisciplinary perspectives* (pp. 355–390). New York: Oxford University Press. Issues associated with aging and work such as older worker stereotypes, aging and training, aging and work attitudes, and aging and work withdrawal are discussed. Organizational changes and the changing nature of careers are also covered in this chapter. The last part of the chapter focuses on definitions of retirement, factors found to predict life-satisfaction in retirement, and retirement issues for men and women.

Warr, P. (1994). Age and employment. In M. Dunnette, L. Hough, & H. Triads (Eds.), *Handbook of industrial and organizational psychology* (Vol. 4, 2nd ed., pp. 487–550). Palo Alto, CA: Consulting Psychologists Press. A comprehensive look at aging and employment is presented in this chapter. The topics discussed include aging and social roles, labor force projections, and research designs in industrial gerontology. A framework for understanding the relationships between four types of jobs and potential age related effects on job performance is also provided. The relationship between aging and many aspects of work behavior such as turnover, absenteeism, and accidents are discussed.

Changing Nature of Work

Hall, D. T., & Mirvis, P. H. (1996). The new protean career: Psychological success and the path with a heart. In D. T. Hall & associates (Eds.), *The career is dead—long live the career: A relational approach to careers* (pp. 15–45). San Francisco: Jossey-Bass. Two types of careers are discussed: organizational and protean. The former describes a career that grows out of one's commitment to an organization, and the latter describes a flexible career that is shaped by an individual's interests and goals. The positive and negative implications of adopting a protean approach to career development are also discussed.

Sterns, H. L., & Huyck, M. H. (2001). Midlife and work. In M. E. Lachman (Ed.), *Handbook of midlife development* (pp. 447–486). New York: John Wiley and Sons. Issues facing working adults at midlife are the focus of this chapter. Special attention is given to models of career development and biological, cognitive, and emotional changes that occur at midlife. Another section of this chapter deals specifically with the importance of work, family, and other social roles in the lives of midlife workers.

Career Development and Training

Kubeck, J. E., Delp, N. D., Haslet, T. K., & McDonnell, M. A. (1996). Does job-related training performance decline with age? *Psychology and Aging, 11*, 92–107. This is one of the most complete and well-done meta-analytic studies on job-related training performance. The analysis results revealed that older adults relative to the younger adults are more difficult to train, learn slower, and take longer to complete the training program. In addition, the results indicated that age differences are substantial when speed of the performance is measured.

Rix, S. E. (1996). Investing in the future: What role for older worker training. In W. H. Crown (Ed.), *Handbook on employment and the elderly* (pp. 304–323). Westport, CT: Greenwood Publishing Group. In this chapter, the author explores the need and benefits of investing human and financial resources in training older workers. In addition, the author examines the issues of who gets trained from both workers and corporate perspective. Further concerns are federal funding for these programs (e.g., availability of funds and who qualifies).

Sterns, H. L., Junkins, M. P., & Bayer, J. G. (2001). Work and retirement. In B. R. Bonder & M. B. Wagner (Eds.), *Functional performance in older adults* (pp. 179–195). Philadelphia: F. A. Davis. Characteristics of the older adult work force are outlined, along with employer-sponsored wellness programs for these workers. Issues regarding older worker performance and training opportunities are discussed. The last section deals with retirement issues and some alternatives to retirement.

Human Factors and Workplace Design

Rogers, W. A., & Fisk, A. D. (2000). Human factors, applied cognition and aging. In F. I. M. Craik & T. A. Salthouse (Eds.), *The handbook of aging and cognition* (pp. 559–592). Mahwah, NJ: Lawrence Erlbaum Associates. The first part of this book consists of chapters devoted to basic principles of cognition and human factors. Chapters in the second part of the book cover applications of human factors in areas such as pilot performance and expertise, designing written instructions, older workers, assistive devices, and robotic technologies.

Sterns, H. L., Barrett, G. V., Czaja, S. J., & Barr, J. K. (1994). Issues in work and aging. *Journal of Applied Gerontology, 13*, 7–19. The section of this article devoted to human factor approaches to work and aging describes how a work environment may be adapted for an older work force. Special attention is given to how training programs may be modified to enhance the performance of older workers.

Job Performance

Avolio, B. J., Waldman, D. A., & McDaniel, M. A. (1990). Age and work performance in nonmanagerial jobs: The effects of experience and occupational type. *Academy of Management Journal, 33,* 407–422. In this study, the authors examine the relative power of years of experience in an occupation in predicting supervisors' ratings of work performance. They test three hypotheses, which can be found on pp. 409–411. Their results revealed that experience was a better predictor of performance than age and that age and experience showed nonlinear relationships with performance.

Salthouse, T. A., & Mauer, T. J. (1996). Aging, job performance, and career development. In J. E. Birren & K. W. Schaie (Eds.), *Handbook of the psychology of aging* (pp. 353–364). San Diego: Academic Press. Methodological issues surrounding the relationship between age and job performance are discussed, along with some possible explanations for the discrepant findings in the literature. Individual factors involved in career development, such as expectations for success and system factors such as social norms are also discussed in terms of their relative importance to aging workers.

Retirement

Sterns, H. L., Matheson, N. K., & Park, L. S. (1997). Work and retirement. In K. F. Ferraro (Ed.), *Gerontology: Perspectives and issues* (pp. 171–191). New York: Springer. This chapter begins with a discussion of definitions of older workers and a model of career development. Retirement is viewed from a life-span perspective, with special attention given to phases one may experience in a retirement role. Several factors that influence the retirement experience are also discussed.

14

INFUSING AGING CONTENT INTO THE PSYCHOLOGY OF DEATH AND DYING

BERT HAYSLIP, JR.

The psychology of death and dying poses many challenges and rewards to the undergraduate student. Students can choose to confront many of their own biases and heretofore unspoken feelings about their own deaths as well as about the often powerful feelings about personal losses in their lives, which they may have put on hold until now. Those who have experienced such losses or whose future livelihood requires knowledge of death and dying tend to make a greater intellectual and emotional commitment to the material. Additionally, students whose parents or grandparents are seriously ill or who have died or those who currently work with older adults tend to embrace the material more fully. Such risks are indeed worth the rewards. Many students come to appreciate how precious life is and value the importance of their relationships to parents, siblings, friends, and grandparents. In the process of doing so, they learn how they really feel about personal choices

Please direct correspondence to Bert Hayslip, Jr., Department of Psychology, University of North Texas, Denton, TX 76203; e-mail: hayslipb@unt.edu.

regarding life and death and about the quality of their relationships with others, which are issues that confront us all irrespective of age. In this light, courses are organized around topics that have as much emotional salience for students as they have intellectual value. This is especially important if the course is open to undergraduates.

Especially relevant to issues of aging is how students learn to appreciate the fact that aging does not equal death, and overcoming such biases often proves to be a powerful obstacle for many. As Robert Kastenbaum (1978) pointed out, "So long as we can believe that old people are ready for death and that it is high time for them to leave the scene, we can hold our emotional responses and professional services within acceptable limits. . . . There is little need to explore precisely what this old man or woman is thinking or feeling" (p. 3).

Courses do vary in terms of specific content (Crase, 1989; Wrenn, 1994; Wrenn & Harada, 1999), but most instructors supplement the text material not only by drawing on lecture material and films but also by inviting guest lectures from professionals who earn a living in certain domains of death and dying. In addition to course examinations based on this information, students should be asked to complete experiential projects that require them to self-disclose. For example, students can write their own obituary, plan their own funeral, or conduct a life assessment (i.e., writing down what is and is not important to them, goals they want to reach, people who are important to them). Moreover, they can actively interact with someone who is a death professional, someone who is grieving, or someone who is dying. In each case, they gain knowledge and insight into their own feelings about death. Some students may prefer to write about a recent personal loss that they have experienced. Listening to music and taking field trips (e.g., visiting a long-term care facility); an intensive care unit (ICU); an emergency room; or a funeral home can each help students develop a personal perspective toward death, diminish unrealistic fears, and change beliefs about such topics as end-of-life care, burial rituals, autopsies, and body preparation (embalming) before burial. Students can also be encouraged to keep a journal detailing their daily interactions with others or specific experiences regarding death, as well as their feelings about and reactions to such. These out-of-class exercises nicely achieve the goal of learning about death in a personal, experiential sense, helping students more fully appreciate the role that death plays in their personal and professional lives.

TOPICS COVERED IN THE PSYCHOLOGY OF DEATH AND DYING

It is common practice to begin the course by discussing students' feelings about death in general and about their own deaths someday, as well as losses they have experienced. This discussion should be conducted in the context of death and dying as a legitimate academic concern but with an appreciation for the personal nature of students' experiences with death. It is crucial to encourage students to share their own experiences and to make certain distinctions clear (e.g., death versus dying, grief versus bereavement versus mourning). Moreover, it is essential to stress the relationships among theory, research, and practice as well as the interdisciplinary nature of thanatology.

Students should be encouraged to come to grips with their own attitudinal biases, fears, and hopes—bringing to light the contradiction between the myths and misbeliefs versus the facts about death. This can be through class discussions or purposefully constructed debates. For many students, this is an uncomfortable experience, and a small number of students may drop the course at this point. Important to this process is exposing students to other cultures' views about death for the purpose of underscoring the impact of Western culture on our own biases versus the facts about death and our own responses to death. It is important that instructors discuss the historical and pedagogical aspects of death education in the context of the many types of and methods by which death education is accomplished, stressing its goals and functions in light of the particular professional context and audience for which it is designed. Such discussion helps students define what is important for them to learn in class.

Most death and dying courses devote some time to what death means and to how people respond to death based on the meaning they ascribe to it. In this respect, it is important to stress variations in the meaning of death, how people respond to such personally constructed meaning(s), and the impact of death on their growth, development, and relationships with family and friends. For this purpose, allowing students to free associate to the term *death* helps illustrate such diversity. Differences in students' perceptions can then be explored in class. In addition, those meanings and responses to death that are jointly determined by individual difference and cultural determinants can be discussed in the context of developmental change and an understanding of other people's feelings, beliefs, and attitudes.

Regardless of who teaches the course, a major emphasis should be placed on the role of the death system (Kastenbaum, 2001), its manifestations, and its impact on individual roles and behaviors. In this case, when people die, how they die, where they die, and how they grieve should be discussed. Topics presented are as diverse as hospice care, the funeral industry, physician-assisted suicide, euthanasia, the legal aspects of death, and the issue of communication about death and how such communication is managed or distorted. Critical here is the input of guest lecturers whose daily experience with death qualifies them as experts, such as physicians, nurses, hospice staff, funeral directors, lawyers, grief counselors, and chaplains. Such experts should also encompass people who are terminally ill and those who are grieving (e.g., older widows, widowers). Although it is rare to have access to individuals who are terminally ill or those who have made the decision to end life support for a loved one, being able to interact with such people can greatly add to students' understanding of the dying process and end-of-life care from a moral, legal, and a spiritual perspective.

Death and dying viewed from a developmental perspective is given a great deal of attention, especially with regard to shifts in the meaning of and response to death, causes of death, and developmentally significant experiences related to coping with illness and the loss of others. Aging-related content is salient with respect to many of the previously discussed topics; however the most central issues are integrity versus despair, the life review, widowhood, chronic illness, and the loss of an adult child. It is especially crucial to stress what is and is not unique about death in late adulthood.

Common to most death and dying courses are the topics of suicide, how individuals cope with terminal illness, and grief and bereavement. The interaction of individual differences and the cultural context are relevant in terms of a discussion of theories and motivations for suicide, models of how people cope with terminal illness and perhaps most important from a student perspective, how to cope with one's own and others' grief. In this respect, having students write a condolence letter to someone they know personally who is grieving is very helpful. Students come to appreciate how important empathic and honest communication is in helping grieving people. In addition, having someone (e.g., a widow) speak about her experiences with the death of her husband gives students "permission" to share their own feelings with others. Students often report having discussed these issues with their families for the first time after such classes. It is vital that interventions of an individual, programmatic, and cultural/societal nature be discussed so that students can understand pathological manifestations of grief and their treatment. Professional grief counselors who are guest speakers are very valuable in this regard.

For many students, the most difficult issue is dealing with their own losses. As noted, many students may choose to discuss publicly or privately significant losses in their lives, such as the death of a child, parent, grandparent, close friend, or pet. There may be the rare student who is terminally ill, has attempted suicide, or has recently experienced the suicide of a family member or friend. Surprisingly, encouraging students to volunteer sharing such experiences is relatively easy when an atmosphere of trust has been established in class. For such people, the opportunity to write down and process what they have experienced is a very important and valuable learning experience. Throughout the class, students should be encouraged to express their opinions and feelings, to the extent that they are comfortable in doing so. They may do so in the context of whatever is being discussed or as a reaction to a public event such as a plane crash, natural disaster, school shooting, or the death of a prominent person.

AGING AND ITS IMPLICATIONS FOR
TEACHING DEATH AND DYING

For many psychologists, the most advantageous approach to late adulthood is that which is grounded in life span developmental psychology (Baltes, 1987). Life span psychology embodies many principles, the first of which is that aging is a complex process. Thus, aging is best viewed along many dimensions (e.g., sensation, perception, intelligence, memory, personality). Each dimension exhibits its own unique pattern of change, of which growth and decline are but one pattern. With regard to death and dying, this view of aging is consistent with distinguishing between concerns about death as an event versus dying as a process and viewing death from the multiple points of view including the dying person, the caregiver or family member, and professional staff. This multi-leveled approach to coping with loss is consistent with Stroebe and Schut's (1999) dual process model of grief, which involves thinking about grief in loss-oriented and restoration-oriented terms.

This preference for complexity is paralleled regarding the antecedents of change in later life, viewed as a joint function of age-graded influences, those that correlate highly with age and are generalizable across people, such as age-related changes in biological/physiological functioning (Whitbourne, 1999). In addition, history-graded influences that co-vary systematically with historical change and nonnormative influences that are idiosyncratic to people and thus not generalizable in terms of their influence are equally important antecedents of change in this respect. Examples of nonnormative influences are natural disasters, unforeseen illness, or unemployment.

With this in mind, it is clear that death can be viewed from multiple perspectives. It can be construed in purely biological terms, such as when one argues that brain death or the failure of critical organ systems constitutes the criteria for legal death. Alternatively, viewing death in sociocultural or interpersonal terms requires a different standard to define it, which is based on the quality of one's relationships with others, societal considerations regarding the worth of an older person's life (Kalish, 1985), or the acute versus anticipated nature of loss (Doka & Gordon, 1996). Moreover, death that is either accidental, stigmatized, or premature in nature requires that it be thought of in terms of the different emotional demands that it makes on a survivor's ability to prepare for and cope with the loss of a loved family member, close friend, or coworker (Corr, 1998; Davidson & Doka, 1996).

That aging is best understood in terms of the context in which it occurs is also a tenet of the life span approach. As cultures and environments change, a certain degree of aging-related change can be attributed to changes in the context in which older people live (and die). With respect to death and dying, acknowledging that our death system has indeed changed and will continue to do so is necessary. For example, such changes are reflected in increased longevity and life expectancy over the last half century, and the development of cures either to prevent the occurrence of or to halt the spread of communicable and debilitating diseases such as influenza, whooping cough, measles, diphtheria, smallpox, and polio (Corr, Nabe, & Corr, 2000). Each affects our perception of how people die, as does the growing importance of factors affecting the likelihood of people's lives being cut prematurely short by accidents or by diseases such as cancer, cardiovascular illness, and acquired immune deficiency syndrome (AIDS; Corr et al., 2000). Moreover, each influences and is influenced by our culture's death system (i.e., how mortality is interpreted and promoting actions that make people more or less vulnerable to death and grief; Kastenbaum, 1999). This, of course, is to say nothing of changes in our orientation toward people who are dying as a function of the growing popularity of hospice care (Hayslip, 1996), the work of Elizabeth Kubler-Ross (1969) relating to the process of coping with terminal illness, or the controversy surrounding Dr. Jack Kevorkian and other proponents of physician-assisted suicide and active euthanasia (Quill, 1996). Work such as this discussing the how, when, or where of dying has, historically speaking, had a profound impact at different times on the experiences of older dying people and their families. Thus, the experience of dying changes not just as a function of age or nearness to death but also because of culturally driven changes in our orientation to dying itself. The impact of cultural change on aging is also reflected in the importance given to cohort or generational effects in aging (Rosow, 1978). Regarding death and dying, cohort effects have been recognized as alternative explanations for age differences in attitudes toward end-of-life issues (Cicirelli, 1997) and for age differences in attitudes toward funeral rituals (Hayslip, Servaty, & Guarnaccia, 1999).

Another life span premise about aging is an emphasis on individual differences (see Hoyer & Rybash, 1994). Such differences increase across adulthood indicating that older adults are more different from one another than are young adults (Nelson & Dannefer, 1992). With regard to older adults and death, such differences are evident whether one focuses on reactions to the loss of a spouse or an adult child (Moss, Moss, & Hansson, 2001), or to other losses that may accompany the aging process, such as the loss of the full-time work role through retirement (Sterns & Gray, 1999). Likewise, there is considerable variation across older people in their concerns about death as a function of health-related, personality, and demographic influences (Cockerel, 1999).

A last dimension of life span psychology that relates to aging is rooted in the dialectical perspective (Lerner, 1996; Riegel, 1976), which emphasizes the continual dynamic among interdependent elements. Regarding death and dying, considering the family as a dynamic system that copes with the loss of one of its members (Share, 1978) would be consistent with such a view. Likewise, dying can be seen from a dialectical perspective as an interpersonal experience with the expectations of both the dying person and a significant other or primary caregiver continually modified as the relationship deepens (Rodabaugh, 1980). In this respect, Rando (1992–1993) has predicted that complicated (abnormal) grief reactions will increase in response to what is predicted to be an "onslaught" of deaths of both adults and children as a result of AIDS. Thus, such effects are intergenerational in nature (Joslin, 2001). Changes in the dynamics of death and grief can therefore be understood in terms of relationships among forces at multiple levels (i.e., those that are intrapersonal, interpersonal, biological, and sociocultural in nature).

INCLUSION OF AGING CONTENT INTO THE PSYCHOLOGY OF DEATH AND DYING

Beyond seeing death and dying in terms of a life span approach to aging, numerous opportunities are available to the instructor to integrate aging into the content of death and dying courses. These revolve around the integration of aging content into a discussion of (a) attitudes toward death and dying, (b) suicide, (c) end-of-life issues, and (d) grief and bereavement.

ATTITUDES TOWARD DEATH AND DYING

Over the past 25 years, an extensive literature has evolved on responses to death and dying, and age differences in such attitudes have emerged as an important dimension of such research. Responses to death cannot be studied independently of the chronic illnesses that kill older people (e.g., heart disease, stroke, cancer; Kastenbaum, 1999) or where such persons die (e.g., in nursing homes, hospitals, or home-based hospices). These topics must be given some attention because of their effects on older people's attitudes toward death and dying (DeVries, Bluck, & Birren, 1993). A number of resources are available to aid the instructor in documenting the extent to which age influences death fears. Although some are more dated (Kastenbaum & Costa, 1977), these references, nevertheless, deserve serious consideration. Relevant here are age-related responses to death and dying that more closely reflect cultural norms and mores regarding how death is viewed (e.g, overcoming versus participating). Also relevant are more indirect ways of thinking about death that unfortunately reflect the manner in which older people are associated with various images of death (e.g, death as a *gentle comforter* or the *gay deceiver*; Kastenbaum, 2001). More recent discussions of the methodological and conceptual issues involved in studying attitudes toward death can be found in Neimeyer (1994) and Tomer (2000), the latter of which comprehensively examines death attitudes in later life from a variety of theoretical perspectives. Reviews of the empirical literature can also be found in journals such as *Omega: Journal of Death and Dying* (Galt & Hayslip, 1998; Neimeyer, 1997–1998) and *Death Studies* (Firestone, 1993). An especially thoughtful discussion of how older people respond to death can be found in Kastenbaum (1999). Moreover, an insightful personal perspective on death can be found in *The Virtues of Aging* by former President Jimmy Carter (1998).

SUICIDE

The topic of suicide in later life was almost unheard of until the publication of Marvin Miller's (1978, 1979) classic studies on suicide among older men. Although qualitative and not quantitative, the studies are extremely thorough and well written, offering numerous clinical insights and speaking powerfully to the worth of human life in later adulthood. Similarly, although dated, worth reading is Gubrium's (1975) work on the centrality of death in nursing homes and Nelson and Farberow's (1980) discussion of indirect self-destructive behavior (ISDB) in nursing homes. Osgood's (1992) and McIntosh's (1992) chapters are also valuable resources in understanding the epidemiology of suicide in later life, as is the chapter by Koenig and Blazer (1992). The volume by McIntosh, Santos, Hubbard, and Overholser (1994) is perhaps the most comprehensive review of the epidemiology of elder suicide; it is a thorough examination of risk factors and treatment approaches to older adults who are depressed and suicidal. Students should learn that older people vary in terms of their risk of attempting and completing suicide and that preventative efforts to lessen the elder's risk of suicide are available. These facts notwithstanding, it is nevertheless important to communicate to students that although people, especially men, over age 65 are at the greatest risk for suicide, the absolute number of completed suicides in later life is actually much smaller than those among young adults or middle-age people (Corr et al., 2000). These facts, and the fact that suicide in later life has a stigma attached to it, suggests that one may have been unhappy, in poor health, recently institutionalized, alcoholic, recently (and forcibly) retired, or unhappily married, but all have important implications for students' ageist assumptions about older adults. These facts also provide valuable information about risk and the lethality of suicide in later life, important in terms of prevention. Sadly, this information also brings to light the plight of many older people who are indeed lonely or depressed, and who wish to exercise what little control they feel they still have over their lives by choosing the time and manner of their death.

END-OF-LIFE CONCERNS

The issues discussed in this chapter regarding the quality of life in late adulthood are clearly reflected in recent debates about euthanasia and physician-assisted suicide—debates that are in part fueled by concerns about the misuse of such practices to end the lives of those who may be deemed less worthy of saving in the first place (i.e., the slippery slope argument;

Corr et al., 2000). Kastenbaum (1999) noted that end-of-life decisions for older people reflect three issues: (1) management of life's final phase (e.g., choosing hospice care, completing advanced directives, attitudes toward prematurely ending one's life); (2) after-death body disposition and memorial services; and (3) distribution of assets. Such decisions even influence one's choice of where to live (Hays, Galanos, Palmer, McQuoid, & Flint, 2001). Cicirelli's (1997) extensive study of older adults' attitudes toward end-of-life choices found support for preferences to maintain life and to end it. Braun, Tanji, and Heck (2001) recently found older people to express more trust in the physician and family in making such decisions, but no direct relationship exists between age and attitudes toward physician-assisted suicide per se. Significantly, however, the Study to Understand Prognoses and Preferences for Outcomes and Risks of Treatment (SUPPORT) project (Lynn et al., 1997; Study to Understand Prognoses and Preferences for Outcomes and Risks of Treatment, 1995) underscores the difficulties patients have in communicating with their physicians at the end of life, based on observations of more than 9,000 adult patients with life-threatening illnesses, where such people's wishes regarding end-of-life care were ignored. Sadly, efforts to improve such communication by educating physicians about their patients' preferences and physical status were not successful. Also important, efforts to define clearly the standards for end-of-life care have been developed through a study by the Institute of Medicine (Cassel & Field, 1997), which provides data and recommendations regarding methods for assessing patient outcomes and preferences and identifies barriers to quality of care at the end of life. This has led to a statement of Core Principles for End-of-Life Care (Cassel & Foley, 1999). These principles have been endorsed and adopted by organizations such as the American Medical Association, the National Kidney Foundation, the American College of Surgeons, the American College of Physicians, and the American Geriatrics Society (Cassel & Foley, 1999).

Recent discussions of this very complex issue can also be found in DeVries (1999), Mishara (1999), and Battin (1994). As mentioned, frank discussion about such decisions can be facilitated through class presentations by lawyers who specialize in elder law, physicians who work with those who are dying, and people who have had to make difficult choices to end life support for a family member.

Interestingly, in light of the idiosyncratic nature of end-of-life decisions, a discussion of postformal reasoning or the pragmatics of later life cognition (Baltes, 1993; Sinnott, 1996) becomes relevant to death and dying.

GRIEF AND BEREAVEMENT

For a variety of reasons, issues of grief and bereavement are relevant to aging. Older people, for example, sometimes experience *bereavement overload* (Kastenbaum, 1978), in which they literally become overwhelmed by grief, having experienced the losses of a spouse, close family members, lifelong friends, or previous co-workers closely spaced in time. Older adults experiencing multiple losses often lack the emotional reserves or social support systems to help them cope, leaving them at risk for depression or chronic illness. Kastenbaum (1999) noted that many older people do move on to integrate the loss into their lives and that successful grief work does not necessarily result in a weakening of the bond between the survivor and the deceased loved one. Yet, in spite of some elders' resiliency, it is also important to recognize that bereavement does leave some older people vulnerable to physical illness, depression, and anxiety within the first 2 years after loss (Hansson, Vanzetti, Fairchild, & Berry, 1999; Zizook, Schuchter, Sledge, & Judd, 1994). In these respects, there is extensive literature bearing on individual differences in grief and bereavement adjustment in later life (Moss et al., 2001) and on the special difficulties faced by older widows and widowers (Lund, 1989, 2001; Sable, 1991).

Because of the unique nature of later life loss, discussions of the deaths of siblings (Hays, Gold, & Pieper, 1997) and about kinship loss (DeVries, 1997) are helpful. Grandparents may be neglected as a viable part of the family system, so the review by White (1999) is especially valuable in pointing out the role that grandparents play when a family member dies and the impact of bereavement on them. If older adults are in a caregiving role, they are faced with the grief that has an effect on caregivers before and after the death of loved ones for whom they are providing such care (Aneshensel, Pearlin, Mullan, Zarit, & Whitlatch, 1995). In later life, new losses can trigger feelings about old losses, so that older people may confront many deaths simultaneously. It is vital that students understand that responses to loss are as variable as the life histories of older people themselves. Timely bereavement support (e.g., Widow to Widow programs, Compassionate Friends) is critical to the health and well-being of older adults. Yet such responses also need to be understood in light of a culture's death system that often works against older adults' ability to cope with loss by stigmatizing them, steering the bereaved to support groups specially constructed for bereaved older people, concealing death and loss in institutionalizing older people, or pathologizing their losses in linking them to later life depression.

SUMMARY

Each of us is at one time healthy and autonomous, whereas at other times, we are ill and dependent. We seek greater meaning and quality in our lives, and being able to be taken seriously as people and to retain control over many aspects of our lives are very important to us. We all eventually die. With this in mind, it is a revelation for students to learn to view parents and grandparents as individuals who happen to be older, with whom we share a personal history, who are capable of change, who are shaped by both their developmental and cultural experiences, and whose attitudes and feelings are shaped by the unique contexts in which they live and die. Through such insights and by listening to one another, not only are students able to grow personally, but valued relationships with parents and grandparents can also be enjoyed now. When death comes to such people, students will be less likely to have regrets, or "unfinished business" (Kubler-Ross, 1969). These are benefits that can be enjoyed for a lifetime.

REFERENCES

Aneshensel, C. S., Pearlin, L. I., Mullan, J. T., Zarit, S. H., & Whitlatch, C. J. (1995). *Profiles in caregiving: The unexpected career*. San Diego: Academic Press.

Baltes, P. B. (1987). Theoretical propositions of lifespan developmental psychology: On the dynamics between growth and decline. *Developmental Psychology, 23*, 611–626.

Baltes, P. B. (1993). The aging mind: Potential and limits. *The Gerontologist, 33*, 580–594.

Battin, M. P. (1994). *Least worst death: Essays on the bioethics on the end of life*. New York: Oxford.

Braun, K. L., Tanji, V. M., & Heck, R. (2001). Support for physician assisted suicide: Exploring the impact of ethnicity and attitudes toward planning for death. *The Gerontologist, 41*, 51–60.

Carter, J. (1998). *The virtues of aging*. New York: Ballantine.

Cassel, C. K., & Field, M. J. (1997). *Approaching death: Improving care at the end of life*. Washington, DC: Institute of Medicine, Division of Health Care Services, National Academy Press.

Cassel, C. K., & Foley, K. M. (1999). *Principles for care of patients at the end of life: An emerging consensus among the specialties of medicine*. New York: Milbank Memorial Fund.

Cicirelli, V. G. (1997). Relationship of psychosocial and background variables to older adults' end of life decisions. *Psychology and Aging, 12*, 72–83.

Cockerel, V. G. (1999). Personality and demographic factors in older adults' fear of death. *The Gerontologist, 39*, 569–579.

Corr, C. (1998). Enhancing the concept of disenfranchised grief. *Omega, 38*, 1–20.

Corr, C. A., Nabe, C., & Corr, D. M. (2000). *Death and dying: Life and living* (3rd ed.). Belmont, CA: Wadsworth.

Crase, D. (1989). Death education: Its diversity on multidisciplinary focus. *Death Studies, 13*, 25–29.

Davidson, J. K., & Doka, K. J. (1996). *Living with grief: At work, at school, at worship*. Levittown, PA: Hospice Foundation of America/Brunner-Mazel.

DeVries, B. (1997). Kinship bereavement in later life [Special issue]. *Omega, 35*, 1–157.

DeVries, B. (1999). *End of life issues: Interdisciplinary and multidimensional perspectives*. New York: Springer.

DeVries, B., Bluck, S., & Birren, J. E. (1993). The understanding of death and dying from a lifespan perspective. *The Gerontologist, 33,* 366–372.

Doka, K., & Gordon, J. D. (1996). *Living with grief after loss*. Levittown, PA: Hospice Foundation of America/Brunner-Mazel.

Firestone, R. W. (1993). Psychological defenses against death anxiety. *Death Studies, 17,* 497–515.

Galt, C., & Hayslip, B. (1998). Age differences in levels of covert and overt death anxiety. *Omega, 37,* 187–202.

Gubrium, J. (1975). Death worlds in a nursing home. *Urban Life, 4,* 317–338.

Hansson, R. O., Vanzetti, N. A., Fairchild, S. K., & Berry, J. O. (1999). The impact of bereavement on families. In B. DeVries (Ed.), *End of life issues: Interdisciplinary and multidimensional perspectives* (pp. 99–117). New York: Springer.

Hays, J. C., Galanos, A. N., Palmer, T. A., McQuoid, D. R., & Flint, E. P. (2001). Preference for place of death in a continuing care retirement community. *The Gerontologist, 41,* 123–128.

Hays, J. C., Gold, D. T., & Pieper, C. F. (1997). Sibling bereavement in later life. *Omega, 35,* 25–42.

Hayslip, B. (1996). Hospice care. In J. E. Birren (Ed.), *Encyclopedia of gerontology* (pp. 318–334). San Diego: Academic Press.

Hayslip, B., Servaty, H., & Guarnaccia, C. (1999). Age cohort differences in perceptions of funerals. In B. DeVries (Ed.), *End of life issues: Interdisciplinary and multidimensional perspectives* (pp. 23–36). New York: Springer.

Hoyer, W. L., & Rybash, J. (1994). Characterizing adult cognitive development. *Journal of Adult Development, 1,* 7–12.

Joslin, D. (2001). *Invisible caregivers: Older adults raising children in the wake of HIV/AIDS*. New York: Columbia University Press.

Kalish, R. A. (1985). Death and dying in a social context. In R. H. Binstock & E. Shanas (Eds.), *Handbook of aging and the social sciences* (2nd ed., pp. 149–170). New York: Van Nostrand.

Kastenbaum, R. (1978). Death, dying, and bereavement in old age: New developments and their possible implications for psychosocial care. *Aged Care and Services Review, 1,* 1–10.

Kastenbaum, R. (1999). Dying and bereavement. In J. C. Cavanaugh & S. K. Whitbourne (Eds.), *Gerontology: An interdisciplinary perspective* (pp. 155–185). New York: Oxford.

Kastenbaum, R. (2001). *Death, society, and human experience* (7th ed.). Boston: Allyn & Bacon.

Kastenbaum, R., & Costa, P. T. (1977). Psychological perspectives on death. *Annual Review of Psychology, 28,* 225–249.

Koenig, H. G., & Blazer, D. G. (1992). Mood disorders and suicide. In J. E. Birren,

R. B. Sloane, & G. D. Cohen (Eds.), *Handbook of mental health and aging* (pp. 380–409). San Diego: Academic Press.

Kubler-Ross, E. (1969). *On death and dying.* New York: Macmillan.

Lerner, R. L. (1996). *Concepts and theories of human development.* Reading, MA: Addison-Wesley.

Lund, D. A. (1989). *Older bereaved spouses: Research with practical applications.* New York: Hemisphere.

Lund, D. A. (2001). *Men coping with grief.* Amityville, NY: Baywood.

Lynn, J., Teno, J. M., Phillips, R. S., Wu, A. W., Desbiiens, N., Harrold, J., et al. (1997). Perceptions by family members of the dying experience of older and seriously ill patients. *Annals of Internal Medicine, 126,* 97–126.

McIntosh, J. L. (1992). Epidemiology of suicide in the elderly. In A. A. Leenaaars, R. W. Maris, J. L. McIntosh, & J. Richman (Eds.), *Suicide and the older adult* (pp. 15–35). New York: Guilford Press.

McIntosh, J. L., Santos, J. F., Hubbard, R. W., & Overholser, J. C. (1994). *Elder suicide: Research, theory, and treatment.* Washington, DC: American Psychological Association.

Miller, M. (1978). Geriatric suicide: The Arizona study. *The Gerontologist, 18,* 488–495.

Miller, M. (1979). *Suicide after 60: The final alternative.* New York: Springer.

Mishara, B. L. (1999). Synthesis of research and evidence on factors affecting the desire of terminally ill or seriously chronically ill persons to hasten death. *Omega, 39,* 1–70.

Moss, M. S., Moss, S. Z., & Hansson, R. O. (2001). Bereavement and old age. In M. Stroebe, R. O. Hansson, W. Stroebe, & H. Schut (Eds.), *Handbook of bereavement research: Consequences, coping, and care* (pp. 241–260). Washington, DC: American Psychological Association.

Neimeyer, R. A. (1994). *Death anxiety handbook: Research, instrumentation, and application.* Washington, DC: Taylor & Francis.

Neimeyer, R. A. (1997–1998). Death anxiety research: The state of the art. *Omega, 36,* 97–120.

Nelson, E., & Dannefer, D. (1992). Aged heterogeneity: Fact or fiction? The fate of diversity in gerontological research. *The Gerontologist, 32,* 17–23.

Nelson, F., & Farberow, N. (1980). Indirect self destructive behavior in the nursing home patient. *Journal of Gerontology, 35,* 949–957.

Osgood, N. (1992). *Suicide in later life: Recognizing the warning signs.* New York: Lexington.

Quill, T. E. (1996). *A midwife through the dying process.* Baltimore, MD: Johns Hopkins University Press.

Rando, T. A. (1992–1993). The increasing prevalence of complicated mourning: The onslaught is just beginning. *Omega, 26,* 43–59.

Riegel, K. F. (1976). The dialectics of human development. *American Psychologist, 31,* 689–700.

Rodabaugh, T. (1980). Alternatives to the stages model of the dying process. *Death Education, 4*, 1–19.

Rosow, I. (1978). What is a cohort and why? *Human Development, 21*, 66–75.

Sable, P. (1991). Attachment, loss of spouse, and grief in elderly adults. *Omega, 23*, 129–142.

Share, L. (1978). Family communication in the crisis of a child's fatal illness: A literature review and analysis. In R. Kalish (Ed.), *Caring for the dying and the bereaved* (pp. 17–31). Farmingdale, NY: Baywood.

Sinnott, J. (1996). The developmental approach: Postformal thought as adaptive intelligence. In F. Blanchard-Fields & T. M. Hess (Eds.), *Perspectives on cognitive change in adulthood and aging* (pp. 358–386). New York: McGraw-Hill.

Sterns, H. L., & Gray, J. H. (1999). Work, leisure, and retirement. In J. C. Cavanaugh & S. K. Whitbourne (Eds.), *Gerontology: An interdisciplinary perspective* (pp. 355–390). New York: Oxford.

Stroebe, M., & Schut, H. (1999). The dual process of coping with bereavement: Rationale and description. *Death Studies, 23*, 197–224.

Study to Understand Prognoses and Preferences for Outcomes and Risks of Treatment (SUPPORT). (1995). A controlled trial to improve care for seriously ill hospitalized patients. *Journal of the American Medical Association, 274*, 1591–1599.

Tomer, A. (2000). *Death attitudes and the older adult.* Philadelphia: Taylor and Francis.

Whitbourne, S. K. (1999). Physical changes. In J. C. Cavanaugh & S. K. Whitbourne (Eds.), *Gerontology: An interdisciplinary perspective* (pp. 91–122). New York: Oxford.

White, D. L. (1999). Grandparent participation in times of family bereavement. In B. DeVries (Ed.), *End of life issues: Interdisciplinary and multidimensional perspectives* (pp. 145–166). New York: Springer.

Wrenn, R. (1994, May/June). What do students value in our death class? *The Forum*, 13–14.

Wrenn, R., & Harada, P. (1999). Literature on death, dying, and bereavement viewed from the basic text. *Omega, 39*, 287–295.

Zizook, S., Schuchter, S., Sledge, P. A., & Judd, L. (1994). The spectrum of depressive phenomena after spousal bereavement. *Journal of Clinical Psychiatry, 55*, 29–36.

ANNOTATED BIBLIOGRAPHY

Cook, A. S., & Oltjenbruns, K. A. (1998). *Dying and grieving: Lifespan and family perspectives* (2nd ed.). Ft. Worth: Harcourt Brace. This text discusses death-related issues from a life span perspective and provides an excellent overview of family bereavement and developmental (child, adolescent, adult) topics. The concluding chapters on caregiving and suicide are timely.

Corr, C., Doka, K. J., & Kastenbaum, R. (1999). Dying and its interpreters: A review of selected literature and some comments on the state of the field. *Omega, 39,* 239–261. This is a comprehensive yet somewhat brief overview of the research on the construct of dying, reviewed with regard to the role of theory development in the enhancement of our understanding of dying both as an event and as a process. A number of issues are argued to be important to the development of a coherent theory of dying, viewed in the context of specific developmental and nondevelopmental theories and as issues particular to dying.

Death Studies. Published 6 times a year, this journal's major focus is on applications of death-related issues in education, counseling, care, law, and ethics. Available from Taylor and Francis Inc.; 1900 Frost Rd., Suite 101; Bristol, PA 19007.

DeSpelder, L. A., & Strickland, A. L. (1999). *The last dance: Encountering death and dying* (5th ed.). Mountain View, CA: Mayfield. This is a classic thanatological textbook covering a broad range of topics from medical ethics to funerals. Using a life span perspective, the book offers diverse opinions and current data on all the key topics in death and dying studies. The book blends theory and research into a method for practical application by professionals in the field.

Hospice Journal. This quarterly journal publishes articles of all kinds involving hospice. Available from Haworth Press; 10 Alice St.; Binghamton, NY 13904.

Howarth, G. (1998). Just live for today. Living, caring, ageing and dying. *Ageing and Society, 18,* 673–689. This qualitative study employed in-depth tape-recorded interviews of older individuals' thoughts on mortality. Their attitudes were divided into two categories: death of self and death of others. Contrary to expectation, many of the participants were not released from fearing their own death or that of others. In old age, many adults are unlikely to be in a position to control the process of dying and to perceive death in an accepting way.

Kramp, E. T., & Kramp, D. H. (1998). *Living with the end in mind.* New York: Three Rivers Press. This book offers an approach to die rationally through leaving a legacy. Erin, a dying person and the coauthor, develops an insightful checklist of things the dying person and family members do together to create a family legacy. The authors advocate cognitive rehearsal of the funeral and the grieving process for family members.

Lund, D. A., & Caserta, M. S. (1997–1998). Future directions in adult bereavement research. *Omega, 36,* 287–304. State-of-the-art article designed to stimulate the development of quality research in adult bereavement and their applications. The authors discuss the importance of integrating theory, research, and practice, and specifically review studies dealing with the efficacy of bereavement interventions. Numerous methodological and measurement issues are discussed.

Moss, M. S., Resch, N., & Moss, S. Z. (1997). The role of gender in middle-age children's responses to parent death. *Omega, 35,* 43–65. This paper investigates the impact of the death of the last surviving parent on middle-age siblings. The authors found sons differed from daughters in bereavement by having more economic resources, more guilt from not caring for their parent, more personal mastery, less grief, more acceptance of the parent's death, weaker ties to the parent, and fewer somatic complications.

Nuland, S. B. (1993). *How we die: Reflections on life's final chapter.* New York: Vintage. Written (as stated by the author) to "demythologize" the dying process, this book is a powerful and frank discussion of the mechanisms by which we die, such as accidents, murder, AIDS, cancer, heart attack, stroke, and Alzheimer's disease. Importantly, the author, who is a surgeon, discusses hope and dying and ways in which the dying experience can be more humane and meaningful.

Omega: Journal of Death and Dying. Founded in 1970 and published eight times a year in two volumes, this is the first journal to focus on death-related issues. It publishes articles on bereavement, the process of dying, grief, suicide, and ethical issues and is largely devoted to research. Available from Baywood Publishing Company; 26 Austin Avenue, Box 337; Amityville, NY 11701.

15

THE AGING DIMENSION IN PERSONAL RELATIONSHIPS COURSES

ROSEMARY BLIESZNER

Typical college students are late adolescents and young adults. They face developmental challenges related to clarifying a sense of their own identity in the context of establishing relationships with intimate others (Erikson, 1963). Their status within the span of life makes courses on personal relationships particularly appropriate for and appealing to them. They are likely to be fascinated with research on romantic relationships, family interactions, and friendship. Capitalizing on their inherent interest by extending the course content to include relationships in old age can give students a complete theoretical and empirical picture of close relationships across the life span, as well as tools to enhance their own family and friend interactions. Discussion of these topics promotes student insight not only into their own

Please direct correspondence to Rosemary Blieszner, Department of Human Development (0416), Virginia Polytechnic Institute and State University, 336 Wallace Hall, Blacksburg, VA 24061; e-mail: rmb@vt.edu.

relational thoughts, feelings, and behaviors, but also into the experiences of their parents, grandparents, and other older relatives.

COURSE OVERVIEW

Personal relationships courses might be organized by type of relationship, relational processes and phases, or some combination of these approaches. Regardless of the preferred organization, a wealth of information on late-life personal relationships exists. As in other stages of life, the two primary sources of close relationships in old age are family and friendships. Old age family relationships entail both intragenerational types (e.g., marital and marital-like, siblings) and intergenerational ones (e.g., parent–child, grandparent–grandchild). Friendships derive from many segments of life and can be casual or close. Naturally, these relationships each have unique features, yet taken together, they serve common purposes of contributing social support and promoting physical and psychological well-being in old age. All of them also have potential to present challenges with which participants must cope.

Objectives

Instructors should expect students to accomplish at least four objectives as a result of reading about, analyzing, and discussing close relationships in late adulthood. These objectives include being able to (a) understand the importance of personal relationships for maintaining physical and psychological well-being throughout the life span; (b) describe similarities and differences in romantic, family, and friend relationships across the life span (or across young adulthood, middle adulthood, and old age); (c) explain reciprocal influences of one's stage of development on close relationships and relational interaction on one's personal development; and (d) recognize changes in personal relationships associated with aging processes and experiences.

A greater appreciation of relational continuity (and change) results from reading about and discussing relationships across all of the life span throughout the entire course, rather than tacking on a small section about relationships in old age at the end of the term. Some interesting comparisons can be made this way. For example, in discussing theories of attraction, a question can be raised about the personal characteristics that are sought in potential friends and romantic partners in adolescence, young adulthood, middle adulthood, and late adulthood. Do perspectives on attractive qualities change over the course of life? Do any endure regardless of age? Similarly, students could consider the ways that social support might be manifested at various times of life, identify similarities and differences over the lifetime, and consider the antecedents and consequences of social support for those of diverse ages.

Recommended Topics

All of the topics that are usually included in a course on personal relationships can be extended to study of relationships across the life span. These include structural features of relationships (e.g., size, homogeneity, equality, status); phases of relationships (e.g., initiation, maintenance, dissolution); relationship goals (e.g., enhancing personal well-being and avoiding loneliness); and interaction processes related to affective, cognitive, and behavioral domains (e.g., physical attraction, self-disclosure, liking and loving, conflict, and so on). (See Adams and Blieszner [1994] for a framework that could be used to organize a course.) Like anyone else, older adults enjoy and are influenced by a wide variety of types and sources of close relationships, including those with deceased family members and pets (Blieszner & de Vries, 2001).

In addition, some special features of middle- and old-age relationships warrant attention. Students with little background in gerontology seem most surprised to discover that long-term married couples are not necessarily bored with each other, that old people enjoy and participate in sexual intercourse and other expressions of sexuality, that caring for aging parents might extend for many more years than caring for offspring typically does, and that friendships can last for many decades. Lively discussions and debates occur when the students consider the implications of the topic at hand for very long-lasting relationships, when their assumptions and stereotypes are challenged, and when they are guided to develop conclusions based on research data rather than personal opinion.

Experience in teaching late teenage and young adult students suggests that they are most curious about several interesting features of relationships. For example, they want to learn about fostering long-term success in marriage or another committed romantic relationship (often in the context of having experienced divorce of their own parents and other adult relatives). Students often seek understanding of parent–child relationships, both between themselves and their parents and also in terms of what their parents are experiencing with their grandparents. They find it fascinating to explore the potential benefits inherent in sibling and friend relationships across the span of adulthood. These topics, combined with those indicated in the objectives noted previously, provide gerontological themes that could be incorporated easily into courses on the psychology of personal relationships.

AGING AND PERSONAL RELATIONSHIPS

The most important overarching concepts about aging and personal relationships to convey to students include the following three core issues.

First, older people enjoy and benefit from family and friend interactions as much as and in many of the same ways as younger people do (Bedford & Blieszner, 2000b; Blieszner, 1994, 2000; Blieszner & Bedford, 1995, 1996). Second, seniors adjust their relational interactions to accommodate the developmental changes they are experiencing (Carstensen, 1992; Hansson & Carpenter, 1994). Third, older adults are a heterogeneous group whose experiences of personal relationships vary by age from young–old to old–old and by gender, racial ethnic group, social class, and sexual orientation (Bedford & Blieszner, 2000a; Stoller & Gibson, 1997; Walker, Manoogian-O'Dell, McGraw, & White, 2001).

Many theories from psychology and sociology can be applied to the study of aging and personal relationships. Examples of theories that are often employed in adult relationship research include attachment, attribution, role, conflict, exchange, equity, symbolic interactionism, various theories related to stress and coping, and perspectives on the contributions of social support to personal well-being. Bengtson's theory of intergenerational solidarity (Bengtson & Roberts, 1991) is useful for examining multiple dimensions of family or friend interaction. It embodies associational, affectual, consensual, functional, normative, and structural influences on solidarity, or degree of emotional closeness. Carstensen's (1992) theory of socioemotional selectivity helps explain changes in relationships with family and friends as individuals move through the years of aging. Building on Baltes and Baltes's (1990) conception that a process of selective optimization with compensation yields successful aging, Carstensen (1992) extended their individual-level theory to the relationship level in a model describing elders' efforts to conserve emotional energy by focusing increasingly on the most meaningful family and friend relationships over the course of development. Empirical tests of these theories and those mentioned earlier can be found in the gerontological literature. Instructors can thus provide examples of the value of theory for advancing knowledge and understanding in particular focal areas.

In the course of covering core topics in aging and personal relationships, it is important to incorporate a realistic perspective on late life close relationships. Although early research on these relationships tended to focus only on the positive aspects of social interaction, a corrective has occurred in the literature recently, such that data are now available on negative aspects of relationships as well. For example, Fingerman (1996) invented the term *developmental schism* to explain possible sources of tension between older adult mothers and adult daughters (namely, differing developmental stages resulting in different concerns and foci). Similarly, studies of difficult aspects of friendship are now available (Adams & Blieszner, 1998; Blieszner & Adams, 1998), to complement the wealth of research on their positive dimensions. Employing a balanced perspective not only reflects reality, but it also achieves greater credibility with students.

Many students will be familiar with common stereotypes claiming that aged people lose physical and mental capacity and thus are lonely, or worse, are abandoned by their family who "dumped" them in a nursing home. As any adult development and aging text will show (Bee, 2000; Cavanaugh & Blanchard-Fields, 2002; Whitbourne, 2001) and as documented in the references cited in this chapter, such characteristics pertain only to a minority of old people. Most elders adapt to and compensate for age-related changes (Baltes & Baltes, 1990), and families remain quite involved in their lives, even among those who are so frail that a nursing home is the safest residence for them (Gaugler, Leitsch, Zarit, & Pearlin, 2000; Pruchno & Kleban, 1993). The friend role can persist and even flourish at a period when older people have relatively fewer responsibilities competing for their attention (Blieszner & Adams, 1992). Thus, personal relationships endure and remain important throughout life. Of course, in old age a person is more likely to be bereaved of a romantic partner, adult child, sibling, or friend than at any other period of life, so grieving the loss of significant others is a common relationship experience (Blieszner & Bedford, 1995).

TEACHING ABOUT LATE LIFE FAMILY AND FRIEND RELATIONSHIPS

The study of personal relationships lends itself well to lively class discussions and other active learning strategies. Besides relying on their personal accounts, it is important to provide students with vicarious experiences beyond their own years of living and beyond their own social networks. Doing so will enable them to engage in meaningful discussion and foster deeper learning. Research reports, case studies, poetry, fiction, educational videos, and commercial films are effective supplements to assigned readings and instructor presentations (see Annotated Bibliography). Writing-intensive (Blieszner & Buffer, 1999; Lytton, Marshall-Baker, Benson, & Blieszner, 1996) and service-learning (Blieszner, 2001) pedagogical approaches give students practice in applying concepts and analyzing the implications of research results in everyday life. A useful approach is to create small-group learning communities within large classes and have students role-play family members of diverse ages and circumstances. During in-class "family meetings," students can respond to case studies that challenge them to apply material from the text to their classroom family in critical thinking and problem solving activities (Jarrott & Blieszner, 2001). Other strategies and resources for teaching about family gerontology can be found in Blieszner (1999).

Brief writing assignments or short small-group discussion sessions can help students acquire insights into complex interactions among multiple variables that affect experiences of aging and close relationships. For example, Nicholas Sparks's (1996) novel about long-term marriage in the context of Alzheimer's disease, *The Notebook*, demonstrates that love can be enduring and resilient despite the many different kinds of challenges that the couple faced over the years. Class discussions often focus on the extent to which the story represents a realistic and accurate depiction of romance, and of Alzheimer's disease, for that matter. Ella Leffland's (1997) short story about caregiving and grief, *The Linden Tree*, shows that shared experiences and strength of love and commitment are more important features of the relationship depicted than the fact that the protagonists are two old gay men. An assignment that prompts good critical thinking asks the students to compare these two works of fiction in terms of the social, cultural, and historical influences on the respective characters as individuals and as relational partners (besides differing by sexual orientation, the characters represent divergent class and racial groups). This approach yields good insights into the ties among societal circumstances, family values and beliefs, long-term romantic commitment, and personal development across the course of life.

An educational video that is particularly effective at illustrating diversity in romantic relationships is *For Better or For Worse* (Collier, 1993). Four very different couples, all of whom have been together for more than 50 years, speak freely about the joys and sorrows that have cemented their unusually long romantic ties. Students are captivated by the varying circumstances these couples faced and anticipate facing in the future. A creative depiction of a mother–daughter bond and the effects of Alzheimer's disease on close relationships appears in *Complaints of a Dutiful Daughter* (Hoffmann, 1994). With warmth, humor, and an honest realism that shows how frustrating interaction with a loved one who has this devastating condition can be, the author (who is also the producer and director) provides an interesting array of situations and coping strategies for audience members to contemplate.

For addressing friend relationships, many print, cinematic, and educational video illustrations are available on the most typical kind of friendship, which is one between individuals who share many characteristics in common. To stretch students' understanding of relational principles, instructors could incorporate examples of unusual kinds of friendships. For example, Mitch Albom's (1997) highly accessible account of intergenerational friendship and caregiving, *Tuesdays With Morrie*, enables students to realize that relationships can be powerful and meaningful influences on the lives of the participants. A documentary depicting a committed intergenerational friendship appears in *When the Day Comes* (Brown & McGowan, 1990). One of the four caregivers featured in this video is a middle-age woman who looks after her deceased mother's close friend, despite the personal cost of doing so to her career advancement and social life. The film, *How to Make an American Quilt* (Pillsbury, Sanford, & Moorhouse, 1996), is an engaging depiction of both intra- and intergenerational friendships that is popular with students. Some might think that friendship in the later years is more women's experience than men's; Tracy Kidder's (1993) book, *Old Friends*, about two old men in a nursing home, belies that assumption. A *20/20* television documentary based on the book is also available, for those who would prefer a visual presentation (American Broadcasting Company, 1994).

Source material for teaching and learning about personal relationships in old age can be found in numerous scholarly and lay books, works of fiction, and journals devoted to developmental and social psychology (*Applied Developmental Science, Developmental Psychology, Journal of Personality and Social Psychology, Psychology and Aging*); family studies (*Family Relations, Journal of Family Issues, Journal of Marriage and Family*); gerontology (*The Gerontologist, Journal of Aging Studies, Journal of Gerontology: Psychological Sciences, Journal of Gerontology: Social Sciences*); and personal relationships (*Journal of Social and Personal Relationships, Personal Relationships*). Excellent sources of educational videos on aging and relationships are Fanlight Productions, Filmakers Library, Films for the Humanities & Social Sciences®, and Terra Nova Films. Course syllabi, text and other print resources, and cinematic and educational video lists can be found in the Resources for Educators section of the Web site for the American Psychological Association (APA) Division 20, available at http://aging.ufl.edu/apadiv20/apadiv20.htm. Some representative and particularly useful print resources are included in the Annotated Bibliography.

REFERENCES

Adams, R, G., & Blieszner, R. (1994). An integrative conceptual framework for friendship research. *Journal of Social and Personal Relationships, 11,* 163–184.

Adams, R. G., & Blieszner, R. (1998). Structural predictors of problematic friendship in later life. *Personal Relationships, 5,* 439–447.

Albom, M. (1997). *Tuesdays with Morrie*. New York: Doubleday.

American Broadcasting Company. (1994). *Old friends* [20/20 television documentary; broadcast December, 23, 1994; segment 3]. Burbank, CA: Author.

Baltes, P. B., & Baltes, M. M. (Eds.). (1990). *Successful aging*. Cambridge, England: Cambridge University Press.

Bedford, V. H., & Blieszner, R. (2000a). Older adults and their families. In D. H. Demo, K. R. Allen, & M. A. Fine (Eds.), *Handbook of family diversity* (pp. 216–231). New York: Oxford University Press.

Bedford, V. H., & Blieszner, R. (2000b). Personal relationships in later life families. In R. M. Milardo & S. Duck (Eds.), *Families as relationships* (pp. 157–174). New York: Wiley.

Bee, H. L. (2000). *The journey of adulthood* (4th ed.). Upper Saddle River, NJ: Prentice Hall.

Bengtson, V. L., & Roberts, R. E. L. (1991). Intergenerational solidarity in aging families: An example of formal theory construction. *Journal of Marriage and the Family, 53,* 856–870.

Blieszner, R. (1994). Close relationships over time. In A. L. Weber & J. H. Harvey (Eds.), *Perspectives on close relationships* (pp. 1–17). Rockleigh, NJ: Allyn & Bacon.

Blieszner, R. (1999). Strategies and resources for teaching family gerontology. *Teaching of Psychology, 26,* 50–51.

Blieszner, R. (2000). Close relationships in old age. In C. Hendrick & S. Hendrick (Eds.), *Close relationships: A sourcebook* (pp. 84–95). Thousand Oaks, CA: Sage.

Blieszner, R. (Ed.). (2001). Service-learning in gerontology education [Special issue]. *Educational Gerontology, 27*(1).

Blieszner, R., & Adams, R. G. (1992). *Adult friendship.* Thousand Oaks, CA: Sage.

Blieszner, R., & Adams, R. G. (1998). Problems with friends in old age. *Journal of Aging Studies, 12,* 223–238.

Blieszner, R., & Bedford, V. H. (1995). The family context of aging: Trends and challenges. In R. Blieszner & V. H. Bedford (Eds.), *Handbook of aging and the family* (pp. 3–12). Westport, CT: Greenwood Press.

Blieszner, R., & Buffer, L. C. (1999). Adult development and aging as a writing intensive course: Student evaluation. *Gerontology and Geriatrics Education, 19,* 65–76.

Blieszner, R., & de Vries, B. (Eds.). (2001). Intimacy and aging [Special issue]. *Generations.*

Brown, C. (Producer), & McGowan, S. A. (Director). (1990). *When the day comes* [Videorecording]. New York: Filmakers Library.

Carstensen, L. L. (1992). Social and emotional patterns in adulthood: Support for socioemotional selectivity theory. *Psychology and Aging, 7,* 331–338.

Cavanaugh, J. C., & Blanchard-Fields, F. (2002). *Adult development and aging* (4th ed.). Belmont, CA: Wadsworth.

Collier, D. (Producer & director). (1993). *For better or for worse* [Videorecording]. Santa Monica, CA: Direct Cinema Ltd.

Erikson, E. (1963). *Childhood and society* (2nd ed.). New York: W. W. Norton & Company, Inc.

Fingerman, K. L. (1996). Sources of tension in the aging mother and adult daughter relationship. *Psychology and Aging, 11,* 591–606.

Gaugler, J. E., Leitsch, S. A., Zarit, S. H., & Pearlin, L. I. (2000). Caregiver involvement following institutionalization: Effects of preplacement stress. *Research on Aging, 22,* 337–359.

Hansson, R. O., & Carpenter, B. N. (1994). *Relationships in old age: Coping with the challenge of transition.* New York: Guilford.

Hoffmann, D. (Producer & director). (1994). *Complaints of a dutiful daughter* [Videorecording]. New York: Women Make Movies.

Jarrott, S. E., & Blieszner, R. (2001). Creating families in the classroom: An active learning approach. *Gerontology and Geriatrics Education, 22*, 15–27.

Kidder, T. (1993). *Old friends.* Boston: Houghton Mifflin.

Leffland, E. (1997). The linden tree. In E. P. Stoller & R. C. Gibson (Eds.), *Worlds of difference: Inequality in the aging experience* (2nd ed., pp. 233–241). Thousand Oaks, CA: Pine Forge Press.

Lytton, R. H., Marshall-Baker, A., Benson, M. J., & Blieszner, R. (1996). Writing to learn: Course examples in family and consumer sciences. *Journal of Family and Consumer Sciences, 88*(1), 35–41, 64.

Pillsbury, S., & Sanford, M. (Producers), & Moorhouse, J. (Director). (1996). *How to make an American quilt* [Videorecording]. Universal City, CA: MCA Universal Home Video.

Pruchno, R., & Kleban, M. H. (1993). Caring for an institutionalized parent: The role of coping strategies. *Psychology and Aging, 8*, 18–25.

Sparks, N. (1996). *The notebook.* New York: Warner Books.

Stoller, E. P., & Gibson, R. C. (1997). *Worlds of difference: Inequality in the aging experience* (2nd ed.). Thousand Oaks, CA: Pine Forge Press.

Walker, A. J., Manoogian-O'Dell, M., McGraw, L. A., & White, D. L. G. (2001). *Families in later life: Connections and transitions.* Thousand Oaks, CA: Pine Forge Press.

Whitbourne, S. K. (2001). *Adult development and aging: Biopsychosocial perspectives.* New York: John Wiley & Sons.

ANNOTATED BIBLIOGRAPHY

Life Span Development Perspective

Bedford, V. H., & Blieszner, R. (2000a). Older adults and their families. In D. H. Demo, K. R. Allen, & M. A. Fine (Eds.), *Handbook of family diversity* (pp. 216–231). New York: Oxford University Press.

Bedford, V. H., & Blieszner, R. (2000b). Personal relationships in later life families. In R. M. Milardo & S. Duck (Eds.), *Families as relationships* (pp. 157–174). New York: Wiley.

Blieszner, R. (1994). Close relationships over time. In A. L. Weber & J. H. Harvey (Eds.), *Perspectives on close relationships* (pp. 1–17). Rockleigh, NJ: Allyn & Bacon.

Blieszner, R. (2000). Close relationships in old age. In C. Hendrick & S. Hendrick (Eds.), *Close relationships: A sourcebook* (pp. 84–95). Thousand Oaks, CA: Sage.

Blieszner, R., Mancini, J. A., & Marek, L. I. (1996). Looking back and looking ahead: Life course unfolding of parenthood. In C. D. Ryff & M. M. Seltzer (Eds.), *The parental experience in mid-life* (pp. 607–637). Chicago: University of Chicago Press.

The chapters cited here encompass two themes: One is a life span perspective on relationships in old age, acknowledging their antecedents in earlier life experiences and their dynamic, changing nature. Also, they illustrate reciprocal influences of stage of development on the nature of relationships and of relationships on personal development. The other theme is diversity, highlighting the ways that elders experience relationships similarly to and differently than individuals at other stages of life, along with the ways that elders from various sociodemographic groups experience close relationships similarly and differently.

Family Relationships

Allen, K. A., Blieszner, R., & Roberto, K. A. (2000). Families in the middle and later years: A review and critique of research in the 1990s. *Journal of Marriage and the Family, 62,* 911–926. The decade review article, fourth in a series dating from 1971, contains a detailed analysis of conceptual and methodological trends along with a wealth of citations to recent family gerontology literature.

Blieszner, R., & Bedford, V. H. (Eds.). (1995). *Handbook of aging and the family.* Westport, CT: Greenwood Press. Reprinted in paperback for textbook use as Blieszner, R., & Bedford, V. H. (Eds.). (1996). *Aging and the family: Theory and research.* Westport, CT: Praeger.

Connidis, I. A. (2001). *Family ties and aging.* Thousand Oaks, CA: Sage.

These two textbooks present a comprehensive array of information about all types of family relationships in the late years and many issues relevant to those relationships. The Blieszner and Bedford volume includes historical and demographic background information, chapters on theoretical frameworks and research methods, and sections on types of family relationships, the context of family life, and turning points and interventions. The Connidis book contains parts on intimate ties, intergenerational relations, siblings, and research and policy directions. It includes excellent coverage of diversity in family experiences according to racial ethnic, sexual orientation, and social class group membership.

Friendship

Adams, R. G., & Blieszner, R. (Eds.). (1989). *Older adult friendship: Structure and process.* Newbury Park, CA: Sage.

Blieszner, R., & Adams, R. G. (1992). *Adult friendship*. Thousand Oaks, CA: Sage.

Fehr, B. (1996). *Friendship processes*. Thousand Oaks, CA: Sage.

Rawlins, W. K. (1992). *Friendship matters: Communication, dialectics, and the life course*. Hawthorne, NY: Aldine de Gruyter.

These resources provide comprehensive information on friendship in adulthood and old age; interactive friendship processes related to cognitions, emotions, and behaviors; friendship initiation, maintenance, and dissolution phases; and conceptual and methodological issues in the study of adult friendship.

Diversity of Relational Experiences

Stoller, E. P., & Gibson, R. C. (1997). *Worlds of difference: Inequality in the aging experience* (2nd ed.). Thousand Oaks, CA: Pine Forge Press.

Walker, A. J., Manoogian-O'Dell, M., McGraw, L. A., & White, D. L. G. (2001). *Families in later life: Connections and transitions*. Thousand Oaks, CA: Pine Forge Press.

These books were designed as companion readers for psychology and gerontology textbooks. They include diverse types of readings, ranging from poetry to short stories to excerpts from journal articles and novels. More than compilations of interesting readings, however, both volumes include extensive narrative by the editors to provide a gerontological context for the entries. They also include discussion questions on the readings and suggestions for additional print and Internet resources. Walker and her colleagues focus exclusively on family gerontology, whereas Stoller and Gibson include other topics with a particular focus on diversity of aging experiences.

Close Relationship Issues

Dykstra, P. A. (1990). *Next of (non)kin: The importance of primary relationships for older adults' well-being*. Amsterdam: Swets & Zeitlinger.

Fingerman, K. L. (2001). *Aging mothers and their adult daughters*. New York: Springer.

Hansson, R. O., & Carpenter, B. N. (1994). *Relationships in old age: Coping with the challenge of transition*. New York: Guilford.

Roberto, K. A. (Ed.). (1996). *Relationships between women in later life*. Binghamton, NY: Haworth.

These books focus on multiple dimensions of close relationships in old age. Dykstra has demonstrated contributions of close relationships in old age to well-being with evidence from Dutch elders. The Fingerman volume focuses on mixed emotions in mother–daughter relationships. Hansson and Carpenter provide empirical support for their theory of relational competence and how possessing this capacity enables elders to meet their needs for social support and other forms of assistance. Roberto's collection addresses both typical and unusual relationships of older women.

INDEX

research methods and statistics course,
8, 44–50, 52–53

resources, 27–28, 50, 52

See also Cognitive functioning, aging
topics in teaching of; Death and
dying, psychology of; Health
psychology, aging topics in teaching of; Introductory psychology
course, aging topics in; Neuropsychology, aging topics in teaching
of; Personality psychology, aging
topics in teaching of; Sensation
and perception, aging topics in
teaching of; Social psychology,
aging topics in teaching of

Emotional functioning

attachment theory, 95

introductory course topics, 22–23

life span development, 96

neuropsychological development, 35

socioemotional selectivity, 96

End-of-life concerns, 209

Endocrine system, 19

Exceptional performance/skill

creativity, 81–82

maintenance of, 81

Exercise, 127

Expertise, 81

External validity, 45

Family relationships, 218, 220, 221–222,
226

Flavor perception, 67

simulating deficits in, 70

Friendship, 218, 222–223, 226–227

Gender differences, 9–10

aging topics in teaching of, 160,
161–170

course objectives, 160–161

in disability risk, 131

gender identity, 161, 165–166

in hearing, 65

household composition, 165

instructional resources, 167–168, 169,
171–172

interpersonal relationships, 164–165

in life expectancy, 161–163

marginalization of women, 160

mortality and morbidity, 161–163,
166–167

public policy, 160

rationale for integrating aging topics in
teaching of, 159–160

role reversal, 168–169

in socioeconomic status, 163–164

stereotypes of aging, 161, 166

in suicide, 161, 163, 168

textbook coverage, 159

in widowhood, 164, 165

Genetic *vs.* environmental influences,
94–95

Grieving, 204, 205, 209–210

Health psychology, aging topics in teaching of, 9, 126–132

biological change, 126

chronic illness, 130–131

compliance with medical regimen, 24

disease processes, 124–125

health behavior, 126–128

individual differences, 124

instructional resources, 136–139

integration of, 132

introductory course, 24

life-span, 124–132

rationale, 123–124, 132

stereotypes of aging, 131–132

stigmatization of disease, 131–132

stress and illness, 128–130

See also Medical health

Hearing, 20, 63

age-related changes, 64–65

assessment, 64, 69

presbycusis, 64

simulating deficits in, 69

sound localization, 65

speech perception, 64, 65

structural changes, age-related, 64

Heritability quotient, 94–95

Historical development of gerontology,
3–4

Household composition, 165

Human factors research, 191–192

Immune function, 128–129

Incontinence, 131–132

Individuation, 95–96

social identity processes, 109–111

ABOUT THE EDITORS

Susan Krauss Whitbourne, PhD, is a professor of psychology at the University of Massachusetts at Amherst. She has published widely in the field of adult development and aging, focusing on personality psychology, and she is actively involved in the field of undergraduate education. Over the past 25 years, Dr. Whitbourne has held a variety of elected and appointed positions in Division 20 (Adult Development and Aging) of the American Psychological Association (APA), including president (1995–1996). She is the Division 20 representative to the APA Council of Representatives. She is a Fellow of Divisions 2 (Teaching), 12 (Clinical), and 20, as well as the Gerontological Society. The recipient of the University Distinguished Teaching Award, she also has been recognized as the Florence Denmark National Psi Chi Advisor and has presented a G. Stanley Hall Lecture on undergraduate education and aging.

John C. Cavanaugh, PhD, is the president of the University of West Florida. He has published numerous articles on adults' self-evaluations of memory and on family caregiving of people with dementia. For more than two decades, Dr. Cavanaugh has held several elected positions in the APA, including president of Division 20 (1996–1997) and member of the Council of Representatives. He also has served on the Executive Board for the Behavioral and Social Sciences Section of the Gerontological Society of America. He is a Fellow of Divisions 1, 2, and 20 of APA and the Gerontological Society of America and is a Charter Fellow of the American Psychological Society.